The Scattered Portions

THE SCATTERED PORTIONS

William Blake's Biological Symbolism

by
Rodney M. Baine
With the assistance of Mary R. Baine

Copyright by Rodney M. Baine 1986
ISBN 0-935265-10-4
Library of Congress Card Number 85-073258

Distributed by the author, Department of English,
University of Georgia, Athens, Georgia 30602

Jacket Plate: The Dance of Albion
National Gallery of Art, Rosenwald Collection

For
William Rion Baine
and
Mark Stevenson Baine

So Man looks out in tree & herb & fish & bird & beast
Collecting up the scatterd portions of his immortal body
Into the Elemental forms of every thing that grows

Contents

A List of Illustrations   xi
A List to Abbreviated Titles   xv
A Note on the Text   xvii
Preface   xix
Chapter One: Introduction   3
Chapter Two: The Carnivorous Beasts   14
Chapter Three: The Herbivorous Animals   37
Chapter Four: The Granivorous Birds   54
Chapter Five: The Birds of Prey   73
Chapter Six: The Insects   84
Chapter Seven: The Reptiles   102
Chapter Eight: Marine Life   121
Chapter Nine: The Trees   134
Chapter Ten: The Plants   150
Notes   173
Illustrations   195
Index   239

A List of Illustrations

Plate numbers accord with those in *The Illuminated Blake,* edited by David V. Erdman.

1. *Jerusalem,* Pl. 98. Copy D.
2. "The Tyger," *Songs of Innocence and of Experience.* Copy O.
3. *Milton,* Plate 46. Copy D.
4. Watercolor for Young, *Night Thoughts,* p. 234.
5. "The Little Girl Lost," *Songs of Innocence and of Experience.* Copy O.
6. "The Little Girl Found," *Songs of Innocence and of Experience.* Copy O.
7. *The Book of Urizen,* Pl. 23. Copy F.
8. *Job,* Pl. 15.
9. "The Shepherd," *Songs of Innocence and of Experience.* Copy I.
10. "The Lamb," *Songs of Innocence.* Copy F.
11. *America,* Pl. 7. Copy E.
12. "The Clod and the Pebble," *Songs of Innocence and of Experience.* Copy O.
13. *Jerusalem,* Pl. 29. Copy D.
14. Watercolor 8 for Gray, "The Fatal Sisters."
15. *Jerusalem,* Pl. 35. Copy D.
16. Watercolor 6 for Gray, "Ode on a Distant Prospect of Eton College."
17. Watercolor title page for *Poems by Mr. Gray.*

18. *America*, Pl. 11. Copy E.
19. *Jerusalem*, Pl. 11. Copy D.
20. *Jerusalem*, Pl. 62. Copy D.
21. *Night Startled by the Lark.*
22. *The Marriage of Heaven and Hell*, Pl. 15. Copy G.
23. *Jerusalem*, Pl. 78. Copy D.
24. *America*, Pl. 13. Copy E.
25. *Europe*, Pl. 14. Copy H.
26. *Milton*, Pl. 42. Copy A.
27. *Visions of the Daughters of Albion*, Pl. 3. Copy G.
28. *Europe*, Pl. 11. Copy H.
29. *Jerusalem*, Pl. 6. Copy D.
30. *Jerusalem*, Pl. 33. Copy D.
31. *The Dance of Albion*, or *Albion Rose.*
32. *For Children: The Gates of Paradise*, frontispiece. Copy D.
33. *For Children: The Gates of Paradise*, Pl. 16. Copy D.
34. *Jerusalem*, Pl. 80. Copy D.
35. *Jerusalem*, Pl. 28, State 1. Copy F.
36. *Europe*, Pl. 12. Copy H.
37. "The Sick Rose," *Songs of Innocence and of Experience.* Copy O.
38. *Jerusalem*, Pl. 2. Copy D.
39. *Jerusalem*, Pl. 14. Copy D.
40. *Jerusalem*, Pl. 44. Copy D.
41. *Jerusalem*, Pl. 53. Copy D.
42. *Jerusalem*, Pl. 63. Copy D.
43. *The Book of Urizen*, Pl. 25. Copy F.
44. *Jerusalem*, Pl. 75. Copy D.
45. *Jerusalem*, Pl. 41. Copy D.
46. *Europe*, Pl. ii. Proof in copy b.

A List of Illustrations

47. *Beatrice Addressing Dante from the Car.* Dante's *Divine Comedy,* Design 88.
48. *The Harlot and the Giant.* Dante's *Divine Comedy,* Design 89.
49. *The Book of Urizen,* Pl. 6. Copy F.
50. *Narcissa and the Ouroboros. Night Thoughts,* p. 78.
51. *Europe,* Pl. 10. Copy H.
52. *America,* Pl. 4. Copy E.
53. *America,* Pl. 5. Copy E.
54. *Jerusalem,* Pl. 40. Copy D.
55. Watercolor 4 for Gray, "Ode on the Death of a Favourite Cat."
56. Watercolor 5 for Gray, "Ode on the Death of a Favourite Cat."
57. *Newton at the Bottom of the Sea of Space and Time.*
58. *Jerusalem,* Pl. 92. Copy D.
59. *The Spiritual Form of Nelson Guiding Leviathan.*
60. "The Little Black Boy," Pl. 2, *Songs of Innocence and of Experience.* Copy O.
61. *America,* Pl. 16. Copy E.
62. "The Ecchoing Green," Pl. 1, *Songs of Innocence and of Experience.* Copy O.
63. *America,* Pl. 1. Copy E.
64. *Jerusalem,* Pl. 9. Copy D.
65. *America,* Pl. 6. Copy E.
66. "The Angel," *Songs of Innocence and of Experience.* Copy O.
67. *America,* Pl. 15. Copy E.
68. "Holy Thursday," *Songs of Innocence and of Experience.* Copy O.
69. "My Pretty Rose Tree," *Songs of Innocence and of Experience.* Copy O.
70. "The Blossom," *Songs of Innocence and of Experience.* Copy Z.
71. *The Botanical Magazine,* Vol. 1, Pl. 30.
72. "The Divine Image," *Songs of Innocence and of Experience.* Copy O.

73. *The Book of Thel,* title page. Copy H.
74. "Infant Joy," *Songs of Innocence and of Experience.* Copy O.
75. *The Book of Thel,* Pl. 2. Copy H.
76. *The Book of Thel,* Pl. 4. Copy H.
77. *The Book of Thel,* Pl. 5. Copy H.

For permission to reproduce these illustrations I am indebted to the courtesy of the following: for Fig. 48, to the National Gallery of Victoria, Melbourne (Felton Bequest 1920); for Figs. 47, 57, and 59, to the Trustees of the Tate Gallery, London; for Figs. 4, 26, and 50, to the Trustees of the British Museum; for Figs. 21, 35, and 46, to the Trustees of the Pierpont Morgan Library; for Figs. 14, 16, 17, 55, and 56, to Mr. Paul Mellon (from his Collection at Upperville, Va.); for Fig. 31, to the Lessing J. Rosenwald Collection, National Gallery of Art, Washington, D.C.; for Figs. 3, 11, 18, 24, 32, 33, 52, 53, 61, 63, 65, 67, 70, 73, and 75-77, to the Lessing J. Rosenwald Collection, the Library of Congress; and for Figs. 1, 2, 5-10, 12, 13, 15, 19, 20, 22, 23, 25, 27-30, 34, 36-45, 49, 51, 54, 58, 60, 62, 64, 66, 68, 69, 71, 72, and 74, to the Houghton Library, Harvard University, Department of Printing and Graphic Arts.

A Key to Abbreviated Titles

AC Emanuel Swedenborg, *Arcana Coelestia: or Heavenly Mysteries contained in the Sacred Scriptures,* trans. John Clowes (London, 1783-1806).

AE _____, *The Apocalypse, or Book of Revelations, Explained according to the Spiritual Sense,* trans. W. Hill and J. Clowes (London, 1811-15).

AR _____, *The Apocalypse Revealed, wherein are Disclosed the Arcana there Foretold,* trans. Nathaniel Tucker. London, 1791.

B Martin Butlin, *The Paintings and Drawings of William Blake* (New Haven: Yale Univ. Press, 1981).

BFIR *The Natural History of Birds, Fish, Insects, and Reptiles* (London, 1798).

CGW David Bindman, *The Complete Graphic Works of William Blake* (New York: G. P. Putnam, 1978).

E *The Complete Poetry and Prose of William Blake,* ed. David V. Erdman (Garden City: Doubleday, 1982).

FQ *The Faerie Queene,* in *The Works of Edmund Spenser, a Variorum Edition,* ed. Edwin Greenlaw et al. (Baltimore: Johns Hopkins Press, 1932-49).

FZ William Blake, *Vala, or the Four Zoas.*

IB *The Illuminated Blake: All of William Blake's Illuminated Works, with a Plate-by-Plate Commentary,* Annotated by David V. Erdman (Garden City: Doubleday, 1974).

JWCI *Journal of the Warburg and Courtauld Institutes.*

MHH Blake, *The Marriage of Heaven and Hell.*

NH George Louis Leclerc, comte de Buffon, and L. J. M. Daubenton, *Natural History, General and Particular,* trans. William Smellie, 2nd ed. (London, 1785).

NT *William Blake's Designs for Edward Young's Night Thoughts,* ed. John Grant et al. (Oxford: Clarendon Press, 1980).

PL *Paradise Lost,* in *The Works of John Milton,* ed. Frank Allen Patterson (New York: Columbia Univ. Press, 1931-38).

PR *Paradise Regained,* in ibid.

TCR Swedenborg, *True Christian Religion, containing the Universal Theology of the New Church,* trans. William Cookworthy, 2nd ed. (London, 1784).

VDA Blake, *Visions of the Daughters of Albion.*

A Note on the Text

I have based my text of Blake upon *The Complete Poetry and Prose of William Blake,* edited by David V. Erdman (Garden City: Doubleday, 1982), herein designated as *E*. Blake's unusual practice of spelling and punctuation I have reproduced from this edition, without adding the distracting *sic*. All brackets with a superior asterisk are those of Mr. Erdman. All other brackets in Blake quotations are my own. Unless otherwise noted, all the brackets in quotations of other authors appear in the edition cited.

Because of its convenience, for the designs I have cited plate numbers as these appear in *The Illuminated Blake,* also edited by Erdman (Garden City: Doubleday, 1974).

Preface

A study of the biological symbols should greatly assist the serious student to understand the poetry and art of William Blake, for these symbols throw light upon many passages, upon even whole poems which have been subject to widely diverse readings, particularly by critics who are too often prone to ignore the symbolic traditions which Blake inherited and to rely, instead, upon impressionistic criticism. Before the student or the critic — traditionalist, structuralist, poststructuralist, or whatever — can understand and evaluate Blake's myth, or myths, he must understand the symbols which help to embody that myth. Though he may reject the aesthetic and critical doctrines of Northrop Frye, he must, like Frye and Erwin Panofsky, study the traditional meanings and implications of the poet's or artist's symbolic language, a language which has been virtually forgot. Otherwise he risks failing to understand an important part of the artist's vocabulary, at least, an important part of William Blake's. Blake's botanical symbolism has been studied by Ms. Elaine M. Kauvar in her "Blake's Botanical Imagery" (Northwestern dissertation, 1971), but the far more extensive zoological symbolism has never been systematically investigated.

For opportunity to pursue my research I am grateful to the University of Georgia, which has provided me with research time and travel funds, including a grant-in-aid from the Research Foundation, and to the American Philosophical Society for a grant-in-aid from the Penrose Fund. To Messrs. William Gaither, Francis Gannon, and Robert Paulk and to Mss. Lucile Clark, Joan Howard, Susan McLain, Patty O'Gwynn, Mary E. Williams, and the late Mary Bledsoe, I am indebted for months of patient help. To Mss. Gina Campbell, Katie Lu, and particularly Millie Norrell, DeAnna Palmer, and Stacie Whiteman I owe typings of several drafts. I am grateful to Mr. Wilbur Duncan, Professor Emeritus of Botany at the University of Georgia, for help in the botanical identifications; to

Northrop Frye and David V. Erdman, for their inspiration and encouragement; and I am especially indebted to Ms. Mary R. Baine, who assisted generously in the research and wrote much of Chapters Two and Three.

In working on Blake I have enjoyed courteous hospitality at several libraries: the University of Georgia Libraries; the Libraries of Harvard University, where Ms. Caroline Jakeman, Ms. Martie Shaw, and Mr. Tom Noonan were especially helpful at the Houghton, Mr. Charles Montalbano at Widener, Ms. Mary Keeler at the Zoological Library, and Ms. Lenore Dickinson at the Gray Herbarium/Arnold Aboretum Library; the Boston Swedenborgian Library; the Library of the Swedenborgian School of Religion, in Newton, Massachusetts, where Ms. Marian Kirven was gracious in her assistance; the Department of Prints and Drawings at the British Museum; the Libraries of the Warburg and Courtauld Institutes of the University of London; and the Fitzwilliam Museum of Cambridge University.

I am grateful to *Philological Quarterly* for permission to quote from "Blake's 'Tyger': the Nature of the Beast," to *Studies in English* for permission to quote from "Blake's Other Tigers," and to the *Colby Library Quarterly* for permission to quote from "Blake's 'Blossom.'"

Rodney M. Baine
The University of Georgia
Athens, Georgia

The Scattered Portions

Chapter One

Introduction

No other English poet or artist used biological images and symbols — beast, bird, insect, reptile, fish, tree, and plant — more often or more meaningfully than did William Blake. They frame the scenes and often occupy the center in *Job* and in *Songs of Innocence and of Experience;* they interlineate *The Marriage of Heaven and Hell* and *America;* they provide enigmatic pictures in *Jerusalem;* they tell a fable of flowers in *Thel*. They provide images and symbols for the wine-press, or printing press of Los:

> Timbrels & violins sport round the Wine-presses; the little Seed;
> The sportive Root, the Earth-worm, the gold Beetle; the wise Emmet;
> Dance round the Wine-presses of Luvah: the Centipede is there:
> The ground Spider with many eyes: the Mole clothed in velvet
> The ambitious Spider in his sullen web; the lucky golden Spinner;
> The Earwig armd: the tender Maggot emblem of immortality:
> The Flea: Louse: Bug: the Tape-Worm: all the Armies of Disease:
> Visible or invisible to the slothful vegetating Man.
> The slow Slug: the Grasshopper that sings & laughs & drinks:
> Winter comes, he folds his slender bones without a murmur.
> The cruel Scorpion is there: the Gnat: Wasp: Hornet & the Honey Bee:
> The Toad & venomous Newt; the Serpent clothd in gems & gold:
> ....
> There is the Nettle that stings with soft down; and there
> The indignant Thistle: whose bitterness is bred in his milk:
> Who feeds on contempt of his neighbour: there all the idle Weeds
> That creep around the obscure places, shew their various limbs.[1]

Most of the flora and fauna which Blake mentioned or depicted, he had ample opportunity to become familiar with. Until perhaps 1795 he often took walking trips of forty or even fifty miles into the countryside, where meadows and woodlands were still alive with trees, flowers, animals, birds, insects, reptiles, and fish. Even in London itself he could have seen most of his trees and plants. The city was gradually encroaching upon the open fields, especially to the north and west, as the population grew from 675,000 in 1750 to 900,000 in 1801; however the royal parks, the pleasure gardens, and the private gardens helped to keep large areas of London in bloom. The flora (the fuchsia, for example) which he could not often see in such places he could have seen in the exhibits of the many nurserymen; in the London Botanic Garden of the Apothecaries, in Chelsea; in William Curtis's London Botanic Garden, in Lambeth and then, after 1789, in Brompton; or, only a few miles away, in the Royal Botanic Garden, at Kew.[2]

Most of his fauna, too, he could have seen in London. Dogs, cats, and caged birds were favorite pets. Horses were necessary means of travel; and at Felpham Blake rode one, his "beloved Bruno."[3] Oxen, cows, sheep, swine, and other animals were herded down the streets of London and butchered in slaughterhouses like that at Carnaby Market, just around the corner from Blake's childhood home in Golden Square. Displayed in the markets also were geese, ducks, turkeys, chickens, pigeons, and even songbirds like larks, as well as eels, lampreys, fish, and shellfish.

The animals which he could not see on the streets or in the markets, Blake could have seen mounted in the museums or private collections or shown in zoos, fairs, or smaller exhibitions. The British Museum collections were gradually being enlarged and made more accessible. Sir Ashton Lever's large museum at Leicester House filled sixteen rooms and included thousands of exhibits.[4] Until the end of the century Salter's Coffee House boasted its zoological collection, with its printed catalogue. From time to time Blake probably also saw the private collections of friends like "Inflammable Gass" (probably William Nicolson) and Henry Fuseli.[5] Indeed Fuseli's delicate use of insects in his illustrations of Shakespeare and Milton may well have suggested to Blake the butterfly headdress on one of the fairies in *Titania, Oberon, and Puck, with Fairies Dancing.*[6] But probably more interesting to Blake than the mounted collections would have been the sparse menagerie at the Tower of London and Gilbert Pidcock's menagerie at Exeter Change in the Strand, where George Stubbs evidently sketched from the life and bought a dead tiger for dissection and study (Altick, p. 39). Strange or

Introduction

trained animals were also exhibited in such fairs as Bartholomew Fair, which lasted a fortnight, and were frequently the attraction for smaller exhibitions. Indeed *The Macaroni and Theatrical Magazine* for January 1773 boasted that there were "'Lions, Tygers, Elephants, &c. in every Street in Town'" (Altick, p. 35). In 1785 or later Blake may have witnessed performances by "the Learned Pig/ Or the Hare playing on a Tabor" (*E,* p. 514).[7]

Doubtless in his depiction of flora and fauna Blake relied in part upon his own observations of nature. At the Royal Academy, however, instruction in drawing from nature evidently concentrated upon the human form, not upon its "scattered portions": there models posed, and there Dr. William Hunter lectured upon human anatomy. For the rest, apparently, students were sent not to the fields or the zoos, but to the Library. And as Blake remarked in his annotations to Wordsworth's *Poems* (1815), "Natural Objects always did & now do Weaken deaden & obliterate Imagination in Me . . ." (*E,* p. 665).

His biological designs were probably based largely upon those of earlier artists whose work he studied and admired and upon the engravings which he found in the scientific works of his day. During the second half of the eighteenth century there occurred rapid advances in the biological sciences, advances due in part to the eminent Swedish botanist Carl von Linné. Blake certainly knew some of Linné's work, for in his *Descriptive Catalogue* (1809), he remarked, "As Newton numbered the stars, and as Linneus numbered the plants, so Chaucer numbered the classes of men" (*E,* p. 533). Blake engraved several plates for the Linnean Erasmus Darwin's *Botanical Garden* (1791-94) and may have borrowed from Darwin some of his botanical imagery and symbolism. But Linné's systematic classifications were as useless to Blake's biological symbolism as were the discoveries of Copernicus and Galileo to Milton's *Paradise Lost.* Just as they displaced man as the center of the universe, so Linné ignored and helped to destroy biological lore and symbolism.

Accompanying these scientific advances, however, were improvements in the depiction of the various species. Twenty-seven volumes of the generously illustrated *Histoire Naturelle* (Paris, 1749-89), by Buffon and his colleagues, were evidently in the Library of the Royal Academy.[8] At the bookstores were such handsomely illustrated works as George Edwards's seven volume *Natural History of Uncom-*

mon Birds (London, 1743-64), Edward Donovan's ten volume *Natural History of British Insects* (London, 1792-1801), and James Sowerby's and Sir J. E. Smith's thirty-six volume *English Botany* (London, 1790-1814). When in 1787 William Curtis began his long-lived *Botanical Magazine,* Blake may have subscribed, for an early issue perhaps furnished the central design for "The Blossom."[9] Interesting, but iconographically useless, however, was their close discrimination between different types. Symbolically the golden eagle does not differ from the bald eagle.

But from whatever sources Blake may have drawn his designs, their emblematic meanings and implications are the subject of our enquiry. For among eighteenth-century artists, none operated more in the emblematic tradition than did Blake. In a study of English artists of the century, Ronald Paulson found him to be "antipathetic" to the empirical and realistic style which was becoming increasingly popular.[10]

For Blake, biological symbolism was inherent, not imposed, for in his myth all forms of life, like the rest of creation, were originally part of man himself. In his address "To the Jews," in *Jerusalem,* he stated, "You have a tradition, that Man anciently contain in his mighty limbs all things in Heaven & Earth: this you recieved from the Druids" (*E,* p. 171). Blake's figure of Albion, the Cosmic Man who embodied the whole earth and heavens, was by no means unique. Blake probably knew, for example, the Druidic version in the prose Edda, available in *Northern Antiquities* (1770), Bishop Percy's translation of Paul Henri Mallet. But Blake's most important sources for his myth were probably Boehme and Swedenborg. According to Boehme, "*All is in Man,* both Heaven and Earth, Stars, and Elements; and also the Number Three of the Deity; neither can there be any thing named that is not in Man; all Creatures, (both in this world, and in the Angelical world,) are in Man."[11] According to Swedenborg, ". . . the whole of heaven, together with it's several Societies collectively, are in the form of a Man, therefore they call heaven the GRAND (MAXIMUM), and DIVINE MAN. . . ."[12]

In Blake's version of the myth, also, Albion in his unfallen state contained within himself all nature. On Plate 25 of *Jerusalem* Albion's Shadow, Vala, along with Rahab and Tirzah, is not only eviscerating him, but is taking away from him the sun, moon, and stars present in his body. When, under the spell of nature, Albion falls from unity, he projects and objectifies what are in imaginative reality only various portions of himself. In observing nature, man is viewing aspects of his own personality:

> So Man looks out in tree & herb & fish & bird & beast
> Collecting up the scatterd portions of his immortal body
> Into the Elemental forms of every thing that grows
> ....
> Screaming in birds over the deep & howling in the Wolf
> Over the slain & moaning in the cattle & in the winds
> And weeping over Orc & Urizen in clouds & flaming fires
> And in the cries of birth & in the groans of death his voice
> Is heard throughout the Universe whereever a grass grows
> Or a leaf buds The Eternal Man is seen is heard is felt
> And all his Sorrows till he reassumes his ancient bliss [.]
>
> (FZ 110.6-28; E, p. 385)

As man falls from vision, he objectifies into separate existence more and more aspects of himself. He stands in awe and horror, wondering where a beast like the tiger comes from, for he does not see in it a portion of his own fallen, divided self.

Every wild beast, bird of prey, wasp, spider, reptile, and weed, however, is capable of being reclaimed into the body of Man. Thus on Plate 85 of *Jerusalem* Enitharmon restores to her Humanity, Los, not only his vines/veins and an intestine-like cloud, but the sun, moon, and stars. When man rejects the domination of nature and reclaims his Emanation the manifestations of selfish malignancy in external nature lose their ferocity. This change Blake represented by the metamorphosis of destructive beasts into creative animals:

> The tygers from the forests & the lions from the sandy desarts
> They sing they sieze the instruments of harmony they throw away
> The spear the bow the gun the mortar they level the fortifications [.]
>
> (FZ 124.16-18)

Similarly, rehumanized tigers and lions draw the wagons of Luvah to the winepresses of the apocalypse. At the close of *Jerusalem* (see Fig. 1) all the animals reunite with Man, as the poet

> heard Jehovah speak
> Terrific from his Holy Place & saw the Words of the Mutual Covenant Divine
> On Chariots of gold & jewels with Living Creatures starry & flaming
> With every Colour, Lion, Tyger, Horse, Elephant, Eagle Dove, Fly, Worm,
> And the all wondrous Serpent clothed in gems & rich array Humanize
> In the Forgiveness of Sins. . . .
>
> (98.40-45)

Here on Plate 98 we see mainly the lowest forms of animal life, but all life is holy and capable of redemption. Beneath the birds, the butterfly, and perhaps a bee, are snail, toad, inchworm (or caterpillar), spider, and a worm apparently casting its skin, defying vermicular limitations, just as the serpent at the top of the page, tied into almost impossible knots, is apparently doing, naturally. (For Blake naturalistic precision was less important than symbolic fitness.) As they shed their skin they enter upon a new life; as all forms of life rejoin Albion they reject the Selfhood which has separated man from man and man from nature and projected all life into an outer void. When Albion accepts the ideas of self-annihilation and forgiveness taught by Jesus, all forms and the affections which they represent "re-humanize," become part of the divine human form again.

One task of the prophet, the poet, as Blake saw it, is to awaken man from his sleep of ignorance and the domination of his Selfhood so that he may read the symbols around him and realize that in Experience his divided state is the cause of the fallen condition of his world; for only through this understanding can he begin to recognize his fragmentation and reintegrate himself into his native unity. Perceiving the projections of his own psyche in various biological forms is obviously an important part of this crucial realization: man readily sees savagery and gentleness, greed and selflessness, innocence and cruelty in animals and even in plants. But he is not always quick to see those qualities in himself. As Henry Fuseli remarked, "Were man and man as easily discriminated as the lamb and the tiger, the Physiognomist's would be a useless science; but since both lamb and tiger may dwell in human frames, he surely deserves our thanks, who points them out to us before we wound the one or sink beneath the other."[13]

In employing his system of biological symbols, especially animal symbols, Blake was following Western traditions in iconography which had begun perhaps with the caveman, been systematized by the Greek philosophers, had been established in the Bible, in Western literature and art, particularly in the emblem books, in natural history and physiognomy, and had been justified and explained by two of Blake's masters, Jacob Boehme and Emanuel Swedenborg. From the time of Paleolithic man, animal emblems have operated powerfully in Western man's art and life. Then with the development of systematic thought, as Francis Klingender noted, "Pythagoras and Plato directed philosophical speculation towards the theory of correspondences in which all spheres of being were related by analogy. . . . In these correspondences the unifying symbols were drawn . . . increasingly again from the animal world."[14] The Aristotelian mode of thought encouraged man to assign human attributes to animals; in his *Natural History* Pliny supplied data to support such attributions;[15] and in his *Metamorphoses* and his *Fasti,* Ovid popularized the practice.

Animal symbolism pervades the Bible and the entire Judao-Christian tradition in art and literature; and to this tradition, especially, Blake owed his emblematic language. Such symbolism is suggested in Genesis and systematized in the division, in Deuteronomy 14.3-20, of the animals and birds into clean and unclean. Though the original purpose of this division was doubtless dietary, this classification, joined with the Platonic justification of symbolism, influenced subsequent biological symbolism throughout the Bible and western civilization. These symbolic idioms and traditions Blake certainly knew. A lover of Ovid, Dante, Spenser, Shakespeare, and Milton, Blake was familiar with their usage of symbols and of the continuation of this traditional iconography by contemporaries like William Cowper. Moreover at Pars's school, Basire's shop, and the Royal Academy he learned to admire Raphael, Michelangelo, Dürer, Giulio Romano, Goltzius, Poussin, and other Renaissance and baroque painters, and learned to use their symbols.

He seems to have owed nothing to the mediaeval bestiary — except in such late derivatives as the animal or flower fables, like

John Gay's *Fables,* for the 1793, Stockdale edition of which he engraved twelve plates, and the *Fables of Flora* of John Langhorne and of John Huddlestone Wynne (1771 and 1773). The emblem books, however, seem to have influenced Blake's symbolism even more than his designs, though most Blake scholars have virtually limited their study of the emblem books to Blake's graphic borrowings. From the time of the Renaissance, emblem books, drawn from the bestiaries, the classics, and the Bible, perpetuated and popularized the symbolic conventions. Such emblem books provided poets and artists with a ready set of well-known biological symbols.[16] According to Erwin Panofsky, the *Iconography* of Caesare Ripa, "that *summa* of iconography," "drawing from classical and mediaeval as well as contemporary sources, has rightly been called 'the key of seventeenth- and eighteenth-century allegory' and was exploited by artists and poets as illustrious as Bernini, Poussin, Vermeer, and Milton."[17] An English translation, much abridged, was published by P. Tempest in 1709; and another, edited by George Richardson, appeared in installments between 1777 and 1779 as *Iconology, or a Collection of Emblematical Figures.*[18] Except for copies of Octavio Van Veen's *Amorum Emblemata* (Antwerp, 1608), and Gabriel Huquier's *Iconologies* (Paris, n.d.), Ripa's was evidently the only emblem book available in the small library of the Royal Academy while Blake studied there.[19] Also the Gravelot *Iconologie par Figures,* which Mario Praz called "the masterpiece of the *genre* for the quality of the workmanship" (p. 201), must have been of particular interest to Blake, because he knew about Gravelot through his own master, Basire.[20] Actually Blake seems to have known and partly to have modelled his *For Children: The Gates of Paradise* and his *Songs of Innocence and of Experience* upon eighteenth-century editions of Francis Quarles's *Emblems* (1635), "modernized" in 1764; John Bunyan's *Book for Boys and Girls* (1686), from 1724 called *Divine Emblems;* and Wynne's *Choice Emblems for the Improvement and Pastime of Youth* (1772).[21] Blake's lyrics, Northrop Frye has suggested, "are in the tradition of the 'emblem books' which used a great deal of the mythological and allegorical material from Christian and Classical sources." ". . . the *Songs of Innocence and Experience* are in the direct tradition of the emblem-books: they are by far the finest emblem-books in English literature."[22]

In this century, moreover, the natural historians, like Buffon and

Introduction

Oliver Goldsmith, in his *History of the Earth, and Animated Nature* (1774), often accepted and perpetuated many of the traditional conventions concerning animals; and Richardson, in turn, seems sometimes to have paraphrased the contemporary naturalists in his *Iconology*. In Blake's day even the popular "science" of physiognomy provided additional justification for traditional animal emblematism. Using the work of Charles Le Brun and the natural historians, especially, Johann Caspar Lavater based his study of physiognomy in part upon animal analogies. Lavater's *Essays on Physiognomy* Blake certainly knew, for he made engravings for the Henry Hunter translation.

More influential than Lavater, Jacob Boehme and Emanuel Swedenborg contributed significantly to Blake's biological symbolism, for in their writings Blake found many of the conventions of biological symbolism justified and, especially in Swedenborg, fully explained. A discussion of these spiritual correspondences Boehme incorporated in his *Mysterium Magnum,* to explain man's Fall:

> Here the Craft and Subtlety of the Serpent was manifest, and the precious Image was corrupted, and became according to the *Limus* of the Earth a *Beast* of all Beasts: Whereupon there are now so many and various Properties in Man; as one a Fox, Wolf, Bear, Lion, Dog, Bull, Cat, Horse, Cock, Toad, Serpent; and, in brief, as Many Kinds of Creatures as are upon the Earth, so many and *various* Properties likewise there are in the earthly Man. . . .
>
> Not that the whole Man is such a [very brute Beast in outward Shape,] but there is such a *Figure* of the Desire in the earthly Essence; and the Man must bear *such* a Beast in the Body, which stirs him up and drives him to the bestial Property; *not* that he has this Form according to the outward [Person,] but *really* in the earthly Essence. . . .
>
> Yet this Beast does somewhat put forth its *Signature* externally in every one; if one does but observe and well mind the same, he may find it: Hence Christ called the Pharisees *a Generation of Vipers, and the Seed of Serpents;* also others he called *Wolves, ravening Wolves, Foxes, Dogs,* and the like; for they were such in the earthly Essence. . . .
>
> For as the Essence is in the Body, so the Spirit figures and *forms* itself internally, and the poor Soul stands in this Prison, bound, and married to such a Beast, unless that a Man be born anew. . . .
> (20.34-37)

His indebtedness to Boehme, Blake himself acknowledged, and it has remained unchallenged. His even greater debt to Swedenborg, at least in his biological symbolism, has not always been fully appreciated, largely because in his *Marriage of Heaven and Hell* (1793) Blake severely attacked some aspects of Swedenborgianism, particularly the apparent predestinarianism and the doctrine of punishment. But his discipleship was not merely an outgrown stage.[23] In *Milton* Blake referred to Swedenborg as "strongest of men, the Samson shorn by the Churches!" (22.50), implying that there was indeed great strength in Swedenborg's ideas even if he had sacrificed himself all too much to conventional religious ideas. Indeed Blake admitted the influence of Swedenborg's system of correspondences in his comments concerning his own *"spiritual Preceptor, an experiment Picture,"* included in *The Descriptive Catalogue* of 1809: "THIS subject is taken from the visions of Emanuel Swedenborg. Universal Theology, . . . No. 623. . . . The works of this visionary are well worthy the attention of Painters and Poets; they are foundations for grand things . . ." (E, p. 546).

Swedenborg maintained that his system of correspondences was not conventional. To the visionary man, at least, in angelic discourse, *"such Things fall into representative Species of Animals; when the Discourse is concerning good Affections, there are exhibited beautiful, tame, and useful Animals . . . as Lambs, Sheep, Kids, She-Goats, Rams, He-Goats, Calves, Heifers, Oxen. . . . But the Discourse of the Angels concerning evil Affections is represented by Beasts of a terrible Appearance, fierce, and useless, as by Tygers, Bears, Wolves, Scorpions, Serpents. . . ."*

> That by Beasts and Animals, in old Time, were signified Affections, and similar Things in Man, may possibly appear strange at this Day; but whereas the Men of old Time viewed Things in a Celestial Idea, and such Things are also represented in the World of Spirits by Animals, and indeed by such Animals as have Resemblance thereto, therefore when they mentioned Beasts and Animals, they had always such a spiritual Meaning: In the Word also, whensoever Beasts are mentioned either in general or in particular, such a spiritual Sense is implied; the whole prophetic Word abounds with this Manner of expressing spiritual Things, insomuch that whosoever is unacquainted with the specific Signification of each particular Beast, cannot possibly understand what the Word containeth in it's internal sense. . . .[24]

So Emanuel Swedenborg warned readers of the Scriptures concerning the animal symbolism there. Few except those of his Church now read the Bible in Swedenborg's manner; but only at the risk of misunderstanding Blake can readers ignore his biological symbolism.

Since all forms of life, except the marine animals, take part in the final reintegration and are thus capable of redemption, I usually ignore their apocalyptic reunion, for their appearance in the new Jerusalem or new Eden in no way nullifies or even modifies their symbolic meaning in the world of Experience. I also ignore those biological images which appear to be merely realistic or decorative. On the other hand I try to examine Blake's usage of all the biological species which frequently appear emblematically in his verse and pictorial art; and I try to illustrate the range of symbolic implications which these species suggest and to provide examples from several periods. I give special attention to those examples in the illuminated canon which present difficulties of interpretation and which the understanding of the biological symbolism helps to clarify; but I also draw from Blake's designs for the Bible, the plays of Shakespeare, and the poems of Dante, Milton, Gray, Young, and Hayley, especially when the examples do more than merely illustrate the text and when they provide additional insight into the biological symbolism.

My arbitrary distribution of the various biological species into nine divisions does not attempt to follow modern scientific analysis or even the biological classifications of Linné. It approximates, rather, the classifications of popular eighteenth century scientists like Oliver Goldsmith, who placed both worm and spider under the general rubric of insect, and follows even more Blake's own iconographic practice. Blake, like Goldsmith, surely knew that the bat is a mammal, but iconographically it seems closer to the owl than to any of its kindred mammals.

Chapter Two

The Carnivorous Beasts

In the world of Experience all Blake's carnivorous animals are, or soon become, aspects of fallen, malevolent man. Since some of them — the ounce, the leopard, and the bear — appear rarely and usually only in conjunction with and ancillary to the important ones, we will concentrate upon the major beasts: the tiger, the wolf, its cousin the dog, the lion, and the apocryphal Behemoth.

From classical literature to Blake's own day the tiger had been singled out to symbolize ferocity and cruelty, for example, in Medea, the tigress who slays her own children. The emblematists exhibited the beast as the epitome of ferocity.[1] In Shakespeare it symbolizes cruelty or inhuman savagery. Of the unrelenting Coriolanus, Agrippa says, "There is no more mercy in him than there is milk in a male tiger." The Duke of York accuses the "She-wolf of France," Queen Margaret, a "tiger's heart wrapp'd in a woman's hide!": "you are more inhuman, more inexorable, / O, ten times more, than tigers of Hyrcania."[2] In *King Lear* the shocked Albany sees Goneril and Regan as "Tygers, not daughters" (IV.ii.40). Blake remembered this passage, for in his *Tiriel* the aged hero twice addresses his sons as "Serpents not sons" (1.21, 4.63). In *The Faerie Queene,* according to A. F. Marotti, "the tiger prefigures the force that despoils the pastoral world and is an indication of an evil which may erupt both in man and in the world in which man lives."[3] Milton could have contributed to Blake's tiger symbolism; for in *Paradise Lost* Satan becomes briefly a tiger; and the tiger (or the ounce) of *Comus* appears in the Huntington version of Blake's *Comus with his Revellers* (B, Pl. 616).[4] Pope and Cowper coupled the tiger with the wolf; and Cowper in his "Table Talk" deplored "the savage thirst a tyger feels."[5] In his *Deserted Village* Goldsmith envisioned the terrors which awaited Oglethorpe's emigrants in the savannahs of Georgia, "Where crouching tigers" (doubtless cougars) "wait their hapless prey."[6]

Even in the novels of Fielding and Smollett the malignant tiger is still a familiar symbol.

Buffon saw the tiger's unslakable thirst for blood as a raging fever: "as blood only augments their thirst, they have often occasion for water, to cool the fervour which consumes them." For Buffon, "the tiger is grossly ferocious, and cruel, without necessity. . . . The tiger . . . though satiated with carnage, seems to be perpetually thirsting for blood. . . . He seizes and tears to pieces a fresh animal with the same rage that he exerted in devouring the first." The tiger exhibits "marks of ignoble malice and insatiable cruelty. He has no instinct but perpetual rage, a blind and undistinguishing ferocity, which often impells him to devour his own young, and tear in pieces their mother, when she attempts to defend them." "They delight in blood, and glut themselves with it till they are intoxicated. They tear the body for no other purpose than to plunge their head into it, and to drink large draughts of blood, the sources of which are generally exhausted before their thirst is appeased."[7] As a naturalist, Goldsmith agreed that the tiger is "fierce without provocation, and cruel without necessity." "In falling in among a flock or an herd, it gives no quarter, but levels all with indiscriminate cruelty, and scarce finds time to appease its appetite while intent upon satisfying the malignity of its nature." Among wild animals it alone is untamable: "'The caresses of the keeper have no influence upon their heart of iron; and time, instead of mollifying its disposition, only serves to encrease its fierceness and malignity.'"[8] In his *Narrative of a Five Year's Expedition against the Revolted Negroes of Surinam* (London, 1796), Blake's friend John G. Stedman, for whose book Blake engraved many of the author's designs, challenged Buffon's assertion that America had no tigers by describing the jaguar and the cougar, or "red tyger," and the *"tiger cat."* According to Stedman, the jaguars "tear and mangle" sheep and goats and even women and children "only for the sake of the blood, with which this ferocious animal is never glutted." ". . . its savage nature, and thirst after blood, is such that it cannot be tamed: it will, on the contrary, bite the very hand that feeds it, and very often devours its own offspring. . . ." The cougar and tiger-cat are "equally ferocious."[9]

In developing his tiger symbol, Blake may well have been influenced also by Lavater: "In the eyes and muzzle of the tiger, what an expression of perfidy! what sanguinary rage! The head of a victorious tiger furnishes the emblem of Satan triumphing over a fallen Saint." Lavater went on to remark on the delight which the cat, like the tiger, finds in tormenting its victim: "They are with respect to birds and mice what the tiger is to sheep; and they even surpass him in cruelty, from the pleasure they take in prolonging the sufferings of their victim" (II, 110). Probably Lavater's emphasis upon the physiognomatic significance of the teeth of the crocodile and the eyes and snout of the tiger and the general practice among physiognomists and natural historians to avoid prominent display of the tiger's fangs in their illustrations led Blake to make his Tyger inadequately ferocious to satisfy some of his commentators. In the quite similar head of the tiger engraved for Holcroft's translation of Lavater, the mouth is closed.[10] "Eyes red and globular," Lavater noted, "whose corners are prominent and lengthened, a large and flat nose, the immediate connexion there is between the nose and the throat, and particularly the line of the latter, all bear an animal and ferocious character" (II, 115).

Swedenborg had pointed out the symbolic significance of the snout which characterizes Blake's tigers: "The natural Man, who is become sensual by Evils and consequent Falses, in the spiritual World in the Light of Heaven does not appear as a Man, but as a Monster, also with a Nose retracted . . . because the Nose corresponds to the Perception of Truth: He also cannot bear a Ray of heavenly Light . . . but what is like that of a Coal-fire."[11] Such suggestions Blake may well have remembered in Tirzah's account of the embodiment of man in *The Four Zoas:* "These nostrils that Expanded with delight in morning skies / I have bent downward with lead molten in my roaring furnaces" (105.36-37). In *Jerusalem* Erin laments "The Nostrils, bent down to the earth & clos'd with senseless flesh. / That odours cannot them expand, nor joy on them exult . . ." (49.38-39).

In one of the paradoxical "Proverbs of Hell" Blake wrote, "The tygers of wrath are wiser than the horses of instruction"; in another, "The wrath of the lion is the wisdom of God" (*MHH* 9.44; 8.24). The tigers and lions of wrath are being true to their natures; the horses of instruction, which Blake evidently associated with Swift's emotionally controlled and rational Houyhnhnms, are not. Throughout this work Blake defended the passions from the attacks of extreme rationalism and championed them as necessary for full life and vision. But though he paradoxically overemphasized this then disparaged aspect of man's personality, he did not advocate, here or anywhere else, the abdication of reason in favor of man's complete domination by the passions, and certainly not by wrath. Occasionally the tiger appears again as an emblem of wrath. But in this fallen world of Experience Blake's tigers almost always symbolize cruel rapacity or the Selfhood. Nowhere short of the apocalypse, where all animals regain their pristine Innocence, do they suggest the noble or divine qualities which some critics see in the Tyger of *Songs of Experience.*

Blake's tigers of wrath he developed more fully in *Europe* and *The Book of Ahania,* and their cruelty becomes even more apparent there. In *Europe,* when Orc finally bursts out in all his fury in France as the Revolution, his passions do not reawaken to vision, but initiate corporeal war characterized by wrath, cruelty, and bloodshed: "The Lions lash their wrathful tails!/ The Tigers couch upon the prey & suck the ruddy tide . . ." (15.6-7). Similarly, in *Ahania,* published after the Reign of Terror and the rise and fall of Robespierre, Blake dramatized through Fuzon the fate of thwarted passions and employed the tiger as a symbol of tyrannizing emotions. Here Fuzon appears as a Moses figure offering to lead his people from the domination of repressive reason; but like his Biblical and French counterparts,[12] he degenerates as soon as he attempts to set up his own tyranny of the passions devoid of reason and imagination:

> While Fuzon his tygers unloosing
> Thought Urizen slain by his wrath.
> I am God. said he, eldest of things!
>
> (3.36-38)

As the immediate death of Fuzon at the hands of Urizen suggests, isolated wrath brings not the return of vision, but the cruelty of the tiger and eventually makes way for an even more repressive tyranny. One recalls from *The Prelude* Wordsworth's view of Paris after the September massacres:" "defenseless / As a fear-haunted wood where Tygers roam."[13] The transition from the tigers of wrath to the tigers of malicious cruelty is inevitable. Blake's first tiger, in "Samson," is linked with the wolf to suggest cruelty. Dalila, in an effort to elicit

Samson's secret, accuses him of being more cruel than the wild beasts, as "'worse than wolves and tygers'" (*E,* p. 444). In "Night" Blake again linked the tiger with the wolf as bloodthirsty beasts, emphasizing their cruelty by opposing to them the Redeemed lion, which in "New worlds" guards "o'er the fold" (*E,* p. 14).

Like the tigers of "Night," which "howl for prey," Blake's subsequent tigers are, except for the apocalyptical tigers, predacious and cruel. Particularly vicious are those of the Selfhood. In *Tiriel* Ijim sees his brother Tiriel successively as a "dreadful lion," a tiger, a cloud "Fraught with the swords of lightning," a serpent, a toad or newt, a rock, and a "poisonous shrub" (4.49-59). Blake may have had in mind here the metamorphosis of Proteus in the *Odyssey* and Satan's similar series of disguises in *Paradise Lost* IV.396-408, 800-14. But as Northrop Frye has pointed out (pp. 242-43), the passage certainly derives in part from Swedenborg's *True Christian Religion.* There a remarkably similar list of noxious animals suggests the disguises of the Selfhood:

> It is in Consequence of this Love, that the various Lusts thereof appear in Hell, at a Distance, like various Kinds of wild Beasts; some like Foxes and Leopards; some like Wolves and Tygers; and some like Crocodiles and venomous Serpents; and that the Desarts where they live consist solely of huge Heaps of Stone, or of barren Sand, with Bogs interspersed, full of croaking Frogs; and that dismal Birds fly, and make a mournful Skreeking over their miserable Abodes. These are the Ochim, Tziim, and Jiim [sic], mentioned in the Prophecies of the Old Testament, where the Love of Dominion arising from the Love of Self is spoken of.[14]

Although Ijim has fallen, he can still recognize hypocrisy, "the corruption by which visionless self assumes masks of ever-increasing meanness and ends as a rock or a poisonous shrub."[15] Like other wild beasts, the tiger thus symbolizes the cruelty caused from domination by the fallen, degraded Self, of which Tiriel, blind and visionless, is a striking embodiment. In the tiger we see not only the cruelty of nature and man, but the malignant and stupid Selfhood.

In the light of the tiger of tradition and of Blake's earlier and subsequent tigers, a reading of "The Tyger" reveals it as the shocked and fascinated reaction of an observer imaginatively visualizing the creation of brutal cruelty in nature and in man.[16] This interpretation is confirmed in the visual design of the poem, the preliminary drafts, the symbolism of the Tyger's contrary — the Lamb — and the implications of the forging process.

In the visual design there is not a single redemptive or hopeful detail. (See Fig. 2.) Here the Tyger is an ugly and foolish-looking beast. The brutal muzzle, with vestigial nose (to indicate spiritual insensitivity) and tiny ears, is tightly joined to a thick-set body and placed in a setting of rank or dead vegetation. An ominously dead or dry tree at the right has markings similar to those of the Tyger and is in some copies similarly colored. Weeds provide the only flourishing vegetation. The Tyger is headed left, the direction recognized as sinister by our Biblical and linguistic heritage and by artistic convention. Indeed, according to Erwin Panofsky, "the strongest of these symbolical laws . . . was the positive nature of the right and the negative nature of the left."[17] The sinister-flying eagle at the top left has already become in Blake a malignant symbol of oppression. Moreover, though not actually a part of the visual design, properly symbolic is the Tyger's natural habitat, the dark forest. For us to see him plain, Blake has brought him into a clearing. But like the owl and the bat, the beast prefers the solitude and the darkness of "the forests of the night," an emblem of his blind stupidity and selfishness.

Some have found the Tyger an "artistic failure."[18] The temptation to ignore or explain away the design is understandable: having come to know the poem originally through the verses only, most of us have visualized the Tyger as embodying "fearful symmetry." Blake could have made the visual image of the Tyger one of fearful symmetry. He did in fact endow with bared fangs the tiger which in 1802 he drew and engraved for William Hayley's "The Elephant" (*CGW*, Pl. 388). But it has the same stupid and ugly profile as does the Tyger. In his *Fall of Man* (*B*, Pl. 869) Blake created a terrifying, Stubbsian tiger and a vulture to illustrate the brutalization of the animals in *Paradise Lost* XI.185-89. Since evidently Blake thought that Milton's lion and eagle alone were symbolically too ambivalent to exemplify man's, or even nature's degeneration, he added the bestial tiger and vulture so that the brutalization would be unmistakable. For his Tyger, however, Blake did not show us the animal's frightening fangs and claws. He wanted us to look at the beast — and at ourselves in the state of Experience — and to see it and ourselves not only as fearful, but as ugly and stupid. That we may at times be terrifying, we are ready to admit; but that we are ever as ugly and stupid as this beast, we will seize upon any pretext to deny.

This interpretation is reinforced by the imagery of the verse and by the drafts of the poem. In the verse two aspects of the creature are unmistakable: its symmetry and its horror. It is "burning bright," and twice its "symmetry" is pointed out. Pictorially considered, the Tyger is "burning bright" because it catches some gleams of light and, more obviously, because its luminous eyes provide a brilliant contrast to the surrounding gloom. About this same time, Blake in his *Visions of the Daughters of Albion* linked "the glowing tyger" (8.5) with other denizens of the dark — the owl and the bat — all of which will be "blotted" by the dawn of the spiritual imagination. Since Blake and his London readers had seen cats and perhaps even tigers enough, this realistic aspect of the tiger demands no literary source; but Goldsmith, borrowing from Buffon, had commented on this practical feature of the feline eye: "In the eyes of cats . . . this contraction and dilatation of the pupil, is so considerable, that the pupil, which by day-light appears narrow and small, like the black of ones nail, by night expands over the whole surface of the eye-ball, and, as every one must have seen, their eyes seem on fire. . . . the animal is thus better adapted for spying out and surprising its prey" (III, 205-06). Swedenborg had commented upon the similarity of the owl and the cat here, "whose Eyes appear like Flame in the Night-time, in Consequence of their burning Appetite for Prey."[19]

Concerning this feature of his Tyger Blake was specific in his Notebook, where he clearly implied in the gleam, the cruelty and the fury of the Tyger — in "The cruel fire of thine eyes" and "thy eyes of fury."[20] This gleam no more assures redemptive force than do the various fires flickering in the murky depths of Dante's Inferno or the fires without light in Milton's Hell. The gleam suggests damnation rather than salvation. Here the traditional story of the naive — or imaginative? — freshman who thought the Tyger on fire is more apt than amusing: the Tyger is on fire from its thirst for blood, as the naturalists pointed out, and raging from its own malice, symbolizing the wrath of nature red in tooth and claw and of raging, fallen man.

No more favorable symbolism for the nature of the Tyger than the gleam is its "fearful symmetry." The tiger as an embodiment of the sublime Blake found in an aesthetic treatise which he read in his youth and clearly remembered even if he did not admire — Edmund Burke's *The Origin of our Ideas of the Sublime and Beautiful* (1757). Burke selected the tiger as an exhibit of the sublime because he is not only strong, but "pernicious": "the sublime . . . comes upon us in the gloomy forest, and in the howling wilderness, in the form of the lion, the tiger, the panther."[21] Although Buffon had commented upon the disproportion of the tiger (*NH,* V, 155), Goldsmith emphasized instead the irony of its beauty:

> "THE antients had a saying, *That as the peacock is the most beautiful among birds, so is the tiger among quadrupedes.* In fact, no quadrupede can be more beautiful than this animal; the glossy smoothness of his hair, which . . . shines with greater brightness than even that of the leopard; the extreme blackness of the streaks with which he is marked, and the bright yellow colour of the ground which they diversify, at once strike the beholder. To this beauty of colouring is added an extremely elegant form. . . . Unhappily, however, this animal's disposition is as mischievous as its form is admirable, as if Providence was willing to shew the small value of beauty, by bestowing it on the most noxious of quadrupedes." (III, 233-34)

But more important than the Tyger's "fearful symmetry" are its "deadly terrors." More detail about the fearful nature of the Tyger exists in Blake's Notebook, where the questioner exhibits the cruelty and fury of the Tyger in "The cruel fire of thine eyes" and asks,

> What dread hand & what dread feet
>
> Could fetch it from the furnace deep
> And in thy horrid ribs dare steep
> In the well of sanguine woe
> In what clay & in what mould
> Were thy eyes of fury rolld. . . .
>
> (p. N. 109 transcript)

The details "horrid ribs," the "eyes of fury," and "well of sanguine woe" leave no doubt that Blake conceived the Tyger not as a redemptive force but a fascinating and horrible symbol of death and destruction. Probably for this reason Blake rejected the penultimate line above: clay and mould suggest a yielding, fruitful unselfishness inconsistent with the hardness and selfishness of the Tyger.

Blake critics who see redemptive qualities in the Tyger should heed Fuseli's remark that "since both lamb and tiger may dwell in human frames, he surely deserves our thanks, who points them out to us before we wound the one or sink beneath the other."[22] The lamb is opposed to the tiger in the poem itself: "Did he who made the Lamb make thee?" (E, p. 25), the observer asks. Since in *Songs of Innocence* Blake had already employed the lamb to symbolize Innocence and unselfishness in nature and in man, the question here posed in "The Tyger" reminds us that now we see its opposite.

Another helpful insight into the nature of the Tyger is the process by which he is created: the imbrutement. The shaping of the Tyger parallels in part Blake's myths of the Fall in *The First Book of Urizen* and *The Book of Los*. But there Los is engaged not only in giving shape and form, but in preparing the avenues into eternity without which fallen man would be self-enclosed. The nearest and aptest parallel of the imbrutement in "The Tyger" Blake etched as "A Divine Image." There Los, or an unhappy demiurge, is hammering into shape a sun with brutalized human features:

> Cruelty has a Human Heart
> And Jealousy a Human Face
> Terror, the Human Form Divine
> And Secrecy, the Human Dress
>
> The Human Dress, is forged Iron
> The Human Form, a fiery Forge.
> The Human Face, a Furnace seal'd
> The Human Heart, its hungry Gorge. (E, p. 32)

Just as the Tyger has its contrary in the Lamb of Innocence, so this ironic "A Divine Image" of Experience has its contrary in "The Divine Image" of *Songs of Innocence*. In "A Divine Image" the furnace and the forge symbols suggest imbruted man, just as they do in "The Tyger." No such symbols are associated with the Lamb or with "The Divine Image," which characterize either a state of Innocence before the fall into the imbruted body, or an imaginative redemption. As Northrop Frye remarked in *Fearful Symmetry*,

> The clearest symbol of the natural body, life imprisoned in death, is the furnace or kiln . . . in which the heat of energy is confined in an abstract husk with its light shut out. This image of the furnace or prison of lightless heat is the core of the orthodox conception of hell, which traditionally has heat without light, and it exactly fits the eternal torment of life in the Selfhood, "the being shut up in the possession of corporeal desires which shortly weary the man," which is Blake's hell. As the natural man is born in this kind of furnace, he is born in hell. . . . (p. 288)

Frye's remarks concerning the fallen world apply equally as well to the Tyger or to "A Divine Image."

Moreover Blake's first important critic, Swinburne, saw the Tyger as evil embodied: "the very stars, and all the armed children of heaven, the 'helmed cherubim' that guide and the 'sworded seraphim' that guard their several planets, wept for pity and fear at sight of this new force of monstrous matter seen in the deepest night as a fire of menace to man. . . ."[23] Swinburne perceived, as many subsequent critics have not, Blake's indebtedness in his "Tyger" to *Paradise Lost;* and his view of the beast may well reflect not only his own perception, but that of someone quite close to Blake himself, like Linnell, whom Swinburne knew.

Like the Tyger, Blake's subsequent tigers also exemplify man in the grip of the Selfhood — malevolent and stupid.[24] The traditional contrary of the lamb, however, is the wolf, "the typical destroyer."[25] In the Bible the wolf often appears as a false teacher or prophet. In the emblem books and Goltzius the wolf (often batwinged in Goltzius) suggests also gluttony, avarice, theft, and cruelty.[26] The poets frequently employed the wolf, a traditional aversion of the sheep-breeding English, to suggest ravenous, insatiable greed or envy, often pairing it with the savage tiger. In Spenser's pageant at the court of Queen Lucifera "malicious *Enuie* rode, / Vpon a rauenous wolfe."[27] Milton used a lupine form for one of the bestial shapes to which the companions of Comus are altered by their lust and gluttony:

>   their human count'nance
> Th' express resemblance of the gods, is chang'd
> Into sum brutish form of Woolf, or Bear,
> Or ounce, or Tiger, Hog, or bearded Goat. . . . (ll. 68-71)

The lupine head appears in both the Huntington and the Boston Museum versions of Blake's *Comus with his Revellers* (B, Pls. 616, 624). Milton also used the beast to characterize false, sectarian teachers and Satan himself.[28] In "Autumn" Pope had Aegon accuse Love, "Wolves gave thee suck, and savage Tygers fed" (l. 90); and in his "Bard" Gray used the wolf to characterize the murderess Isabel as the "She-wolf of France."[29] Cowper pleaded for "just restraint" to "Chain up the wolves and tigers of mankind" and mourned "the pride / And av'rice that makes man a wolf to man."[30] With such views the naturalists fully agreed;[31] and Lavater found in the wolf "a character ferocious, passionate, treacherous, and sanguinary" (II, 111). The wolf, Boehme remarked, is "a churlish Dog, crafty, fierce, and greedy" (*Three Principles* 16.21). According to Swedenborg, a wolf signifies "the Avidity of seizing" and "those who are against Innocence" (*AC*, Par. 6441, 3994). "Spiritual hypocrites," especially, walk "like wolves" (*TCR*, Par. 381).

Blake used the wolf in this conventional fashion to suggest gluttony, cruelty, hypocrisy, jealousy, and envy, but developed it particularly as a symbol of rapacious empire and the Selfhood.[32] In annotating Lavater's *Aphorisms* (1789) he used the traditional Biblical contrast to characterize the hireling shepherd: "Hipocrisy. is as distant from superstition. as the wolf from the lamb" (*E*, p. 591). And in annotating Francis Bacon's *Essays* several years later, he indignantly rejected one of Bacon's aristocratic pronouncements concerning clergymen: "What Shepherds does he mean Such as Christ describes by Ravening Wolves[?]" (*E*, p. 624). In *Milton* the poet castigates those

> Whose pretence to knowledge is Envy, whose whole Science is
> To destroy the wisdom of ages to gratify ravenous Envy;
> That rages round him like a Wolf day & night without rest[.]
>   (41.16-18)

In "The Mental Traveller" the "Labyrinths of wayward Love" evidently include jealousy, for there the wolf roams (*E*, p. 485). In *Jerusalem* the wolf helps to complete the animal pattern of jealousy, blindness, and selfishness, here qualities of the Shadow: "behold ye the Jealous Wife / The Eagle & the Wolf & Monkey & Owl & the King & Priest were there" (94.26-27).

Just before the Chorus of "A Song of Liberty," which closes *The Marriage of Heaven and Hell*, Blake adopted the wolf as a symbol of ruthless empire to accompany the hitherto ambivalent lion: "Empire is no more! and now the lion & wolf shall cease" (*E*, p. 44). For the same purpose, in *America* he used the identical line (6.15). In *Jerusalem* he used the wolf to emblematize the Selfhood: there the Spectre of Los pants over him "like a frighted wolf, and howling," "A horrible Shadow of Death" (7.1, 4). As the natural enemy of the lamb, the wolf is fittingly employed as a symbol of the Selfhood, the Spectre warring upon the divine human imagination.

Toward the wolf's cousin the dog, a carnivore long tamed, but still a carnivore, a sentimental attitude gradually prevailed in the eighteenth century. The shepherd's loyal companion had always been approved, and in the emblem books the dog became a symbol of fidelity, obedience, memory, and humanity.[33] In Pope's *Essay on Man* the poor Indian expects that in Heaven "His faithful dog shall bear him company" (I.111); and Goldsmith, paraphrasing Buffon (*NH*, IV, 3-4), maintained that the dog gives us "a lesson of courage, temperance, and fidelity" (III, 274). While Blake was working for Hayley, he included the valiant and loyal dog in designs for two poems in Hayley's *Ballads* — "The Dog and the Crocodile" and "The Dog defending his Dead Master from the Vultures," where the new master, the Hermit, insists that Hero is not his servant: "'A noble, independent friend,/ He deigns to live with me!'"[34] Blake's dog is sometimes a realistic component in a pastoral scene, accompanying the piper.[35] Certainly Blake was sensitive to the animal: "A dog starvd at his Masters Gate / Predicts the ruin of the State." "The Beggers Dog & Widows Cat / Feed them & thou wilt grow fat" (*E*, pp. 490, 491). Urizen prefers to feel sentimental pity: when the dog howls "at the wintry door" "he wept, & he called it Pity" (*Urizen* 25.2-3). In the following plate a pathetic child with clasped hands and a supine dog vainly beg for shelter at a closed door.

In previous centuries, however, the dog seemed little better than the wolf. In the Bible he is almost invariably hateful and contemptible, usually as street dog and scavenger. Isaiah, for example, characterized Jehovah's lazy or false prophets as "dumb dogs . . . sleeping, lying down, loving to slumber" (56.10). The Psalmist envisioned his enemies as dogs "bellowing with their mouths, and snarling with their lips" (59.6-7). Dante, in his *Inferno*, presented his gluttons as dogs. In Goltzius and in some of the emblem books dogs appear as symbols of envy, greed, gluttony, and lust.[36] For the dog the major English poets had few kind words. Chaucer had none.[37] Spenser gave a canine body both to his Blatant Beast (the "hellish Dog") and to the monster Gerioneo: "The body of a dog she had, / Full of fell rauin and fierce greedinesse" (*FQ* VI.vi.12.2; V.xi.24.1 2). In *Titus Andronicus* the villain Aaron ironically agrees with his accusers that he is like "a black dog" (V.i.122); and in *King Lear* Regan and Goneril become for the plain-spoken Kent "dog-hearted daughters" (IV.iii.45). In *Paradise Lost* the only dogs are the spawn of Sin and Death, "these Dogs of Hell" (X.616), and these Blake depicted vividly (*B*, Pls. 108, 633, 646). For Isaac Watts, dogs continued to furnish object lessons:

> LET dogs delight to bark and bite,
> For God hath made them so. . . .
> If we had been ducks we might dabble in mud,
> Or dogs, we might play till it ended in blood,
> So foul and so fierce are their natures.[38]

Satan sometimes appears, Boehme maintained, as a snarling dog; and man is "often like a Dog, snappish, envious, malicious." "Now if thou hast had an envious [spiteful] dogged Mind, and hast grudged every Thing to others, as a Dog does with a Bone which himself cannot eat, then there appears such a doggish Mind . . ." (*Three Principles* 16.21, 45). For Swedenborg the dog represented "the lowest of all." "Dogs in the spiritual World appear from those who have indulged their Appetite and Palate . . ." (*AC*, Par. 84; *AR*, Par. 952).

Blake's dogs also suggest stupidity, greed, insincerity, violence, or lust. In Dante's *Purgatory*, for the fraudulent Cianni Schicchi, Blake in his Design 59 invented a canine head.[39] He also used the dog as an emblem of stupidity. Oothoon asks ironically of Urizen, ". . . wilt thou take the ape / For thy councellor? or the dog, for a schoolmaster to thy children?" (*VDA* 5.8-9); and in *The Four Zoas* Enion admits that she has chosen "the dog / For a schoolmaster to my children" (35.3-4).[40]

In the most complicated symbol of folly and selfishness masquerading as widsom, a Cerberean Urizen (see Fig. 3) opposes the return of Milton to the world of Death to free his Emanation, Ololon. Here the dragon-bodied monster has a canine head as well as a chicken head with forked tongue, with a third head only partly glimpsed behind the trunk of a tree. Doubtless the Cerberean figure symbolizes in part the materialistic, Egyptian worship of nature in the canine headed Anubis, a possibility strengthened by the fact that in one touched proof copy of the title page of *Europe* (B, Pl. 372), where the serpent of materialism dominates the page, Anubis is seated upon one of its coils.[41] An analogous myth suggested in Figure 3, a myth still quite popular in the art and music of the century, is that of Orpheus, an earlier poet who, confronting Cerberus, seeks to enter the world of Death to redeem his Emanation. In his Dante illustrations Blake devoted two of his designs to Cerberus, for the monster there too opposes a journey which ultimately reunites Dante with his Emanation, Beatrice. Other myths are also implicit in this motif — those of Hercules subduing both Cerberus and the hydra of Lerna, the many-headed dragon whose heads in the various editions of Ovid are usually canine. This conflict was adapted in some of the emblem books, like Boudoin's (Pl. 73), to symbolize the battle between virtue, as a weaponless strong man, and a hydra vice. Earlier in *Milton* Blake had linked himself with Hercules just as he identified Milton with Samson and with himself, for Los deplores

> Lambeth ruin'd and given
> To the detestable Gods of Priam, to Apollo: and at the Asylum
> Given to Hercules, who labour in Tirzahs Looms for bread [.]
> (25.48-50)

For Blake lived at 13 Hercules Buildings in Lambeth from 1790 until 1800, when he moved to Felpham.

Often in Blake the dog is vicious, sometimes a hellhound of destruction. In *Night Thoughts,* to denigrate the brutally strong — "Their Arts, and Conquests, *Animals* might boast" (see Fig. 4) — Blake depicted a wolfish dog tearing a supine man while another man scrambles desperately up a tree in order to escape.[42] The scene is doubtless modelled in part upon the popular artistic depiction of Actaeon torn by his own dogs when he is changed into a stag, in *Metamorphoses,* Book XIV. In this fallen world man's energies are not creative, but are occupied in war and hunting. Hounds bred to the pursuit of man and thus, like the warhorse and the elephant, perverted, are linked with Nimrod, the evil king of war, pursuit, and oppression. For Young's line "Till *Death,* that mighty Hunter, earths them all" Blake exhibited Death wearing a spiked crown and brandishing his spear while one of his dogs springs at the throat of a helpless man, and others, hair bristling and fangs ready, prepare to join (I, *NT* 117). When Tiriel invokes the earthquake as a curse, Blake must have had such hellhounds in mind, as well as Cerberus: "let his fiery dogs / Rise from the center belching flames & roarings" (5.6-7). The same symbol in *The Four Zoas* heralds the resurgence of the Satanic Orc:

> As when the Earthquake rouzes from his den his shoulders huge
> Appear above the crumb[l]*ing Mountain. Silence waits around him
> A moment then astounding horror belches from the Center
> The fiery dogs arise[.] (91.6-9; *E,* p. 363)

The similarity between Orc and the earthquake at this point makes a significant statement about him: he is not the redemptive, apocalyptical force he at first appeared to be. His wrath is mere rage which, like the power of the earthquake, brings only destruction. The hounds of Nimrod also appear in *Jerusalem:*

> Great is the cry of the Hounds of Nimrod along the Valley
> Of Vision, they scent the odor of War in the Valley of Vision.
> All Love is lost! terror succeeds & Hatred instead of Love. . . .
> (22.8-10)

The dog suggests also a usually degraded aspect of sexuality, particularly as the dogs of Leutha. From primitive times to the present the dog has symbolized lust, from the Anubis cult in Egypt and the use of the term in Deuteronomy 23.18 down to the term "bitch" in our own. In some of the emblem books lust is presented in animal heads in which that of the dog is prominent; and perhaps Milton had this emblem in mind in the hell-hounds which inhabit the womb of their mother, Sin. In his Design 59 for Dante, Blake invented a canine head for Myrrha, who lusted for her father; and in his own *Judgment of Paris (B,* Pl. 964), probably borrowing from Marcantonio Raimondi's engraving of Raphael's *Judgment of Paris,*

Blake included a dog, his collar marked "Paris," to reinforce the suggestion that Venus is seducing Paris by lust. In *Visions of the Daughters of Albion* Leutha appears as the healthy spirit of sexuality: it is her marigold — the acceptance of sex — which Oothoon plucks on her way to meet Theotormon. In *Europe* Leutha has evidently degenerated: Enitharmon addresses her as her "lureing bird of Eden!" as "Sweet smiling pestilence!" (14.9,12). Her role there seems to be that of the alluring female sexuality which tempts man and then snares him in a web of "Female Will," or nature. Then in *Milton* Leutha appears as the daughter-consort of Satan, springing from her parent's breast in the way in which Sin springs from Satan's head in *Paradise Lost*. In her own accounts of events, Satan, "in selfish holiness demanding purity" (12.46), has cast her out as Sin. Thus she seems to be the spirit of female sexuality which the prudish, conventional morality of Satan or the Spectre regards as "impure."

Her dogs make a final appearance with Los in *Jerusalem:* "With him went down the Dogs of Leutha, at his feet / They lap the water of the trembling Thames then follow swift" (83.82-83). These sexual passions can destroy their masters when they represent aspects of Orc, or of Satan — aspects of fallen Luvah — of love turned to hate or perverted to lust. When controlled by Los, the divine imagination, however, they are healthy, rather than degrading. The passage above comes just after the conversion of the Daughters of Albion from complete selfishness to an unselfish devotion to their children, so that an acceptance of Leutha's sexuality would here be especially appropriate, for sexuality is now playing a creative role in the reintegrated life.

If the growing humanitarian attitude toward animals gradually changed the symbolic meaning of the dog, the lion offered a traditional symbolic ambivalence; for from times remote the lion had suggested destructiveness on the one hand and fearlessness, protectivity, and magnanimity on the other. In Scripture his qualities can be either royal power, courage, or cruelty.[43] In I Peter the Devil appears as "a roaring lion" (5.8),[44] yet in Revelation Christ is the "Lion of the Tribe of Juda" (5.5). In Ezekiel 1.10 and Revelation 4.7, finally, the lion is one of the four beasts, or zoas, the emblem, subsequently, of St. Mark. At the outset of Dante's *Inferno* we meet him as a symbol of pride or ambition, or so Cary identified him;

and so Blake probably intended to suggest in his Designs 1 and 3. In iconographic convention the lion's skin is a far more reliable emblem than is the lion himself, for his skin suggests courage; but the lion can be, on the one hand, a symbol of justice, magnanimity, clemency, and generosity, or on the other hand, of anger, fury, pride, or even revenge, for he is "remarkable for returning injuries."[45]

In England particularly the lion exhibited this ambivalence. As an emblem of protective magnanimity, he was emblazoned on the royal coat of arms, impaled there by Richard I. Some of the favorable symbolism in English poetry and art was doubtless prompted by this heraldic convention. There is ample courage, but apparently no magnanimity, only fierceness, in Chaucer's lions.[46] The heraldic usage appears, however, in *The Faerie Queen* (V.ix.33.4; V.ix.27,9); and it doubtless prompted Spenser to create the protective lion which guards Una when she is deserted by the Redcrosse Knight and which accompanies her in Blake's *Characters in Spenser's 'Faerie Queene'* (B, Pl. 879). Yet throughout *The Faerie Queene*, A. F. Marotti asserts, except for Una's protector, "Spenser uses lion similes to indicate that a character is acting in a wrathful or animal manner";[47] and in the procession of the Seven Deadly Sins "fierce reuenging *Wrath*" rides upon a lion (*FQ* I.iv.33.1). In Shakespeare also this duality appears. In *Twelfth Night* Olivia remarks, "how much the better / To fall before the lion than the wolf!" (III.i.128-29). Yet as Henry VI comments of regal ambitions, "Whiles lions war and battle for their dens, / Poor harmless lambs abide their enmity."[48]

In Milton's symbolism the lion loses this emblematic ambivalence and becomes uniformly malignant. In *Samson Agonistes* the hero tears the lion "as the Lion tears the Kid" (l. 128). In *Paradise Lost,* while stalking his prey, Satan assumes as his first animal disguise the appearance of a lion; and as the first visible demonstration of the fall of the world of nature, the now savage lion pursues the hind (IV.402; XI.187-89), a scene which Blake depicted in *The Ghost of Abel*. In *Paradise Regained* the lion is coupled with the "fierce" tiger. (I.313).

Most of the naturalists praised the lion. Brookes did not: he regarded his small brain as an indication of "want of wit and judgment" and "a cruel disposition."[49] Buffon thought the lion magnanimous (*NH,* V. 69); and Lavater thought that the prominent nose indicated intellectual capabilities (II, 110). According to Boehme, however, in his *Three Principles,* the sinful mind "stands in the Figure of a Serpent, Wolf, Lion, Dragon, or Toad" (19.48). Man is often like "a Lion, stern, cruel, sturdy and active in devouring of his Prey" (16.21). For Swedenborg the lion was, again, an ambivalent symbol: ". . . by a lion is signified divine truth, wherefore the Lord is also called a lion in the Word; hence, in the opposite sense, a lion signifies the infernal false as to the power of destroying divine truth, and thus the Word, which is especially done by falsifications and adulterations thereof; and whereas a lion is the most powerful of all animals, and his power increaseth according to his appetite for devouring, and thus of seizing his prey and tearing it in pieces, therefore by a lion is also signified the lust of destroying the truths of the Word."[50]

In Blake's earliest poetry the lion is occasionally an ennobling emblem. In "King Edward the Third" the Prince is a "young lion" (iii.26); and the minstrel sings, to inspire the soldiers, "Your ancestors came from the fires of Troy, / (Like lions rouz'd by light'ning from their dens . . .)" (vi.7-8). In the redeemed world of Higher Innocence, the lion especially suggested for Blake the qualities of generosity and magnanimity. Thus in "The Little Girl Lost" and "The Little Girl Found," which were etched for and at first included in *Songs of Innocence,* the kingly lion, "A spirit arm'd in gold," represents a state of Higher Innocence:

> On his head a crown
> On his shoulders down,
> Flow'd his golden hair.   (E, p. 22)

In this poem Lyca, the antitype of Thel, willingly encounters the wild animals of her adolescent and adult passions, particularly of her sexual nature, and finds that they can be unselfish and creative. (See Figs. 5 and 6.) The embracing of the lovers at the right of the first plate is replaced by the entwined elms in the same position on the last — an emblem of enduring love. Leopards and tigers play a limited part in the action and none in the designs for the poem. The lioness conveys Lyca to the lion's palace, and the lion reassures her parents. In the plates we see only the protective lion and lioness, together in the final plate, as Lyca sleeps, her nude children playing around them. In the second plate the lioness, alone, lifts her long nose to indicate, as Lavater and Swedenborg suggested, spiritual sensitivity. Here the lions of Higher Innocence suggest the passions creatively utilized, not an afterlife after Lyca, and presumably her parents also, have met their deaths, for her three children would then be virtually inexplicable.

Even in Blake's very earliest poetry, however, the lion occasionally suggested merciless cruelty: in "Samson" Dalila accuses the obdurate Samson, "'a lioness suckled thee'" (*E,* p. 443). After *The Marriage of Heaven and Hell,* moreover, the lion is in Blake's world of Experience never the protector of the lamb against the wolf; both are his devourers. Blake thus early adopted the malignant leonine symbolism of Milton and Boehme. In order to show that his lions of Experience are indeed malignant, Blake frequently coupled the marauding wolf with the lion, especially when he wished to suggest the selfish passions of domination, of empire. In *The French Revolution* the Governor of the Tower "stalk'd like a lion from tower / To tower," "Panting over the prisoners like a wolf gorg'd" (ll. 21-22, 26). In *Tiriel,* as John Beer has suggested, "Ijim's description of himself as a lion establishes him as the highest form of selfhood . . ." (p. 65). In *Europe* Blake only slightly modified the symbolism for the advent of the revolutionary terror in France, substituting malicious tiger for malicious wolf: "The Lions lash their wrathful tails! / The Tigers couch upon the prey & suck the ruddy tide . . ." (15.6-7). Though Rintrah is again given his lions, they and he have degenerated. "O lion Rintrah," Enitharmon invokes, in her role as Female Will and nature, "raise thy fury from thy forests black" (8.2). Since Rintrah, "furious king," has divided from his Emanation and is therefore dominated by his Spectre, fallen Rintrah's lions of his black forests represent the stupid, malicious, predatory passions, especially the terrors of empire. Both brutal lion and tiger illustrate Young's line "In quenchless *Passions* violent to crave" (I, *NT*246). In *Christ's Troubled Dream* (*B,* Pl. 691), for the *Paradise Regained* series, the lion at the lower right suggests the temptations of empire, its brutality reinforced by the tiger at the left and the accompanying serpents.

In *The Four Zoas,* except in the final, apocalyptical Night, Urizen's lions again symbolize man's fallen or misdirected energies. These lions, or energies, degenerate after Urizen usurps dominion over the other Zoas and after he, like Rintrah, forgets his Emanation, who is now "distant far" (16.17). As Urizen begins to construct the Mundane Shell, his various beasts — lions, leopards, "tygers of wrath," and "horses of instruction" — stand "round Urizen prince of Light / Petrifying all the Human Imagination into rock & sand" (25.3, 5-6). At this moment Albion "gave his loud death groan" and "the stars of heaven Fled" (25.9, 12), just as in "The Tyger" they relinquish their protective spears and weep at the advent of the Selfhood. Here in *The Four Zoas* the visionless reason, degraded to abstract science and allied with wrath, petrifies the sublime Humanity. When the cold, calculating reason enlists and falls prey to the malevolent and cruel emotions characterized by the wild beasts particularly associated with the fallen Luvah, or Orc, then the human imagination becomes a spiritual wasteland where no vision can exist. Ahania pleads with Urizen to resume his "fields of Light," for now the intoxicated "steeds of light," she says, "call thy lions to the fields of blood, they rowze thy tygers / Out of the halls of justice" (39.1, 3, 8-9). Similarly when Orc is first bound down with the chain of jealousy, he still retains potentialities of creative life, symbolized by tame animals. However, as he begins to vegetate upon the rock the innocent animals disappear, and only the predatory beasts and brutalized horses remain: "fierce his lions / Howl in the burning dens his tygers roam in the redounding smoke . . ." (77.8-9). In the visionless wrath of the Spectrous Orc, Urizen's horses, which originally drew the chariot of light, have maddened into warhorses among the raging tigers and lions of Orc's den.

These brutalized animals represent another aspect of the Selfhood: man bestialized in his fallen senses. As Albion degenerates deeper into Selfhood and the bestial qualities take more control, he loses his visionary capability and becomes increasingly locked up in the cavern of his fallen senses. Exploring his dens or caverns of the fallen world, Urizen encounters his "Children ruind in his ruind world." Earlier, in *Urizen,* we see him as he begins this journey. (See Fig. 7.) The lion, headed left, with brutal snout, shaggy mane, and downcast, uncomprehending eyes, is no more visually terrifying than the Tyger. Neither master nor beast seems to recognize the other, and the lion even seems unaware of his master's presence. Here the lion suggests "vast enormities," "Dread terrors! delighting in blood" (23.2, 7) which annoy Urizen as he explores his fallen world with his fallen sun. But here again, as with his Tyger, Blake has revealed the terror in the verse; the beast's stupidity, in the design. In *The Four Zoas* the verse reveals both aspects of the Selfhood:

> Then he beheld the forms of tygers & of Lions dishumanizd men
> Many in serpents & in worms stretchd out enormous length
> Over the sullen mould & slimy tracks obstruct his way
> Drawn out from deep to deep woven by ribbd
> And scaled monsters or armd in iron shell or shell of brass
> ....
> His voice to them was but an inarticulate thunder for their Ears
> Were heavy & dull & their eyes & nostrils closed up[.]
>
> (70.31-40)

In contrast Urizen appropriately recalls the lion and lamb of organized, or internal Innocence,

> in Climes of happy Eternity
> Where the lamb replies to the infant voice & the lion to the man of
>   years
> Giving them sweet instructions. . . .
>
> (71.5-7)

These Spectres, or Selfhoods refuse to expand their senses and rise from Ulro, the abyss of the merely sensuous:

> The eyelids expansive as morning & the Ears
> As a golden ascent winding round to the heavens of heavens
> Within the dark horrors of the Abysses lion or tyger or scorpion
> For every one opend within into Eternity at will
> But they refusd because their outward forms were in the
>   Abyss. . . .
>
> (73.37-74.2)

To these wild beasts let us add the apocryphal embodiment of the wild beast incarnate, Behemoth. What the Biblical model may have been is not clear:[51] the elephant, some thought, including Swedenborg, but more likely the hippopotamus, as Blake represented him in his *Job*. Behemoth was the Biblical embodiment of animal power

(Job 40.15-24). For the emblematists, the hippopotamus was malevolent enough and certainly carnivorous: "he devours his father," Richardson informed us, "from a desire to cohabit with his mother."[52] Lavater wrote, "The throat of the Sea-horse is a profound and horrible gulph, formed only to crush and swallow" (II, 126). For Swedenborg, Behemoth represented "the natural man as to good" (*AE*, Par. 455).

In presenting *The Spiritual Form of Pitt Guiding Behemoth* (B, Pl. 877), painted in 1809 and exhibited in 1812, Blake was probably deliberately ambiguous.[53] He explicated somewhat disingenuously, in Addisonian terms, that Pitt *"is that Angel who, pleased to perform the Almighty's orders, rides on the whirlwind, directing the storms of war: He is ordering the Reaper to reap the Vine of the Earth, and the Plowman to plow up the Cities and Towers"* (E, p. 530). Knowing how Blake used the term "Angels" in *America*, we can easily read "The Almighty" here as George III and perceive Pitt's pleasure in holocaust. In the painting the shape of the beast, patently a carnivore, is somewhat obscured by the deterioration caused evidently by dampness and subsequent attempts at restoration. But the transparent upper part of the beast, filled with human bodies, hardly seems like that of a hippopotamus; and the head looks quite similar to that of an engraved monster which Blake might have seen in the Library of the Royal Academy, in a scene where Esione is being delivered by Hercules from a sea monster.[54]

Just what Blake really meant by his Behemoth, however, is clear in *Jerusalem*, where the Spectre, defying Los, "builded stupendous Works,"

> forming Leviathan
> And Behemoth: the War by Sea enormous & the War
> By Land astounding: erecting pillars in the deepest Hell,
> To reach the heavenly arches. . . .
>
> (91.32, 38-41)

Here no creative forces are implied, only destructive, selfish ones. When later Blake engraved Behemoth and Leviathan on Plate 15 of his *Job* (see Fig. 8), he engraved in the margin, following Job 40.19, that Behemoth is "the chief of the ways of God." The irony of this description is apparent from Blake's previous use of the beast and from the massive and stupid animal which he engraved in *Job*. Resembling here Dürer's famous woodcut *Rhinocerus*, Behemoth represents not intellectual warfare, but corporeal; not creative energy or imagination, but the stupid Selfhood. This muscle-bound animal is given virtual plate armor to suggest not only imperviousness to attack, but also to sensation and thought. Like the Tyger, but perhaps even more stupid, he represents the ultimate Selfhood.

Chapter Three

The Herbivorous Animals

The herbivorous animals often dominate the scene in *Songs of Innocence* and appear frequently and significantly throughout Blake's work. Some of them, especially the members of the flock and herd, generally symbolize man in a state of childish innocence or of childlike, imaginative creativity. Others, like the goat, suggest aspects of fallen man.

Among these herbivores, sheep and lamb are the most innocent, as iconographic convention had long established. From the very advent of pastoral poetry, sheep and lambs have symbolized simple childish innocence, meekness, patience, purity, Christ, and the Christlike principle of self-sacrifice. Most of this pattern was doubtless set by the Bible.[1] Christ himself adopted the allied symbol: "I am the good shepherd: the good shepherd giveth his life for the sheep" (John 10.11). In the emblem books, art, and poetry the lamb was "the established symbol of innocence" and suggested also humility, purity, and patience.[2] This symbolic convention was reinforced for Blake by Boehme and Swedenborg. In *Three Principles of the Divine Essence* Boehme warned that the Christian "is a Sheep, in the Midst among Wolves, and must be in the Form and Mind of a Sheep, and not of a Wolf" (20.3). In one of his "Gates" in his *Threefold Life of Man* he directed the Christian, "If you Light off" the Beast "and pull off your Dressing, and go in the form of a *Child* to the *Lamb,* then you may catch it, it goeth willingly with you, if you play like a child with it in simplicity." ". . . incline your ear to the *voice* of the Lamb, go forth from your outward Man, into the Inward Man, and so you *shall come* to your true Native Country, *into Paradise*" (6.15, 16). Such a passage surely contributed to the symbolism in Blake's "The Lamb" and "Spring," for there the child hears the voice of the lamb, takes off his dress, and plays with the lamb in simplicity. For Swedenborg also sheep signified "they who are endowed with Charity" (*AC,* Par. 294): "when the lamb is named or read of in the Word, then the angels . . . perceive the good of innocence, and when the Lord is thus called, they perceive his divine human [principle], and at the same time the good of innocence which is from him" (*AE*, Par. 314).

From his earliest poetry Blake used sheep and lambs, in traditional fashion, to suggest innocence.[3] In *Songs of Innocence* sheep and lambs help to establish a pastoral setting which includes Christlike as well as simple Innocence. At the very outset, the child requests the Piper, "Pipe a song about a Lamb" (*E*, p. 7). Child, lamb, and Christ are clearly identified in "The Lamb":

> He is called by thy name,
> For he calls himself a Lamb:
> He is meek & he is mild,
> He became a little child:
> I a child & thou a lamb,
> We are called by his name. (*E*, p. 9)

In "The Shepherd" the role of the shepherd is not only protective, but sacramental. (See Fig. 9.)

> He shall follow his sheep all the day
> And his tongue shall be filled with praise.
>
> For he hears the lambs innocent call,
> And he hears the ewes tender reply. . . . (p. 7)

The paradisaical nature of the scene is provided in the design by the flock of sheep and their shepherd and by the overarching, flourishing tree, around which twines the honeysuckle, emblem of innocence and plenty. The bird of paradise, always a sign of promise, flies up and to the right; three other birds fly in the distance; and two songbirds, perhaps doves, rest on a limb below them. The peaceful attitudes of the sheep and the glances of several towards their shepherd show their trust; and his downward glance here suggests his concern for them, though ordinarily, as Swedenborg remarked, "the real rational Man . . . is spiritual or celestial when he looketh upwards, but merely animal when he looketh downwards" (*AC*, Par. 1702). In the comparatively neglected "Spring" some of the details suggest an even higher form of innocence than do those in "The Lamb." There (see Fig. 10) the boy is usually, though not always nude, has pulled off his "Dressing," but though a glance unites the boy and one of the lambs, he holds himself apart from and above them. In "Spring" the union is far more intimate, for as sheep and two angels watch and approve, the nude child embraces and kisses — unites with the lamb amid the budding "*Spring Grass.*"[4]

Sheep and shepherds reappear in *Thel, America, The Song of Los,* the designs for *Night Thoughts,*[5] *The Four Zoas,* and *Jerusalem,* but as reminders of a prelapsarian Innocence or as a hope for an apocalypse. On Plate 7 of *America* (see Fig. 11) the naked children, the protective ram, the rainbow colors of the sunrise from behind them, the overarching, protective flowering birch, the birds of paradise, the butterfly, the other, distant birds — all the symbolic details combine to suggest an almost paradisaical world of Innocence. But the guardian ram, which should be alert, and the children still sleep, a minatory fallen oak leaf appears at bottom right, and the grapevine seems to be trying to entwine itself rather than the nearby birch. Despite the reinforcing butterflies, the sheep and shepherd on Plate 3 of *The Song of Los* give little reason for optimism, for they are threatened by a lizard and a sinister boa-constrictor and are also evidently asleep, spiritually as well as physically. The verses as well as the design treat of the degeneration of man. In *The Four Zoas* Los laments "those blessed fields/ Where memory wishes to repose among the flocks of Tharmas" (34.39-40). Similarly, bemoaning his division from Enion, Tharmas recalls a time when she in "Eternal fields in comfort wanderd with my flocks" (51.21). Jerusalem also looks back with longing to the time "Among my lambs & brooks of water, among my warbling birds: / Where we delight in innocence before the face of the Lamb" (*Jerusalem* 20.8-9). Only in the closing moments of the poem does Albion realize that the shepherd embodies the unselfishness of man's Humanity and his divine imagination:

Then Jesus appeared standing by Albion as the Good Shepherd
By the lost Sheep that he hath found & Albion knew that it
Was the Lord the Universal Humanity, & Albion saw his Form
A Man.   (96.3-6)

However, the symbol of Christ the sacrificial lamb often resulted in a major deception, for the symbol was frequently perverted through ignorance, misunderstanding, or wilfulness into its exact opposite — from an example to be emulated into a scapegoat merely requiring recognition and acceptance. Swedenborg warned, "It is believed in the world that the Lord is called a Lamb from this circumstance, that the continual burnt offering . . . was from lambs, and especially on the days of the Passover, when a lamb was also eaten, and that the Lord suffered himself to be crucified: But this reason of his being so called, is only for those in the world, who do not think beyond the sense of the letter of the Word; nevertheless, in heaven no such thing is perceived, when a lamb is predicated of the Lord . . . " (*AE,* Par. 314). In *The Four Zoas,* Rahab, "thinking to destroy the Lamb," "cut off the Mantle of Luvah from/ The Lamb of God." It rolls apart and becomes Satan; and Rahab weaves from it "Her web of Religion."[6] In *Jerusalem* also this scapegoat is worshipped by the degenerate sons of Albion — Hand and Hyle — who are gratified "That the Perfect, / May live in glory, redeem'd by Sacrifice of the Lamb" (18.26-27).

But in his self-sacrifice the Lamb exhibits and encourages emulation of his essential nature:

Then sang the Sons of Eden round the Lamb of God & said
Glory Glory Glory to the holy Lamb of God
Who now beginneth to put off the dark Satanic body [.]
                                                                                  (*FZ,* 104.5-7)

For Blake the lamb suggested not the scapegoat, but the divine creative imagination. This association of the lamb symbol Blake may have intended in his first illuminated work: several sheep appear immediately below the poet's assertion in *All Religions Are One:* "all are alike in the Poetic Genius" (*E,* p. 1). A year later, in the frontispiece to *Songs of Innocence,* the grazing sheep reinforce the presence of the naked, soaring child to suggest the poetic genius of the piper; and in the frontispiece to *Songs of Experience* they all appear together again. Blake's symbol of the lamb as the poetic imagination is perhaps most explicit in the union of Jesus with Jerusalem as that of the Lamb with his Bride, for Jerusalem recognizes Jesus as "the Divine Lamb," "O Human Imagination" (*Jerusalem* 60.50,

57). Later, when the Good Shepherd appears to Albion, "the Divine Appearance was the likeness & similitude of Los" (96.7). The example of Christ the Lamb thus becomes for man the pattern for rejecting this vegetable world of illusion for the eternal world of the imagination.

Not only the scapegoat, but the goat in its other aspects symbolized almost the opposite of the sheep. For centuries the goat had emblematized fertility, lust, or even Satan himself, who in popular imagination and the literature of witchcraft sometimes assumed this form. Both the symbol of the evil goat and the convention of the sinister left and the spiritual right were confirmed when Christ announced that at the Last Judgment he will separate the souls "one from another as a shepherd divideth his sheep from the goats: And he shall set the sheep on his right hand, but the goats on the left" (Matthew 25.32-33). For the emblematists, the artists, the poets, the naturalists, and Swedenborg the goat was a symbol of lust.[7] In the triumphal procession of the Seven Deadly Sins at the Court of Queen Lucifera, "lustful *Lechery*" rides upon a "bearded Gote" (*FQ* I.iv.24.1). Shakespeare used the goat to suggest lust in several plays, but with especial effectiveness in *Othello*.[8] In *Comus* Milton associated goat and hog with predatory animals to suggest the human form debased by lust and gluttony.

Sometimes Blake's goats may be merely goats. According to his *Descriptive Catalogue,* in a lost painting, the goats which strip the ivy leaves from the native girls who board the Missionary ship are, Blake would have us believe, not lustful sailors, but hungry goats (*E*, p. 546). In *The Marriage of Heaven and Hell* Blake paradoxically used the convention of the lustful goat to praise the "sin": "The lust of the goat is the bounty of God" (*E*, p. 36). In this attack upon the characteristic eighteenth century puritanical, Urizenic suspicion of passion, Blake was stressing its essential health. However, Blake's only reference to the lusty goat-man, the satyr, places him with manifestations of fallen Urizen, with the wolf, the tiger, the bear, and the lamia (*FZ* 106.48-107.1). Another passage involving the goat is more complex. In the Notebook Blake recorded a sentimental criticism of Christ: "Jesus does not treat [?all?alike]* because he makes a Wide Distinction between the Sheep & the Goats consequently he is Not Charitable" (*E*, p. 695). Here Blake was not using the symbol paradoxically, but directing his irony toward those who fail to discriminate.

In *The Marriage of Heaven and Hell* he contrasted the prolific and the devourer:

> These two classes of men are always upon earth, & they should be enemies; whoever tries to reconcile them seeks to destroy existence.
> Religion is an endeavour to reconcile the two.
> Note. Jesus Christ did not wish to unite but to seperate them, as in the Parable of sheep and goats! (*E*, p. 40)

Here Blake sounds rather like the predestinarian Swedenborg he was so violently rejecting. These classes he later abandoned for his doctrine of States. He also refined his basic opposition between prolific and devourer atop Plate 3 of *Jerusalem:*

SHEEP   GOATS

Here the sheep, presumably at Christ's right hand, and the goats at his left are no longer the sinless and the sinners, but the sheep who follow Christ the selfless human imagination and the goats who refuse to do so, bound up in the bonds of materialism and the Selfhood.

No member of the flock, the stag appears several times in Blake's designs and occasionally in the verse, sometimes ominously. Although the stag could suggest solitude, purity, and the thirst of the soul for God,[9] Goldsmith observed that when pursued, the stag "tries every artifice to put off some other head for his own" (III, 117); and Wynne made the stag an emblem of false friendship (pp. 59-62). In *Paradise Lost* the stag appears in suspect company, immediately after the malevolent ounce, leopard, and tiger and before Behemoth and the crocodile (VII.466-74). There Milton was following the same tradition as did the German artists who in their representations of Paradise placed the stag among the carnivores (Tervarent, col. 67). In his *Adam Naming the Beasts* (*B*, Pl. 890), similarly, Blake placed the stag at Adam's left, with the lion and the wolf. The stag is in similar company when in *The Four Zoas* Urizen, "No longer now Erect," arises "in his pride," "Calling the Lion & the Tyger the horse & the wild Stag / The Elephant the wolf the Bear the Lamia the Satyr" (106.41, 43, 48-107.1). Moreover, as Erdman has suggested, the two stags on Plates 8 and 22 of *The Marriage of Heaven and Hell* may represent respectively "a base man" and "a jealous king" (*IB*, p. 123). Similarly in "The Mental Traveller" the "Female Babe," the apparently innocent stag, is an emblem of nature, or the Female Will, for the stag was an attribute of Diana (Tervarent, cols. 65-66). It creates thickets and labyrinths infested with the wild beasts of the violent and selfish passions.

After the sheep and lambs, not the stag, but the cattle, particularly the ox and the bull, provided Blake with symbols for the innocent and constructive qualities in man. The patience of the ox was proverbial. Moreover it adores the Christ child in partically every Nativity. The winged calf or ox was also the emblem of St. Luke, and Blake apparently adopted it for Luvah in the second title page for his illustrated *Genesis* (*B*, Pl. 975). The emblematists, poets, and natural scientists used the ox to suggest work, patience, humility, and suffering.[10]

The presence of sheep and cattle clarifies the meaning of the much debated "Clod and the Pebble," of *Songs of Experience* (see Fig. 12):

> Love seeketh not Itself to please,
> Nor for itself hath any care;
> But for another gives its ease,
> And builds a Heaven in Hells despair.
>
> > So sang a little Clod of Clay,
> > Trodden with the cattles feet:
> > But a Pebble of the brook,
> > Warbled out these metres meet.
>
> Love seeketh only Self to please,
> To bind another to Its delight;
> Joys in anothers loss of ease,
> And builds a Hell in Heavens despite, (*E*, p. 19)

Since both views receive precisely equal time, many are tempted to think that Blake meant these views to be contraries of love, equally true and equally necessary, even though Blake told us throughout his poetry and art that he rejected the pebble's view. But the frequently ignored symbolism of the design makes this poem quite clear. The upper part, affirming unselfish love, is given almost three times the space afforded to the selfish view; and it is exemplified not only by the cattle mentioned in the verses, which are in Blake usually emblems of fertility and patience, but by families from the flock, which, like the clod itself, are emblems of innocence and self-sacrifice. The willow above them suggests suffering. The inferior view, at the foot of the page, is associated with a worm and two coldblooded frogs, which in the eighteenth-century view were a type of virulent reptile, as we shall see in Chapter Seven. The vine-like water plant shows no blossoms.

Blake's inspiration for the poem may well have been John Bunyan's "Upon the Flint in the Water," in his *Divine Emblems*. Here the flint has the same imperviousness as Blake's pebble:

> This Flint, time out of mind, has there abode,
> Where Chrystal Streams make their continual Road;
> Yet it abides a Flint as much as 'twere,
> Before it touch'd the Water, or came there.
> Its hard obdurateness is not abated,
> 'Tis not at all by Water penetrated.
> Though water hath a softening vertue in't
> This Stone it can't dissolve, 'cause 'tis a Flint:
> Yea though it in the water doth remain;
> It doth it's fiery nature still retain.
> If you oppose it with it's Opposit,
> At you, yea, in your face it's fire 'twill spit.[11]

In the Clod of Clay, Blake has opposed the flint with its opposite. This interpretation of "The Clod and the Pebble" is substantiated both earlier and later in Blake's verse. The Clod of Clay in *The Book of Thel* voices the same view to the unwilling ears of the heroine:

> O beauty of the vales of Har. we live not for ourselves,
> Thou seest me the meanest thing, and so I am indeed;
> My bosom of itself is cold. and of itself is dark,
> But he that loves the lowly, pours his oil upon my head.
>
> (4.10-5.1)

In *Jerusalem* the symbol of the clod of clay is used derisively, but by the selfish Daughters of Albion, so that the symbol is itself not invalidated. They reject the notion that they will ever be anything but pebbles of the brook. They "laugh," "Gwendolen / Is become a Clod of Clay! Merlin is a Worm of the Valley!" (56.27-28). Ironically, the fulfillment of this mockery in their subsequent fruitfulness leads to their redemption and to Albion's reawakening.

Cattle continue to be emblems of patient suffering.[12] Thus in "Auguries of Innocence" Blake singled out the patient ox: "He who the Ox to wrath has movd / Shall never be by Woman lovd" (*E*, p. 490). In *The Four Zoas* fallen man is depicted "moaning in the cattle & in the winds" (110.23); and at the apocalypse "the cattle gather together / Lowing they kneel before the heavens" (118.28-29).

The bull, however, was an ambivalent symbol. It was sometimes an emblem of uncontrolled strength or even violence, as in Psalms 22. 12-13. Shakespeare and Spenser often referred to its power, sometimes as uncontrollable, and occasionally Prince Arthur and his Squire perform like "wylde," "fierce," or "saluage" bulls.[13] In his *Mysterium Magnum* Boehme even named the bull among man's evil natures (20.34). But the bull can also suggest virility, sometimes without the implications of lust which accompany the goat. For example, Dürer used the bull to suggest temperance as well as virility;[14] and Spenser's "fresh *Aprill* full of lustyhed" (*FQ* VII.vii.33.1) rides upon a bull. Lavater usually saw the animal as an emblem of strength and courage (II, 111).

Blake associated the bull with both Luvah, the zoa of emotional and sexual energy, and with Urizen, for reason has its energies as well as does passion. When in *The Four Zoas* Luvah vanishes from the scene, "the plow of ages" is "held in Urizens strong hand / In many a valley, for the Bulls of Luvah dragd the Plow" (28.9-10). However when in *Jerusalem* Urizen is dominated by his Spectre, Satan, in this fallen, abstract state, his energies are impotent. (See Fig. 13.) Here Urizen stupidly concentrates upon the plow, apparently trying to push it mentally. The bulls, his energies, their hair and beards mocking those of their master, look up abstracted and bewildered. Urizen is obviously getting nowhere, for no furrows appear on this still unplowed surface. Without the vision of Los, the instincts of Tharmas, and the passions of Luvah, the coldly analytic and scientific energy of fallen Urizen is unproductive. These attributes he has, however, when at the end of *Jerusalem* he is compelled "to his Furrow" (95.16).

But the bulls of Luvah are in the wrong hands when they are left to Luvah's fallen counterpart, Orc, Satan's alter ego. Before his degeneration, the newly chained Orc still retains some of unfallen Luvah's productivity: "His loins inwove with silken fires are like a furnace fierce / As the strong Bull in summer time when bees sing round the heath" (*FZ* 62.1-2). But after Orc degenerates into sheer wrath, his bulls begin to madden and snort flames in a landscape of hellish fire and marauding tigers: "The bulls of Luvah breathing fire bellow on burning pastures / Round howling Orc . . ." (77.16-17). In the Boston Museum version of *Comus with his Revellers* (B, Pl. 624) Blake even gave a bull's head, to suggest violence and lust, to one of the revellers, though Milton included no such metamorphosis.

Blake occasionally used the ass to suggest humility or dullness, but perhaps the most complex of the herbivorous animals in Blake's symbolism is the horse. For the Psalmist, Goltzius, Aldegrever, and the major English poets, the horse, especially the warhorse, suggested pride or stupidity. The Psalmist warned, "Be ye not as the horse, *or as the mule, which* have no understanding . . ." (32.9). In Goltzius's engraving *Casting Out Evil* the horse is not only clearly marked as pride, but given a headdress of peacock feathers.[15] Chaucer showed no affection or admiration for the horse; and in Shakespeare's *Troilus and Cressida* it suggests stupidity, especially apt for the slow-witted Ajax.[16] In *Paradise Lost* Satan "like a proud Steed reind, went hautie on, / Chaumping his iron curb" (IV.858-59). For Swedenborg the horse was an ambivalent symbol. Horses were attributed to the sun to signify "intellectual Things" from celestial love (*AC*, Par. 4966); yet the horse could also represent "false scientifics which are things imaginary" (*AE*, Par. 654); and the "Captivity of the Horse denotes the intellectual Principle deprived of it's Power" (*AC*, Par. 2799).

Blake's remarks in *A Descriptive Catalogue* show Swedenborg's influence here. Concerning Picture No. 8, "*The spiritual Preceptor, an experiment Picture*," he explained: "THIS subject is taken from the visions of Emanuel Swedenborg. Universal Theology, No. 623. The Learned, who strive to ascend into Heaven by means of learning, appear to Children like dead horses, when repelled by the celestial spheres" (*E*, p. 546). Some details from Swedenborg's vision will help to elucidate Blake's remarks. A teacher explains to the children, "Horse signifieth the Understanding of Truth derived from the Word . . . for when a Man is engaged in meditating on the Word, his Meditation appears at a Distance like a Horse, generous and lively, in Proportion as he meditateth spiritually, but on the contrary wretched and dead, in Proportion as he meditateth materially" (*TCR*, Pars. 623, 624). Picture No. 6, another in Blake's exhibit, seems to have been drawn partly from Swedenborg's equine correspondences. It contrasts Pegasus, the horse of inspiration, with a horse of instruction: "*A Spirit vaulting from a cloud to turn and wind a fiery Pegasus — Shakespeare. The Horse of Intellect is leaping from the cliffs of Memory and Reasoning; it is a barren Rock: it is also called the Barren Waste of Locke and Newton*" (E, p. 546).[17]

Blake's usage of the horse symbol follows that of Swedenborg, but exhibits an even wider range. For he used the horse to suggest the vehicular energies of three of the Zoas: not only fallen Urizen and unfallen Los, but unfallen Urizen and both the unfallen and the fallen Luvah. Although in the early poetry the horses of the sun are not given to Urizen,[18] in *The Four Zoas* the horses of intellectual energy, which Ahania calls "the immortal steeds of light" (39.3), are specifically given to him. He remembers his primitive and proper role as plowman and the rest which Ahania provided, when, as he recalls, "I laid my head in the hot noon after the broken clods / Had wearied me. there I laid my plow & there my horses fed" (43.15-16). In the apocalyptical "Night the Ninth" they again cooperate with Urizen in their proper work.

Though the horses of intellectual energy should suggest a quest for spiritual truth, they frequently represent a debased or depraved form of intellect, sometimes guided by fallen Urizen, sometimes by his surrogate Satan. The horse then becomes the emblem of debased intellectualism — Swedenborg's dead horse of scientifics, or horse "of instruction." When these horses of instruction appear in *The Four Zoas* they are suffering the consequences of the fall and separation of the Zoas:

> The tygers of wrath called the horses of instruction from their mangers
> They unloos'd them & put on the harness of gold & silver & ivory
> In human forms distinct they stood round Urizen prince of Light
> Petrifying all the Human Imagination into rock & sand[.] (25.3-6)

Similar symbolism occurs in *Milton:* when fallen Urizen's surrogate Satan, the spirit of rationalism, mechanism, and conventional morality, assumes control of the horses properly guided by Palamabron, "Palamabrons horses. / Rag'd with thick flames redundant, & the Harrow maddend with fury" (7.43-44). When as a poet Milton allowed his self-righteous spectre Satan, "the reasoning negative," to take over control of the Apollonian horses of creative imagination and the Harrow of Pity, then forgiveness, Blake thought, turned to accusation; for the "Eternal Life" (4.18) of the imagination was then guided by abstract reason.

Also important is Luvah's horse of passion, at first unfallen, but in later myths degraded in his fallen hands or depraved in the warhorses of Orc. The horse of fertility or passion played a prominent role in myth and was known to Jeremiah: "They were *as* fed horses in the morning: every one neighed after his neighbor's wife" (5.8).[19] The horses of the unfallen Luvah appear rarely. In *Thel* the Cloud informs Thel that "our steeds drink of the golden springs / Where Luvah doth renew his horses" (3.7-8). The horse of unrestrained passion appears also where the lily "Revives the milked cow, & tames the fire-breathing steed" (2.10). In *The Marriage of Heaven and Hell* Blake depicted such a horse of passion on Plate 4 above the rejected error "That God will torment Man in Eternity for following his Energies" (*E,* p. 34). On the final plate two large horses, rampant, flank the word "Chorus" and evidently exhibit the advent of unrestrained desire. They remind one of Cowper's horse "That skims the spacious meadow at full speed, / Then stops and snorts" and throws "high his heels" (*The Task* IV. 332-33), or of Buffon's South American horses whose "motions are neither constrained nor measured" and which "wander and frisk about in immense meadows" (*NH,* III, 308).

Just as the sterile coldness of fallen reason petrifies everything it touches, so the fallen, raging emotions, bursting forth in wrath and hatred, craze whatever they touch. The horses of war, particularly, are no better than the horses of instruction; and they are not being true to their natures, either. The horse had long been perverted into the warhorse. The Jews apparently "used the horse only for military riding, and but two instances occur in the Bible of persons without military rank being mounted on horseback."[20] In a passage in Job which Blake ignored in his *Job,* God glorified the warhorse (39.22-

29). Buffon admired the warhorse: "This noble animal . . . seems to feel the glory of victory. . . . He delights in the noise and tumult of arms, and annoys the enemy with resolution and alacrity" (*NH*, III, 306).

This perversion of horse to warhorse, Blake roundly condemned in his "Auguries of Innocence": "He who shall train the Horse to War / Shall never pass the Polar Bar" (*E*, p. 491). In his illustrations for the poems of Gray the warhorses seem particularly cruel. In Design 9 for "The Bard" the warriors battle one another under a red sky upon horses whose hooves help to color the scene symbolically. In Design 7 for "The Fatal Sisters" several warriors are being trampled under the hooves of the sisters' horses, emblems of the will of the cruel sisters and of nature. In the following design (see Fig. 14) the three armed sisters, pointing accusatory hands, are oblivious of the carnage they are wreaking beneath them among the dead and dying, where one warrior is actually biting the ground in his agony. Since the horses, as Buffon maintained, have learned to delight in the noise and carnage of battle, they spurn the dead beneath them and trample the living into death. Design 10 shows similar slaughter.

One of the central themes of *The Four Zoas* is the betrayal of intellectual energy, the horses of Urizen, into the hands of fallen Luvah, love turned to hate. They then become warhorses.[21] Ahania understands the consequences of Urizen's abandonment of his energies, his horses:

> No longer now obedient to thy will thou art compell'd
> To forge the curbs of iron & brass to build the iron mangers
> To feed them with intoxication from the wine presses of Luvah
> Till the Divine Vision & Fruition is quite obliterated[.]
>
> (39.4-7)

In lines repeated in *Jerusalem* (65.47-49), even the "demons of the deep" lament this perversion:

> How ragd the golden horses of Urizen bound to the chariot of Love
> Compelld to leave the plow to the Ox to snuff up the winds of desolation
> To trample the corn fields in boastful neighings.
>
> (93.11-13)

Perhaps the most malignant of these warhorses are those in Plate 35 of *Jerusalem* (see Fig. 15), their malignancy and stupidity suggested by their bat wings. Bestridden by "Satan's Watch-fiends," as the sun sets, "they search numbering every grain / Of sand on Earth" for the Gate of Los (35.1-2). Though we see only one of the watchfiends, the drawn bows of the other two and the bat wings of the other horses appear behind the first.

The elephant Blake saw as another herbivore degraded, like the horse, into an instrument of war and oppression. For the elephant also there existed a disparity of attitude. The emblematists, Thomson, Lavater, and Goldsmith made him a symbol of gratitude, temperance, meekness, humanity, and intelligence.[22] In his *Essay on Man* Alexander Pope found him "half-reas'ning" (I.222). Only once, perforce, did Blake follow this tradition, when he engraved his elephant for William Hayley's ballad honoring the quadruped which "nobly vies / In virtue with mankind" (p. 13). Elsewhere Blake followed the major English poets and some of the naturalists. In Spenser's "Visions of the World's Vanity" the elephant, bedecked with bells and bosses and a tower, "Was puffed vp with passing surquedrie, / And Shortly gan all other beasts to scorne" (8.105-06). In *Troilus and Cressida* the elephant is not only proud, but stupid (I.ii.21; II.iii.2). Beilby deplored, "From time immemorial this animal has been employed either for the purpose of labour, of war, or of ostentatious parade...." "They are likewise made use of as the dreadful instruments of executing condemned criminals — a task which they perform with great dexterity."[23] Such a report on the elephant had already made its way into poetry, for in his "Elephant and the Bookseller" John Gay noted "How they perform the law's decrees, / And save the state the hangman's fees" (I. 46). In *The Four Zoas* the elephant is a subject of fallen Urizen, "King of Pride," along with lion, tiger, "the wolf the Bear the Lamia the Satyr" (107.1). In equally disreputable company, an elephantine reveller appears as an accessory to tyranny in the Boston Museum version of *Comus with the Lady Spellbound* (B, Pl. 628), though Milton did not include the beast in his group of revellers. In *The Marriage of Heaven and Hell* the Urizenic, jealous king falls among warhorses and elephants (25.15). Although the elephant does not appear there in Plate 5, he does in a similar illustration for Young's

Night Thoughts: there an elephant accoutered for battle hurtles downward with a warrior, apparently Lucifer (II, *NT*508).

To descend from the largest land mammal to one of the smallest, we find in the mole a rodent universally used to emblematize blindness. In Isaiah it is linked with the bat as a creature of darkness; and in the emblem books it represents blindness of the mind.[24] Bunyan lamented its preference for darkness: "Poor silly Mole, that thou shouldst love to be, / Where thou, nor Sun, nor Moon, nor Stars can see" (p. 26). Its blindness was frequently contrasted with the keen vision of the eagle.[25] Lavater remarked, for example, "Examine every other eye downward to that of the mole — where will you find that penetrating, firm and rapid glance which seizes the whole horizon at once?" (II, 120). In his "Expostulation" Cowper wrote sarcastically, "The moles and bats in full assembly find, / On special search, the keen-eye'd eagle blind" (ll.630-31). In his *Emblemata* Sambucus also contrasted the two, but his eagle is quite willing to leave unclaimed the domain of the mole:

> *Talpae conniuet Iouis ales, dum videt illam*
>   *Visu priuatem cernere posse nihil:*
> *Non tamen immemor officij est, sublimia pensat,*
>   *Nec se credit humo quin reuolare queat.*[26]

The mole makes an important appearance only twice in Blake, in identical verses used as the motto for *Thel* and repeated in *Visions of the Daughters of Albion:*

> Does the Eagle know what is in the pit?
> Or wilt thou go ask the Mole:
> Can Wisdom be put in a silver rod?
> Or Love in a golden bowl?
>
>   (*Thel* i.1-4)

This contrast is in part later explained by Oothoon: "Does not the eagle scorn the earth & despise the treasures beneath? / But the mole knoweth what is there, & the worm shall tell it thee" (*VDA* 5. 39-40). In using the eagle-mole contrast Blake was thus not contrasting the soul which follows imagination with that which has only Ulro sight, or spiritual blindness. The eagle knows and cares little about what transpires in the pit; the mole does. He lives there, experiencing and suffering what cannot be understood when viewed from afar or measured by such instruments as silver or platinum rod or golden bowl.

But the motto has suggested to many a partly sexual interpretation; and though this view is not substantiated by emblem writers or poets, it may be by the natural historians. In 1693, in his *Synopsis Methodica Animalium Quadrupedum et Serpentini Generis,* John Ray made a few observations about the astounding sexual equipment of the mole; and Buffon quoted the Latin original, elaborated on it, and explained that nature, to recompense the mole for its virtual blindness "has bestowed on it a prodigious proportion of the sixth sense, remarkable vessels and reservoirs, a prodigious quantity of seminal fluid, enormous testicles, a penis of immoderate length." "Of all animals the mole is most amply endowed with generative organs, and consequently with their relative sensations. It has, besides, a delicate sense of touch . . . and a perpetual vigour" (*NH,* IV, 310-11). In his adaptation of Buffon, Goldsmith was content delicately to quote Ray's Latin and to add, "non mihi apparet magnitudinem partium talem voluptatem augere. Maribus enim salacissimis contrarium obtinet" (IV, 93, n.). Thomas Pennant, however, was offended: modestly quoting only the opening remarks of Buffon, he suggested that "To make amends for the dimness of its sight, the mole is amply recompensed, by the great perfection of two other senses, those of hearing and of smelling."[27] Whether or not Blake intended the mole to represent the sexual aspects of Experience, in the dichotomy of the motto the eagle suggests the abstract, rational view of life; the mole exemplifies the emotional.

An omnivore, the swine appears in Blake as wild boar only in "The Mental Traveller," and here only to accompany the wolf and the lion. As domesticated hog, it appears more often in the verse and the designs. An unclean animal forbidden the Jews as food (Leviticus 11.7), it is into the hog that the companions of Odysseus are turned by Circe; and artists and poets like Milton kept the legend alive.[28] The emblematists used the swine to suggest obstinacy, lust, sloth, stupidity, and especially gluttony.[29] In Spenser's procession of the Seven Deadly Sins, Gluttony rides on a "filthie swyne" (*FQ* I.iv.21.2); and Circe's charmed cup and swine reappear in Milton's *Comus* (ll. 52-53). The naturalists and Lavater found the hog, of all the quadrupeds, "the most rude and brutal."[30] In his *Three Principles* Boehme asserted that he had "written nothing for the Swine, and other bestial Men . . . seeing they will bear no angelic Image" (8.15).[31]

To suggest this general depravity and particularly gluttony, Blake in *Night Thoughts* used four or five swine to epitomize Young's line "'For sensual Life *They* best Philosophize . . . '" (II, *NT*309). A swine's head, moreover, crowns a reveller in both the Huntington and the Boston Museum versions of Blake's *Comus with his Revellers* (*B*, Pls. 616, 624). In Design 6 for Gray's "Ode on a Distant Prospect of Eton College" (see Fig. 16) a rooting pig emerges from behind the left thigh of the shadowy figure at the left, to suggest gluttony as one of the "fury passions" (p. 58), though Gray did not mention it. And in the draft of "I Saw a Chapel" the imaginative viewer is so revolted by the desecration of true religion by the state church and the clergy that, like Lemuel Gulliver when he returns to England after residing with the Houyhnhnms, he prefers the company of animals: "I turnd into a sty / And laid me down among the swine" (*E*, p. 468).

Chapter Four

The Granivorous Birds

Just as Blake distinguished sharply between the symbolism of the carnivorous beasts and that of the herbivores, so did he, following traditional iconography, differentiate between that of the birds of prey and the granivorous birds, the songbirds. ". . . intellectual Truths," Swedenborg had suggested, are signified "by the gentle, beautiful, and clean Fowls, but Falses by ravenous, ugly, and unclean Fowls" (*AC,* Par. 866). We can generally assume that when Blake wrote "birds" he meant to indicate songbirds and that a flock of birds on a design is usually a flock of songbirds. In his *Divine Emblems* Bunyan had suggested of flying birds:

> These Birds are Emblems of those men, that shall
> Ere long possess the Heavens, their All in All.
>   They are each of a divers shape, and kind;
> To teach, we of all Nations there shall find.
>
> (p. 52)

Sometimes, as in *The Marriage of Heaven and Hell,* Blake's bird in flight emblematizes aspiration: "No bird soars too high. if he soars with his own wings" (7.15); and for Young's "'Breathing high Hope!'" (II, *NT* 307) Blake depicted several soaring birds. Blake's songbirds frequently suggest happiness. In "Laughing Song" "the painted birds laugh in the shade" (*E,* p. 11). Children, the Little Vagabond feels, would be "as happy as birds in the spring" (*E,* p. 26) if they were better treated by the Church; and in *Visions of the Daughters of Albion* Oothoon invokes the songbirds, "Arise you little glancing wings, and sing your infant joy!" (8.9). Such symbolism, as Erdman suggests, is frequently found also in the designs. On Plate 8 of *The Marriage of Heaven and Hell,* for example, the birds evidently suggest, along with the animals and grapes, "immense joys" (*IB,* p. 105). Moreover, just as the caged bird is frequently a symbol of the imprisoned mind or soul, so the flying songbird was by emblem writers recognized as a symbol of liberty.[1]

The direction of a bird's flight is sometimes, but not always significant. Flight toward the right is far more likely to be optimistic than flight toward the left; but sometimes a descending bird may be needed in a design largely to balance an ascending one. In "Laughing Song" the swallows flying downward both above and below the verses of the poem probably carry no pejorative significance. And on Plate 14 of *Europe* there is no symbolic difference between the two predatory eagles, one rising to secure his prey, the other diving for his. Although in the designs the birds are sometimes too minute for precise identification, we must, however, discriminate, by context as well as by visual detail, between the songbirds and the birds of prey and must understand the traditional symbolism of each important species.

A bird which sang only at his death, the swan was the king of the waterfowl. In the artistic and literary tradition which Blake inherited, the best known swan was that in which the disguised Zeus seduced Leda.[2] This perennial artistic and literary favorite Blake depicted, with batlike wings, on Plate 71 of *Jerusalem,* still purple with passion after his conquest. Apart from the Leda motif, however, the swan was an emblem of good fortune, beauty, sincerity, and purity.[3] For Buffon it was the peaceful monarch of the waterfowl, the contrary of the eagle and vulture: ". . . la violence fit les tyrans, la douce autorité fait les Rois: le lion & le tigre sur la terre, l'aigle & le vautour dans les airs, ne règnent que par la guerre, ne dominent que par l'abus de la force & par la creauté: au lieu que le cygne règne sur les eaux à tous les titres qui fondent un empire de paix, la grandeur, la majesté, la douceur; avec des puissances, des forces, du courage & la volonté de n'en pas abuser. . . ."[4] The swan as an emblem of good fortune Blake evidently used just above the text of the first plate of "The Little Boy Lost," to promise his rescue. Sometimes Blake's swan suggests beauty and purity. Thus Oothoon proclaims the sweetness of

> The new wash'd lamb ting'd with the village smoke & the bright swan
> By the red earth of our immortal river: I bathe my wings.
> And I am white and pure to hover round Theotormons breast.
> (VDA 3.18-20)

The swan also suggests beauty and innocence when Urizen contrasts the beauty of the pristine world of Innocence with the ugliness of the present one: "My fountains once the haunt of Swans now breed the scaly tortoise" (*FZ* 63.28).

Sacred to Apollo and Orpheus, the swan was also an emblem of music and poetry. Even the naturalist Thomas Pennant recognized "the twofold character of the poet, *Vates* and *Poeta*, which the fable of transmigration continue to the bird" (III, 569). Following the models of Plato, Euripides, and Horace in transforming the poet to a swan, in his "Ruins of Time" Spenser portrayed Sir Philip Sidney as "a snowie Swan of heavenly hiew" (l. 590); and Ben Jonson celebrated Shakespeare as the "Sweet swan of Avon!"[5] Cowper, among others, saw Virgil as "the Mantuan swan" ("Table Talk," l. 557). Several times Blake also used the swan as a symbol of poetic genius. On the title page of Gray's poems (see Fig. 17) the poet, accepting his lyre from above, is astride a rising and openmouthed, evidently lyrical swan. This swan is Blake's own contribution here. Nowhere did Gray suggest the swan as a symbol of poetic inspiration; indeed the swan does not appear in Gray's established canon. Instead, in "The Progress of Poetry" he implied in his lines on Pindar that for him the eagle was the bird of genius. Although in *The Marriage of Heaven and Hell* the eagle symbolizes genius and vision, for Blake it came early to suggest the terrors of empire as a bird of prey and was therefore unacceptable to him here as a symbol of poetic inspiration. On Plate 11 of *America* (see Fig. 18) the swan and its rider evidently suggest the prophetic voice of liberty which has been heard in the American Revolution and is now apparently, like Shelley's West Wind, spreading its influence to Europe. The rider, the "scribe of Pensylvania" who "casts his pen upon the earth" (14.15), is doubtless either Franklin, or, more probably, Tom Paine. The direction of the swan is felicitiously to the right, also toward Europe; thus the rider may be looking back at the home which he is temporarily leaving: Franklin represented the American cause in France; and Paine continued to be a voice of liberty in England and France. The spirit of liberty which the thirteen coastal states exhibited seems aptly symbolized by the peaceful monarch of waterfowl and symbol of the poetic imagination. Propitious also are the waxing moon, the swallows, and the serpent of Higher Innocence, now harnessed and ridden toward the right by three nude infants.

The most puzzling of Blake's swans appears on Plate 11 of *Jerusalem*. (See Fig. 19.) Here we may see, as Erdman has suggested, the "androgynous form" of the poet himself, "more than half turned into a snowy swan like Horace" (*IB,* p. 290). But in contrast with the sinisterly swimming Sabrina below, the spirit of the Severn (as we shall see in Chapter Eight), above is Shakespeare as the sweet Swan of Avon, a river which flows into the estuary of Sabrina's Severn. The swan is in iconographic tradition almost invariably benign; and it is travelling right — the spiritual direction which is taken by all three of Blake's swans of poetic genius. The Swan of Avon, the spirit of poetry, is lamenting what he sees as he moves upriver towards Stratford, also toward a willow of sorrow and sterility.

Of the granivorous land birds, the most obvious paradox is the cock. Although his song is limited to his clarion call and his flight is severely restricted, he belongs by nature to the innocent, granivorous group; by training, the imported fighting cock almost belongs among the birds of prey, for not only is he trained to maim and kill, but according to Buffon's English adapter, "he devours greedily . . . both fish and flesh."[6] It is this perverted cock that particularly horrified Blake: "The Game Cock clipd & armd for fight / Does the Rising Sun affright" (*E,* p. 490). In iconographic tradition the native cock was ambivalent: on the one hand he was an emblem of vigilance, diligence, and even wisdom;[7] on the other hand — and in this direction Blake inclined — he symbolized anger, pride, jealousy, and lust.[8] As the shepherd's clock, the clarion of the morn, the cock had been popular with English poets ever since Chaucer's Chantecleer. Lavater, however, thought the English cock "more haughty, more jealous — perhaps also, more passionate" than the eagle (II, 121); and in his *Conjugial Love* Swedenborg held that cocks are jealous "because they are vain-glorious lovers, and the glory of that love cannot endure an equal; that they are vainglorious lovers, above every genus and species of birds, is manifest from their gestures, nods, gait, and tone of voice."[9]

Only once, in "Spring," did Blake make the cock, like the little boy, an emblem of Innocence: "Cock does crow / So do you" (*E,* p. 15). Elsewhere Blake, like Lavater and Swedenborg, made the cock a type of braggart. In "Edward III" Dagworth uses the cock, with obvious irony, to characterize the French braggarts who, he fears, are dismaying the English invaders: "The Lion flees, and fear usurps his heart; / Startled, astonish'd at the clam'rous Cock . . ." (iii. 114-115). The symbol is, of course, especially appropriate because the cock had long been an unofficial national emblem of France. The paradox was a common one among emblem writers: Sir Thomas Browne reported that the lion's fear of the cock "is related by many, and believed by most."[10] In his Notebook, Blake wrote, apparently concerning Robert Cromek, "He is a Cock would / And would be a Cock if he could" (*E*, p. 503). In *Milton* Theotormon and Sotha frighten the yet unborn Spectres into accepting human forms by first creating for their reception "the crested Cock." Terrified at this bird of battle, "the Spectre screams & rushes in fear into their Net" (28.24, 25). Moreover one of the revellers seated by the Lady in the Huntington version of *Comus with the Lady Spellbound* (*B*, Pl. 620), where Blake replaced Milton's animal metamorphoses with avian ones, looks like a cock, doubtless as a symbol of lust.

Like the gamecock an importation from the East, the peacock early became a major emblem for pride. Although as the bird of Juno it occasionally suggested sheer beauty or marital bliss, it generally betokened vanity and arrogance. For Chaucer it was an emblem of pride; and Spenser had Queen Lucifera drawn by "faire Pecocks, that excell in pride" (*FQ* I.iv. 17.8). Shakespeare used the peacock to mock the arrogant stride of a haughty Ajax or Talbot. "'Fly pride,' says the peacock," warns Dromio of Syracuse.[11] Cowper also found the bird unbearable: "The self-applauding bird, the peacock, see — / Mark what a sumptuous pharisee is he!" ("Truth," ll. 58-59). Goldsmith objected not only to its "horrid scream," but its pride, fickleness, lust, and gluttony (V, 171, 174). In his *Mysterium Magnum* Boehme commented that man's bestial self "exalts itself . . . as a proud Peacock" (21.12); and the designs and comments of Dionysius Freher featured the peacock as an emblem of pride, directly opposed to the heavenly dove.[12]

A casual examination of Blake's peacocks might lead the unwary to believe that Blake rejected this whole pejorative tradition. With the paradoxical irony that characterizes *The Marriage of Heaven and Hell* Blake took the traditional pride of the peacock and there made a cardinal sin into a virtue: "The pride of the peacock is the glory of God" (*E*, p. 36). But nowhere else in Experience does such a view characterize the peacock. When in *The Four Zoas* "the far beaming Peacock waited on the fragrant wind / To bring her [Vala] fruits of sweet delight from trees of richest wonders" we have a return of the Golden Age, when all beasts regain their innocent natures and "the Strong Lion deignd in his mouth to wear the golden bit" (94.51-52, 50).

In *Jerusalem,* however, the peacock appears as the traditional emblem of pride. (See Fig. 20.) In emblematic tradition a wreath or fan of peacock feathers serves to suggest pride as well as does the bird itself. Such a wreath and fan appear in Blake's sketch entitled by Butlin *Enitharmon as Iris* (*B,* Pl. 795). Here in *Jerusalem* Albion is tormented as his head is crushed by a coiling serpent from which extrude peacock feathers. The constricting serpent is surely the brazen serpent of the Selfhood. The peacock feathers represent the pride and insolence conventionally assigned to the bird. Here Albion is a parody of the true Christ, whom we see nailed to the Cross and crowned with thorns on Plate 76. Albion is not being tortured, despite his protruding tongue. He is tormenting himself. Both his hands, as Blake takes special pains to make us see, are free, free to tear the serpent and the peacock feathers from his head. But he is possessed by his own Selfhood. From the use of the peacock here, we can be sure that on Plate 2 of *Job* the peacock in the left margin is an emblem of Job's pride. It warns us not to trust the apparent serenity of the lower part of the scene.

A third Eastern importation important in Blake's symbolism, a bird which rivalled or even sometimes exceeded the peacock in beauty, is the bird of paradise. Except in the *Emblemata* (1566) of Joannes Sambucus, the bird of paradise was practically ignored by the poets and the emblematists.[13] It was quite popular, however, with the natural historians; and for Goldsmith birds of paradise were "God's birds, as being superior to all others that he has made" (V, 260). Swedenborg placed it with the dove "in the spiritual World, where there are also seen Birds of every Genus and Species, in Heaven such as are most beautiful, Birds of Paradise, Turtle Doves and Pigeons" (*AR,* Par. 757). In *Divine Love* he suggested that "some have thought the spiritual Principle to be like a Bird which flieth above the Air in the Aether where the Eye-sight doth not reach, when nevertheless it is like a Bird of Paradise" (Par. 374).

Although Blake mentioned the bird of paradise only once, it appears, always with its Swedenborgian implications, fairly often in his designs. Probably it was only at some museum or in the plates of some natural historian like George Edwards that Blake could have seen anything of this exotic bird, which had a voice both "loud and harsh."[14] Otherwise he might not have, at least twice, shown it singing. But for Blake the bird of paradise was a songbird. With its gorgeous colors and its long, bifurcated tail, it appears from *Songs of Innocence* through *Jerusalem*. Two beautiful birds of paradise, with impossibly elongated but graceful necks, fly towards each other in an Edenic scene in the Huntington version of *Raphael Warns Adam and Eve* (B, Pl. 637); and another appears above in *The Creation of Eve* (B, Pl. 512). In *Songs of Innocence* that in "On Another's Sorrow" flying left alongside the verses "He doth give his joy to all. / He becomes an infant small" (E, p. 17) helps to suggest a paradise in this world when Christ and men relieve suffering and share in others' joy. Perhaps Blake felt that since the dove traditionally emblematized the Holy Ghost or God's love for the Son, he needed a different symbol for such a human assurance. The bird of paradise suggests a paradise of Higher Innocence in "The Little Girl Lost" (see Fig. 5): "In futurity / I prophetic see" "the desert wild / Become a garden mild" (E, p. 20). Here Lyca helps the reader to anticipate her own attainment of this Higher Innocence by pointing to the ascending bird of paradise. At the optimistic final stanza of "The Little Vagabond" Blake added a bird of paradise; and even for the chill "A Little Girl Lost" birds of paradise flank the opening lines to reassure us that for *"Children of the future Age"* (E, p. 29) love will not be thought a crime. On Plate 48 of *Jerusalem* the bird of paradise accompanies the reassurance which in their despondence Erin offers to the Daughters of Beulah; and in Plate 79, just before the peripety, grapes and a bird of paradise singing an annunciation give assurance of a new birth. In his nonce use of the bird in his verse, in *Europe*, Blake seems to suggest that, like the peacock, the bird of paradise can be also an emblem of vanity or of sexual seductivity. There Enitharmon asks,

> Where is my lureing bird of Eden! Leutha silent love!
> Leutha, the many coloured bow delights upon thy wings:
> Soft soul of flowers Leutha!
> Sweet smiling pestilence! I see thy blushing light. . . .
>
> (14.9-12)

But Blake's usage of the bird of paradise remained constant: it is Enitharmon here who distorts the symbol.

In addition to these Eastern importations, Blake's important granivorous birds include several native songsters: the sparrow, the swallow, the robin and the wren, the goldfinch, the pigeon and the dove, the nightingale, and the lark. All embody various aspects of Innocence. Of all these English songbirds, the sparrow is supposedly the least melodious; and traditionally it has not been highly regarded, especially in America. In England, however, the numerous varieties include such songsters as the "hedge," or "house" sparrow, or sparrow finch. Indeed it is difficult to be sure just what bird any particular "sparrow" designated in Blake's day. Brookes discussed more than a score of varieties. Goldsmith had no separate discussion of the sparrow, but included among the "sparrow kind" the bullfinch, goldfinch, and linnet. The English adapter of Buffon lumped practically all the English songbirds under this label, including as sparrows even the robin, nightingale, and lark.[15]

In Psalms the sparrow is linked with the swallow: "Yea, the sparrow hath found an house, and the swallow a nest for herself . . . at thy altars, O LORD of Hosts . . ." (84.3). Perhaps Christ remembered this Psalm when he used the sparrow as an emblem of God's concern for the lowly: "Are not two sparrows sold for a farthing? and one of them shall not fall on the ground without your Father" (Matthew 10.29). Shakespeare recalled this saying in three of his plays.[16] For Richardson the sparrow suggested solitude, loquacity, and passing friendship.[17] Though the accepted avian symbol of lust was the partridge, for some of the poets and naturalists the sparrow implied lasciviousness or infidelity;[18] and today the rhyme "sparrow / arrow" seems automatically to evoke sexual implications, even though these did not become clear to us before Freud. In "The Death and Burial of Cock Robin" the sparrow is, from his very name, perhaps, the shooter of the arrow; but the arrow there is a lethal weapon, not a sex symbol. If any of Blake's sparrows are Freudian symbols, they are, I believe, those in "The Fairy." There the fairy invokes the sparrows as an audience, however, to advocate not sexual fulfillment, but chastity and the repression of sex. In contrast with the sorrowing robin in "The Blossom" the loquacious sparrow is a "Merry Merry Sparrow," representing happiness just as most songbirds do in Blake, and meriting the notice of the "blossom" child just as it had won the concern of Christ himself.

In his Notebook, however, Blake varied the Biblical association of sparrow with swallow in a quite novel fashion for an attack upon a favorite target, Sir Isaac Newton: "Reason and Newton they are quite two things / For so the Swallow & the Sparrow sings" (E, p. 501). Here the sparrow, like Newton, evidently sings natural truth, or scientific fact. Blake evidently gave this role to the sparrow because Vincent Bourne had in his "Sparrows Self-Domesticated in Trinity College, Cambridge," given the sparrows a home not at the altar of God, but "Beneath the celebrated dome / Where once Sir Isaac had his home," as Cowper translated the poem, in 1799. It was first published by Hayley in 1803, while Blake was assisting with the edition.[19]

Unlike the sparrow, but like the bird of paradise, the swallow has a forked tail and is in some of Blake's plates virtually indistinguishable from the more glamorous bird. Like the sparrow, the swallow sometimes appears in the emblem books as a symbol of inconstant friendship and solitude, and sometimes as an emblem of justice.[20] Occasionally, as in Spenser, Shakespeare, Pope, and once in Blake, she is merely a bird swift in flight. But renowned in classical legend as Procne, the sister of the nightingale Philomela, and popular as the joyous prophet of summer, the melodious swallow seems to have been a universal favourite. According to Herbert Friedmann, the barn swallow was, next to the goldfinch, "the bird most frequently depicted in early paintings of the Madonna and Child," and "the bird most intimately bound up with the theme of Resurrection."[21] In his *Divine Emblems* Bunyan praised her:

> This pretty Bird, oh! how she flies and sings!
> But could she do so if she had not Wings?
> Her Wings, bespeak my Faith, her Songs my Peace;
> When I believe and sing, my Doubtings cease.
>
> (p. 11)

In Cowper's translation of Madam Guion's "The Swallow" the bird becomes again an emblem of love for God: "She dwells in the skies, she is ever above" (p. 484).

Usually Blake's swallow, like his other songbirds, suggests merely joy or optimism.[22] Twice in the Notebook, however, the swallow is an emblem of imaginative perception. As we have just seen, Blake contrasted the enlightened reason with the narrowly scientific by using these emblems: "For so the Swallow & the Sparrow sings" (*E,* p. 501). "The Swallow sings in Courts of Kings / That Fools have their high finishings" (*E,* p. 513). Empire and aristocracy encourage pretentious, shallow art, not the imaginative art of the swallow. Sometimes also the swallow may symbolize this imaginative perception in the designs. Thus in the "Introduction" for *Songs of Innocence* a swallow flies in the upper right medallion of the Tree of Jesse design.

Although Blake mentioned the goldfinch by name only twice and then in lists of birds, it is probably the goldfinch which he more than once lamented as the type of caged bird. In his *Emblems* Quarles presented the caged bird as a symbol of the imprisoned soul:

> Imprison'd in this Cage of Flesh,
> We earnestly Enlargement wish;
> In Hope that GOD Relief will bring,
> The caged Bird its Song will sing.

As Erdman has implied,[23] Blake may have borrowed from the design here. He seems also to have remembered some of the verses on the following page:

> My Soul is like a caged Bird,
> ....
>   And there she hops about.
> From Perch to Perch she skips and sings. . . .

Probably Blake, as Quid, recalled the lines ironically in his wry praise of "Matrimony's Golden Cage":

> It makes them smile it makes them skip
> Like Birds just cured of the pip
> They chirp & hop away[.]
>
> (*E,* p. 460)

In the song "How Sweet I Roam'd," from *Poetical Sketches,* Blake surely visualized an imprisoned goldfinch, for the jailor, the bird complains, "stretches out my golden wing" (*E,* p. 413). Here Blake lamented the bird's imprisonment — and imprisonment in any form, especially marriage. Rather incongruously for visualization, but with flowers emblematically appropriate, the imprisoned goldfinch, or woman, is given, she recalls, "lilies for my hair, / And blushing roses for my brow," and the cage becomes, like the ironic "Matrimony's Golden cage" of "An Island in the Moon," the jailor's "golden cage" (*E,* pp. 413, 460). Much simpler is the symbolism of constraint conveyed by the caged bird in "The School Boy."

Another songbird sometimes caged, like the goldfinch, was the robin, the most beloved of all English songbirds.[24] Traditionally the redbreast had stained itself with its own blood when it attempted to pluck thorns from Christ's head or when it carried water to assuage his sufferings on the Cross.[25] In *The Owle* Drayton presented the redbreast as an emblem: "Covering with Mosse the deads unclosed eye, / The Little Red-breast teacheth Charitie."[26] In *Cymbeline* Arviragus promises that the robin will deck the grave of Imogene (IV.ii.224-29); and in his "Song from Shakespear's Cymbelyne" William Collins reiterated this promise:

The Redbreast oft at Ev'ning Hours
   Shall kindly lend his little Aid:
With hoary Moss, and gather'd Flow'rs,
   To deck the Ground where thou art laid.[27]

In the late sixteenth century ballad "The Children in the Wood" the robin again cares for the dead:

No burial 'this' pretty 'pair'
   Of any man receives,
Till Robin-red-breast piously
   Did cover them with leaves.[28]

This popular ballad was printed by Bishop Percy and was often separately reprinted into the nineteenth century. Robins and other similar birds were also becoming popular objects of benevolence in children's books. In 1786 Mrs. Sarah Trimmer published her *Fabu-*

lous Histories designed for the Instruction of Young Children respecting their Treatment of Animals, later known simply as *The History of the Robins.* Stories concerning these birds Mrs. Trimmer "intended to convey moral instruction . . . at the same time that they excite compassion and tenderness for those interesting and delightful creatures . . . and recommend *universal benevolence.*"[29] When shortly thereafter, in 1787 or 1788, Mary Wollstonecraft, a friend of Mrs. Trimmer and Blake, wrote her *Original Stories from Real Life,* a book which Blake illustrated, she too utilized birds in order to dramatize lessons of sympathy and benevolence.

In Blake's verse the robin several times merely accompanies other songbirds as they begin their song; but the captive robin is lamented by the outraged Blake in his "Auguries of Innocence": "A Robin Red breast in a Cage / Puts all Heaven in a Rage" (*E*, p. 490). Quite important for the meaning of the poem is the symbolism of the robin in "The Blossom" (see Fig. 70):

> Merry Merry Sparrow
> Under leaves so green
> A happy Blossom
> Sees you swift as arrow
> Seek your cradle narrow
> Near my Bosom.
>
> Pretty Pretty Robin
> Under leaves so green
> A happy Blossom
> Hears you sobbing sobbing
> Pretty Pretty Robin
> Near my Bosom.
>
> (*E*, p. 10)

The speaker in "The Blossom" is surely a mother with her infant. At the top of a lily stalk (as we shall see in Chapter Ten) a mother holds her child, madonna-like. The "blossom" is surely the child. The other actors in the poem, both addressed by the mother, are the sparrow and robin. The "happy" sparrow may be represented in the design by any of the four winged *putti* paired off; the robin is perhaps the winged cherub reading — could it be the demise of the robin in "The Death and Burial of Cock Robin"?[30] In "The Blossom" the child too is happy, but the mother is preparing her child to experience the traditional altruistic suffering of the robin as well as the joy which characterizes the sparrow.

The theme implicit in "The Blossom" is quite similar to that in "On Another's Sorrow":

And can he who smiles on all
Hear the wren with sorrows small,
Hear the small birds grief & care
Hear the woes that infants bear —

And not sit beside the nest
Pouring pity in their breast. . . .

(E, p. 17)

In England there was a "reciprocity" of the traditions of wren and robin.[31] In this poem Blake again used infant and bird to suggest the universal need for sympathy. Here the sorrows of the wren are combined with those of the weeping infant; and both are pitied by Christ, just as in "The Blossom" the sobbing robin anticipates the inescapable sorrow of the infant, both pitied by the madonna-mother. One other appearance of the wren deserves attention, the lines in "Auguries of Innocence": "He who shall hurt the little Wren / Shall never be belovd by Men" (E, p. 490). Here Blake was varying a popular folk verse, *Kill a robin or a wren, / Never prosper, boy or man.*[32] In many parts of England, including Sussex, Surrey, and Essex, the wren was still ritually hunted and killed at Christmas, possibly because it had for centuries been known as king of the birds.[33]

The dove, which Blake used far more extensively and variously, has served as a common symbol of love, especially married love, ever since doves were supposed to draw the chariot of Venus.[34] Only rarely did Blake use the dove to suggest simply romantic or marital love;[35] but with obvious irony, in his *Canterbury Pilgrims* (*CGW*, Pl. 477) he placed several doves on or near the roof of the Tabard Inn, centering over his Venus — the Wife of Bath. The dove also served Christ, the emblem writers, the poets, and Lavater as an allied symbol of innocence and sincerity.[36] The dove appropriately suggests, in "The Land of Dreams," an innocent child's love for his dead mother: "I wept for joy like a dove I mourn" (E, p. 486); and dovelike innocence also characterizes the child of "Cradle Song." It is this beauty and childlike innocence of life which Enion laments as she accuses herself: "I have blotted out from light & living the dove & nightingale" (*FZ* 35.5). It is also this quality of protected innocence which characterizes Beulah:

> Into this pleasant Shadow all the weak & weary
> Like Women & Children were taken away as on wings
> Of dovelike softness. . . .
>
> (*Milton* 31.1-3)

The dove also suggested peace, divine grace, and divine or prophetic inspiration. The dove of peace was of course a classical symbol; and the dove functioned as messenger of reassurance and peace from a formerly angry God to the inhabitants of the Ark. The dove also symbolized the spirit of the Father, the Holy Spirit, as in Matthew 3.16-17. Thus in "On the Morning of Christ's Nativity" the dove, "crown'd with Olive green, came softly sliding," "With Turtle wing the amorous clouds dividing" (ll. 47, 50).[37] In the *Olney Hymns* Cowper transferred the symbol to Christ: "The Lamb, the Dove, set forth / His perfect innocence" (p. 446). In his *Mysterium Magnum* Boehme explained that Genesis 8.9 meant that when God's children "can find *no Rest* in the earthly Dominion, then they come again before the *Ark* of *Noah,* which is set open in *Christ,* and *Noah* receives them again in Christ, into the first Ark, whence Adam departed." ". . . the *Dove* denotes the *Gospel* of Christ, which brings us again into the Ark, and *saves* the Life" (32.40, 41). Swedenborg asserted, "Doves often appear in Heaven, and the Angels know, when they observe them, that they are Correspondencies of the Affections and Thoughts relating to Regeneration, and Purification in some Persons not far off . . ." (*TCR,* Par. 144).

Blake several times used the Christian, imaginative dove,[38] especially as messenger to the Ark, where man and animals still dwell together in unity. The dove appears prominently on the title page of *Jerusalem* as an emblem of hope and reassurance in a scene of apparent mourning. On Plate 24, where in copies B and E it is given a human face, the dove outstretched over the Ark provides assurance just after the relapsed Albion has reasserted a "God in the dreary Void" (23.29). On Plate 39 only the wings are visible above the Ark as the friends of Albion attempt vainly to bear him back, evidently to that Ark of reintegration which, as Boehme explained, opens in Christ. Later man, engulfed in the Sea of Space and Time, sends "the Dove & Raven: & in vain the Serpent over the mountains" (66.70), searching for some sign of hope. A complex example of this symbol appears when Enitharmon, the Emanation of Los, and his Spectre escape the chaos which attends the fall of Albion. Here Blake seems to have combined God's assurance to Noah with the reassurance in Isaiah 60.8: "Who *are* these *that* fly as a cloud, and as the doves to their windows?" For "the Divine hand was upon them," Blake explicated, "bearing them thro darkness / Back safe to their Humanity as doves to their windows" (44.12-13). Here the dove returns to the ark, or body of Los, to suggest that Los is reintegrated, for he now reincorporates his formerly alienated Emanation and Spectre.

In another complex example of this symbolism, in *Milton* Ololon resigns her separate existence as Shadow and reunites with her Humanity:

> Away from Ololon she divided & fled into the depths
> Of Miltons Shadow as a Dove upon the stormy Sea.
>
> Then as a Moony Ark Ololon descended to Felphams Vale
> In clouds of blood, in streams of gore, with dreadful thunderings
> Into the Fires of Intellect that rejoic'd in Felphams Vale. . . .
>
> (42.5-9)

Milton has just cast his own Spectre into the sea, explaining that it is a "Negation," a "false Body" which "must be destroyd," "which must be put off & annihilated away" (40.33-36). Similarly Ololon rejects her own Selfhood, her Shadow, in order to reunite with her Humanity; and the dove is here an emblem of self-sacrifice.[39] The dove probably suggests divine inspiration in the final plate of *All Religions Are One*, where the wings alone hover just above the water and just below the assertion that "The true Man" is the source of prophecy and religion, "he being the Poetic Genius" (*E,* p. 2).[40]

The swallow's sister, the nightingale, had long been a special favorite of the English poets and naturalists.[41] The poets differed only about the implications of her song. Shakespeare, Milton, Coleridge, and others found it melancholy.[42] Indeed, some, like Thomas

Lodge, envisioned the nightingale singing with its breast against a thorn (Armstrong, pp. 188-190). Blake's nightingales differ. As Oothoon ceases to lament and to macerate herself, and as day begins symbolically to break, "the nightingale," she says, "has done lamenting" (*VDA* 2.24); and in "Spring" it sings "Merrily Merrily to welcome in the Year"(*E*, p. 15). In *Milton* it leads all the songbirds in their chorus of praise for the return of spring, for the annual rebirth of nature: "Thou hearest the Nightingale begin the Song of Spring" (31.28). After the lark essays his more spiritual song, the nightingale again leads the chorus, but a sadder one, a lament rather than a paean:

> The Nightingale again assays his song, & thro the day,
> And thro the night warbles luxuriant; every Bird of Song
> Attending his loud harmony with admiration & love.
> This is a Vision of the lamentation of Beulah over Ololon!
>
> (31.42-45)

Beulah, even at its best in the melodious nightingale, cannot understand the joyous implications of the lark's song, for it is unwilling to face the wars of Eden. It can only lament and admire Ololon's self-sacrifice.

The bird which for Blake transcends the nightingale is the lark, the joyous herald of the morn. Though most of the poets, like Milton, preferred the nightingale, the "chearfull" or "merry" lark was also a favorite.[43] In "L'Allegro" the cheerful man is promised "To hear the Lark begin his flight, / And singing startle the dull night" (ll. 41-42). In Blake's *Night Startled by the Lark* (see Fig. 21) the lark is, except for his wings, completely human and male, a radiance around his face. His is "an Angel on the Wing" (*E*, p. 682). The wings, a conflation of angelic and avian, like those in "The Blossom," seem more symbolic than functional, making him angel rather than bird. In much of Blake's early poetry the lark carried cheerful connotations. Thus in "The School Boy"

> When the birds sing on every tree;
> ....
> And the sky-lark sings with me.
> O! what sweet company.
>
> (*E*, p. 31)

In "The Ecchoing Green" the skylark sings "To the bells chearful sound" and in "Spring" sings joyfully, along with the nightingale, "to welcome in the Year" (*E,* pp. 8, 15). In *Visions of the Daughters of Albion* the lark becomes a symbol of spiritual daybreak: "The lark does rustle in the ripe corn" as Oothoon attains a more imaginative vision (2.25).

The lark was also the ascending singer and melodious dweller in the skies. Here it was a favorite of the emblem writers, the poets, and the naturalists alike.[44] "Thy nature is to soar up to the sky," Bunyan marvelled. "This simple Lark's a shadow of a Saint" (pp. 30, 31). In *Cymbeline* "the lark at heaven's gate sings, / And Phoebus gins arise . . ." (II.iii.20-21). In Sonnet 29 the return of hope "(Like to the lark at break of day arising / From sullen earth) sings hymns at heaven's gate." In *Hamlet* Marcellus reports that some view the lark as a divine protection against evil, for at Christmas time "This bird of dawning singeth all night long, / And then they say no spirit dare stir abroad" (I.i.160-61). At times the towering song becomes a religious symbol, as in "To Some Children Listening to a Lark," by Cowper's friend Nathaniel Cotton:

> SEE the Lark prunes his active wings,
> Rises to heaven, and soars, and sings.
> His morning hymns, his mid-day lays,
> Are one continued song of praise.[45]

This skylark Blake developed into a symbol of divine, poetic inspiration. In "Auguries of Innocence" he wrote: "A Skylark wounded in the wing / A Cherubim does cease to sing" (*E,* p. 490). The symbolism is most fully developed in *Milton:*

> The Lark sitting upon his earthy bed: just as the morn
> Appears; listens silent; then springing from the waving Corn-field!
>   loud
> He leads the Choir of Day! trill, trill, trill, trill,
> Mounting upon the wings of light into the Great Expanse:
> Reechoing against the lovely blue & shining heavenly Shell:
> His little throat labours with inspiration; every feather
> On throat & breast & wings vibrates with the effluence Divine[.]
>
> (31. 29-35)

The Granivorous Birds

Although nature, in Beulah and the nightingale, is unable to understand how the song of the lark can be joyous when Ololon annihilates her own Selfhood, the lark does not lament, for in its flight of prophetic vision it transcends the restricted understanding of the limited world of Beulah and celebrates the impending reunion of Humanity and Emanation. This song of the birds in *Milton* resembles not so much the avian concert in Thomson's *Seasons* as it does that which heralds the reunion of Beatrice with Dante and Milton's nuptial song for the union of Adam and Eve (*PL* VIII.515-19).[46]

> The Lark is Los's Messenger thro the Twenty-seven Churches
> That the Seven Eyes of God who walk even to Satans Seat
> Thro all the Twenty-seven Heavens may not slumber nor sleep[.]
> (35.63-65)

As the prophetic imagination, the lark nests at the gate of Golgonooza, for here it helps to inspire the creation of a Heavenly City in this world, a "spiritual fourfold London" (20.40). As poetic messenger, or as poet-prophet, the lark ranges through the twenty-seven heavens, through all the "churches," or civilizations in all ages, so that the Eyes of God, or spiritual imagination, may not slumber or sleep, so that the prophetic "Poetic Genius / Who is the eternal all-protecting Divine Humanity" (14.1-2) may reawaken moribund religions or dormant or decadent spiritual ideals.

> When on the highest lift of his light pinions he arrives
> At that bright Gate, another Lark meets him & back to back
> They touch their pinions tip tip: and each descend
> To their respective Earths & there all night consult with Angels
> Of Providence & with the Eyes of God all night in slumbers
> Inspired: & at the dawn of day send out another Lark
> Into another Heaven to carry news upon his wings
> Thus are the Messengers dispatchd till they reach the Earth again
> In the East Gate of Golgonooza, & the Twenty-eighth bright
> Lark. met the Female Ololon descending into my Garden
> Thus it appears to Mortal eyes & those of the Ulro Heavens
> But not thus to Immortals, the Lark is a mighty Angel.
> (36.1-12)

In this epiphany Blake identified Milton as the twenty-seventh lark, the poet-prophet who reawakened the Protestant Church of Luther and the Protestant civilization to their spiritual mission. Here as Milton and Blake "touch their pinions tip tip," we have the promise of an apocalyptical reawakening, for the twenty-eighth lark is Blake-Los, the poetic imagination in Blake which heralds the apocalypse and presents it in *Jerusalem*. Blake is "the Twenty-eighth bright / Lark" (36.9-10) who meets Milton's Emanation as she descends into his garden, a scene which he depicted at the bottom of Plate 40. For Humanities must converse by their Emanations: Blake can know Milton and be inspired by him only through his song — the poetry which he has created. Immediately after this promise of an apocalypse, after Blake's "Resurrection & Judgment in the Vegetable Body," he as "Lark mounted with a loud trill from Felphams Vale" (42.27, 29).

Chapter Five

The Birds of Prey

"The analogy between the structure of rapacious birds and carnivorous quadrupeds is obvious," Ralph Beilby remarked; "both of them are provided with weapons which indicate destruction and rapine; their manners are fierce and unsocial. . . ."[1] The predatory birds had long been used to emblematize man's fallen, perverted faculties; and in *The French Revolution* "the seven diseases of earth," in "the den nam'd Religion," were for Blake "like birds of prey" (ll. 35-36).

Of all these carnivorous birds, the universal favorite was the eagle. Associated by the Greeks with Zeus, it usually appears in the Bible as the noblest of the birds, high soaring and keen of sight, and came to symbolize the evangelist St. John.[2] The awakener of Dante in the *Purgatorio* and the genial instructor of Chaucer in *The House of Fame,* the eagle was for the emblem writers a symbol of the sun, royalty, understanding, generosity, youth, virtue, and vision.[3] It was the favorite not only of the poets,[4] but the naturalists. "The first rank in the description of birds," Goldsmith wrote, "has been given to the eagle; not because it is stronger or larger than the vulture, but because it is more generous and bold" (V, 107). Swedenborg, however, discriminated: *"they, who are like to eagles as to rapaciousness, are wicked, but . . . they, who resemble them as to sharpsightedness only, are good"* (AC, Par. 9970).

Following the popular convention, Blake in his early work used the eagle to suggest liberty and courage.[5] In *The Marriage of Heaven and Hell* appears also the eagle of poetic imagination: "When thou seest an Eagle, thou seest a portion of Genius. lift up thy head!" (*E,* p. 37). It is this eagle which, evidently, we see on Plate 15 (see Fig. 22): "In the third chamber was an Eagle with wings and feathers of air, he caused the inside of the cave to be infinite, around were numbers of Eagle like men, who built palaces in the immense cliffs" (*E,* p. 40). In the design his vision is directed upwards; and he clearly transcends the viper which he clutches in his talons. Although the winged serpent may sometimes, as Kathleen Raine has suggested, be an "Alchemical emblem of the contraries" (I, 119), surely the imaginative process is Blake's central concern. Here in paradoxical style, Blake has the eagle of enlightened reason and the serpent of the passions cooperate rather than combat, although the eagle-serpent confrontation usually suggests a struggle, frequently between good and evil.[6] The eagle of vision reappears in *Visions of the Daughters of Albion*. After the invoked eagles have macerated her, Oothoon attains a purified vision and announces to Theotormon,

> the Eagle returns
> From nightly prey, and lifts his golden beak to the pure east;
> Shaking the dust from his immortal pinions to awake
> The sun that sleeps too long. Arise my Theotormon I am pure.
>
> (2.25-28)

The eagles prey upon Oothoon as long as she accepts the code of society and willingly suffers the evil of Experience. When she rejects this code and proclaims her own purity, she transforms the eagle from a bird of prey to a bird of vision, embodying a form of Higher Innocence for her just as the lions do for Lyca. The eagle continues occasionally to suggest courage and reason. Though the last of these far-ranging eagles, in *The Four Zoas* (29.8-13), are strong and brave, they represent there the energies of a fallen Urizen.

A final and special eagle of genius appears on Plate 78 of *Jerusalem*. (See Fig. 23). Here one must not be misled by the lines immediately beneath into identifying the eagle-headed contemplative with a Spectral son of Albion; for this plate serves as a chapter heading, and in the four plates so used Blake was concerned in his design more with the chapter and whole poem than with the verses on the particular plate. This is the head of Los, whom Blake associated with St. John the visionary,[7] as well as the evangelist, whom he pictured (and doubtless Los) with eagle head on the second title page for his *Genesis* (*B*, Pl. 975). Here in *Jerusalem* Los seems to be quite melancholy at the prospect before him: the sun is sinking behind clouds, added in the only copy which Blake completely colored; and the future of Albion seems quite bleak. Something of Dürer's engraving *Melencolia I* may very well appear here, as Judith

Ott has argued: Samuel Palmer asserted that Blake was so fond of the print that he had a copy hanging by his engraving table.[8] But apart from the eagle-headed Los, the eagle of genius or vision does not reappear in Blake's illuminated canon after *The Marriage of Heaven and Hell* and *Visions of the Daughters of Albion* — until, like the rest of creation, it is reincorporated in man himself.

Perhaps because it was Jove's bird and was the emblem of the Roman legions, the eagle also symbolized empire, oppression, and war.[9] In *Paradise Lost* it becomes the original bird of prey: "The Bird of *Jove,* stoopt from his aerie tour, / Two Birds of gayest plume before him drove . . ." (XI. 185-86). Lavater regarded the eagle as the contrary of the dove, "the Wolf and Lamb of the feathered race." "Is it possible to look upon him," he asked, "without discerning in his external form . . . the fiery rage of this formidable ravisher?" (II, 124, 120).

Blake developed his predatory eagle early. The scavenger eagle is often accompanied in Blake by less noble birds or beasts of prey; and together these frequently symbolize the bloodshed and suffering which attend empire and war. The scavenger eagle appears alone in "Gwin, King of Norway" (l. 112), but is coupled with the lion in *The French Revolution.* The ruthless Burgundy urges the King: "Stretch the hand that beckons the eagles of heaven; they cry over Paris, and wait / Till Fayette point his finger to Versailles; the eagles of heaven must have their prey" (ll. 103-104). Ironically Burgundy fears "the eternal lion and eagle" (l. 97) he is himself invoking. In *America* this eagle of empire appears again (see Fig. 24) to prey upon Oothoon, "the soft soul of *America* (*VDA,* 1.3), ripping flesh from the supine Emanation above, just as the vultures of the deep feed upon the Humanity below. We see its victims upon the frontispiece, though without the screaming eagle which hovers over the dead bodies in *A Breach in a City the Morning after a Battle* (B, Pl. 195). In *Europe* (see Fig. 25) Blake's eagle of empire implies also the Female Will and nature-worship. Enitharmon, whose benighted vision commends this worship, invokes Manathu-Vorcyon: "I see thy lovely eagles round; / Thy golden wings are my delight, & thy flames of soft delusion" (14.7-8). Although the eagles are not prominent in the design, they are preying there. Two "lovely" eagles on the right are headed, one downward, one upward toward flies and caterpillars; and on the following plate another eagle is about to devour a fly. There is nothing of genius in these eagles. Eagles of empire also appear in the bottom corners of Plate 15 of *Job* (see Fig. 8) to accompany Behemoth and Leviathan, war by land and war by sea. This predatory eagle reappears in *Jerusalem* in apparently odd company when Brittannia awakens and confesses, "behold ye the Jealous Wife / The Eagle & the Wolf & Monkey & Owl & the King & Priest were there" (94.26-27). Empire feeds upon the pomp and cruel power of the eagle, the ruthlessness of the wolf, and the blind stupidity of the monkey and owl. This predatory eagle of empire and slaughter reappears in Design 2 for Gray's "Bard." There against an ominous red glare "'The famish'd eagle screams, and passes by'" (p. 98), hovering momentarily above the dead bodies.

In *The Four Zoas* in the "night of Carnage" "the Eagles cry & the Vultures laugh" (96.24, 23). Ahania tells of Albion,

> Of Man who lays upon the shores leaning his faded head
> Upon the Oozy rock inwrapped with the weeds of death
> ....
> And the Strong Eagle now with num[b]ing cold blighted of feathers
> Once like the pride of the sun now flagging in cold night
> Hovers with blasted wings aloft watching with Eager Eye
> Till Man shall leave a corruptible body he famishd hears him groan
> And now he fixes his strong talons in the pointed rock
> And now he beats the heavy air with his enormous wings[.]
> (108.29-109.6; E, p. 384.)

Albion is aroused, at least partly, by the "sound of rage of Men drinking each others blood" (120.11). In *Jerusalem* an analogous scene includes Albion's Emanation Brittannia:

> Albion cold lays on his Rock: storms & snows beat round him.
> ....
> The weeds of Death inwrap his hands & feet blown incessant
> And washd incessant by the for-ever restless sea-waves foaming abroad
> Upon the white Rock. England a Female Shadow as deadly damps
> Of the Mines of Cornwall & Derbyshire lays upon his bosom heavy
> ....
> Over them the famishd Eagle screams on boney Wings and around
> Them howls the Wolf of famine deep heaves the Ocean black
>   thundering[.]
> (94.1-16)

Here "England who is Brittannia" (94.20) reawakens, realizing that she has "slain" Albion. Her realization and admission then reawaken Albion himself.

In a similar scene on Plate 42 of *Milton* (see Fig. 26) the pair on the rock must be Milton and Ololon, but may well represent Albion and Brittannia as well. Both pairs are awakened and reintegrated in large part by the realization of the Emanation that she must give up her independence as Shadow; but the bird of awakening has long ceased to be the eagle. Still under the spell of the eagle of genius in *The Marriage of Heaven and Hell,* some critics have ennobled this scavenger eagle of empire into an eagle of awakening inspiration, but Blake's eagles of inspiration died about a quarter of a century before *Milton* appeared. In his illustrations for Gray, Blake substituted the swan for the eagle of genius; and here in *Milton* he developed that role specifically for the lark. If the cry of the eagle and the howl of the wolf (who is invisible here) help to awaken, they do so to help Ololon, or Brittannia, realize the ruthlessness of empire, of the Female Will, or nature. In Copy A, here represented, the erect penis of Albion confirms his creative reawakening from his spiritual sleep.

A predator hated by poets and naturalists alike, the vulture was used by the emblematists and poets to suggest fraud, jealousy, remorse, and unrequited love.[10] Doubtless pointing to his heart, Lear complains of Goneril, "O Regan, she hath tied / Sharp-tooth'd unkindness, like a vulture, here" (II.iv.135-36). In Design 6 for Gray's "Ode on a Distant Prospect of Eton College" (see Fig. 16) Blake portrayed at least one vulture. Here Blake's three grotesque birds embody the "fury Passions," "the vultures of the mind," as Gray called them (p. 58), perhaps remembering *Titus Andronicus* V.ii.31-32. Gray's subsequent lines recall the vultures of unrequited love:

> Or pining Love shall waste their youth,
> Or Jealousy, with rankling tooth,
> That inly gnaws the secret heart. . . .
>
> (p. 59)

For Blake the vulture was, with one realistic exception (*VDA* 5.36), invariably malignant. Although in his *Comus* Milton did not include avian metamorphoses for his revellers, in both of his versions of *Comus with the Lady Spellbound* Blake seems to have included a vulture. In the Boston Museum version (*B,* Pl. 628) it has a long and crane-like beak, like that of a waterfowl, but it is unmistakably a bird of prey. In the Huntington version (*B,* Pl. 620) it is seated with two other birds, one probably a crow and the other perhaps a raven, perhaps a cock. In this scene Blake evidently drew upon the similar situation in Jonson's *Volpone,* where Volpone, an earlier Comus, exploits the predatory natures of Voltore, Corvino, and Corbaccio and attempts to seduce a lady by his lavish displays. Here Comus's Mosca is represented by two predatory owls. On Plate 14 of *Europe* (see Fig. 25) a vulture, apparently, its long neck outstretched, at the middle right, is about to gobble up a caterpillar. Several times Blake used the vulture as an emblem of carnage. Thus at the prospect of fire and death "the Eagles cry & the Vultures laugh" (*FZ* 96.23). At the Fall of Adam, as we have seen, Blake added a vulture to reinforce the predatory nature of the eagle as they contend for the lamb. He even adopted the vulture as a symbol for carrion-eating fish and marine monsters, for the Spectre of Urthona boasts to Tharmas, "I protected thy ghastly corse / From Vultures of the deep" (*FZ* 50.25-26). On Plate 33 of *Jerusalem* he gave a vulture-like beak to the malignant bat Spectre which hovers over the recumbent, sleeping Jerusalem.

An especially interesting conflation of verse and design occurs in *Visions of the Daughters of Albion.* (See Fig. 27.) After Oothoon has been seduced or raped by Bromion, "The Eagles at her call descend & rend their bleeding prey" (2.17). The eagle here, Ms. Kostelanetz has suggested,[11] looks much like a vulture. Like the eagle, the vulture is an apt instrument of tyrannical punishment, as it was for Prometheus; and part of Oothoon's suffering comes from the society which demands bridal virginity, along with its other codes of good and evil, and which exacts suffering of those who neglect or violate the codes, or even the victims of the codes. But another part of her pain comes from her eventual realization of wronged love, and the vulture of this realization also tears at her heart, just as at Lear's.

Another scavenger, the raven was from Biblical times a malignant and ominous bird. In Isaiah 34.11 it is an ill-omened symbol of desolation and approaching destruction; and it was used by the emblem writers as a symbol of superstition, and by the poets as an evil omen.[12] For Boehme it was the contrary of the dove. In his *Mysterium Magnum* he suggested that the raven of the Ark "denotes the *earthly Man,* and shews how that he would . . . advance himself in his Selfhood and earthly Lust." "And though he came forth out of the Ark, yet he would fly to and fro in the Kingdom of his Selfhood . . ." (32.38, 39). Citing Psalms 147.9, Swedenborg suggested that "sons of the raven" signify "natural men who are in a dark lumen arising from fallacies concerning truth divine" (*AE,* Par. 650).

Sometimes Blake used the raven as the malignant scavenger, along with other birds of carrion, on the field of battle. In *The Four Zoas* "the drunken Raven shall wander / All night among the slain & mock the wounded that groan in the field" (96.26-27). It is even more indurated than the vulture. At the apocalypse "moping terrors" come "from the Eagle / And raven" (122.33-34). For him the black raven also suggested the priest. In "The Human Abstract" Blake wrote of the Tree of Religion, of mystification, that "the Raven his nest has made / In its thickest shade" (*E,* p. 27). In *The Marriage of Heaven and Hell* the priests are adjured, "Let the Priests of the Raven of dawn, no longer in deadly black, with hoarse note curse the sons of joy" (*E,* p. 45). Some symbolism of this sort, as well as unrelieved gloom, may be suggested by the two birds "painted so black they must be ravens" (*IB,* p. 177) on Plate 4 of *The Song of Los.*

Among the predatory birds, the most contemptible is the crow. For the emblem writers it suggested misfortune;[13] and Shakespeare several times contrasted the black crow with the white dove.[14] Latham and Pennant even accused the crow of pecking out the eyes of "young defenseless lambs" or even "of horses when engaged in bogs."[15] In *The Marriage of Heaven and Hell,* where the eagle is ennobled, he "never lost so much time. as when he submitted to learn of the crow" (*E,* p. 37). In *The Four Zoas* Blake suggested the fall from harmony to discord by the contrast between music and corvine chatter. "The houses of my harpers," Urizen laments, "are become a haunt of crows" (63.29). In *Jerusalem* a similar contrast marks the change from beauty and innocence to ugliness and nocence, from music to discord: "The birds of song" have changed "to murderous crows" (19.11). In Plate 10 of *Job,* finally, Blake coupled the crow with the owl as emblems of malice and spiritual darkness.

If the diurnal predatory birds were rapacious, the nocturnal ones were just as malign and were even more stupid. Since the owl was Athena's bird, the emblem writers sometimes used it to suggest prudence, vigilance, and wisdom. Yet in the Bible it was an unclean bird; and some of the same emblematists used it to symbolize lust, superstition, or blindness. For Dürer it suggested "the Old Faith that did not recognize the Messiah"; and for Aldegrever, gluttony. For Shakespeare it was malign and stupid.[16] In *The Dunciad* it suggests intellectual, spiritual, and artistic blindness. Its malevolence Ovid had reported in the *Fasti,* where screech owls attack and snatch unprotected children from their cradles (VI. 135-68); and, Pennant confirmed, "'*Hasselquist* describes a species found in *Syria,* which frequently in the evening flies in at the window, and destroys the helpless infant'" (I, 209). For Swedenborg owls were *"they who have used the sciences as means of annihilating the things which are of faith, have totally destroyed their intellectual principle, and see in thick darkness like owls, mistaking what is false for what is true, and what is evil for what is good"* (*AC,* Par. 8628).

Never in Blake's designs or verse is the owl anything but baleful and stupid. In the *Hecate,* of 1795, the owl is perched at the left of the main group, accompanied by bat, frog, lizard, ass, and weeds to suggest spiritual darkness (*CGW,* Pl. 334). To illustrate Young's lines "Dreams / Thro' senseless Mazes hunt Souls *un-inspir'd*" (II, *NT* 521) Blake placed an owl atop the page, a hunting scene by the sleeper, and a bat above his head to suggest his benighted soul. Similarly, in *Dunciad* fashion, he placed an owl atop another design to comment upon Young's lines "But you are learn'd; in Volumes, deep you sit; / In Wisdom shallow: pompous Ignorance!" (I, *NT* 199); and on Plate 10 of *Job* one clutches a victim. In "Auguries of Innocence" it suggests a special consequence of this spiritual blindness: "The Owl that calls upon the Night / Speaks the Unbelievers fright" (*E,* p. 490). The owl of spiritual blindness is also present, we recall, when in *Jerusalem,* as Brittannia confesses, she "Murdered" Albion (94.23).

To suggest lack of vision, however, Blake usually preferred the bat, a mammal then popularly regarded as a bird. In the Bible merely an unclean bird, the bat was for emblem writers a symbol of envy, superstition, or "the rapid progress in a vitious course of life" (Richardson, II, 8). Ever since the Middle Ages, moreover, Satan had been represented with bat wings after his fall. For most poets the bat forboded evil, misery, or death. For Spenser it was "dayes enimy" (*FQ* II.xii.36.6). In *The Tempest* Caliban curses Prospero, "All the charms / of Sycorax, toads, beetles, bats, light on you!" (I.ii.339-40); and in *Macbeth* the witches add to their envenomed brew "Eye of newt and toe of frog, / Wool of bat and tongue of dog" (IV.i.14-15). For the naturalists and Lavater the bat was not only a lover of darkness, but a vicious predator. For Buffon it was "imperfect or deformed," "monstrous" (*NH,* IV, 317, 318); and for Goldsmith the vampire bats, especially, were "deformed, greedy, uncleanly, and cruel." They often attack people "in the face, and inflict very terrible wounds," being "'the most expert blood-letters in the world'" (IV, 143). Blake must have read John Stedman's account of his awakening to find himself "weltering in congealed blood" from the work of a "*vampire* or *spectre* of Guiana"; and as Sir Geoffrey Keynes suggests, he may have been indebted to Stedman in his development of the bat symbol for his Spectre.[17] For Lavater the features of the bat "are expressive of violent passion, but confined to very narrow bounds, an ignoble passion which shuns the light. These little eyes, concealed and sunk, these large ears, erect and fearful, these small teeth, sharp and pointed, have, in my opinion, the impress of a passion ardent, mean, malicious and concentrated." "The tail, and the extremity of the wings characterize its malevolence" (II, 125). For Swedenborg ". . . the Light of Infatuation is the Light arising from the Confirmation of what is false, and that Light corresponds to the Light which Owls and Bats see by, to whom Darkness is Light and Light Darkness . . ." (*AR,* Par. 566).

Blake similarly used bats, bat wings, and bat ears to suggest gloom, envy, and intellectual or spiritual blindness, especially as this blindness appears in Satan and in the Selfhood. In *The Marriage of Heaven and Hell* (Pl. 10), he perversely gave bat wings to the instructing devil there who apparently became the narrator's "particular friend" (*E,* p. 44). There only, however, are bat wings a sign of spiritual perception. Occasionally the bat, along with the owl, is merely a traditional emblem of melancholy and gloom. It suggests a "vitious course of life" in the designs for others' poetry, mainly for *Night Thoughts*. To illustrate Young's phrase "A mere Froth of Joy" Blake pictured a scene of revelry dominated at the top by large green bat wings, upper bat face, and bat ears. Another jovial bat with angelic wings at the right center is, with wine and women, doubtless also developing bat wings (II, *NT* 409). This bat figure, apparently, tops the following design at the end of the revelry. Blake also gave bat wings to several other figures and abstractions in *Night Thoughts:* to "'some *Passion,*'" "Disguise," "blind *Industry,*" and "*Appetite* and *Passion.*"[18] In his design for *Mirth* (*CGW,* Pl. 601), for Milton's "L'Allegro," bat wings characterize a figure which John Grant has identified as "Wanton Wiles."[19]

Blake's far more characteristic bat of intellectual and spiritual blindness appears as early as "An Island in the Moon" with Suction's disrespectful attack upon Dr. Johnson: "Lo the Bat with Leathern wing" (*E*, p. 458). Blake's famous bloodthirsty flea, in *The Ghost of a Flea*, has impossibly bat-shaped wings in a preliminary, full-length drawing.[20] At the bottom of Plate 1 of *Europe* bat wings characterize, doubtless, some blind political figure (*IB*, p. 159). In Plate 11 (see Fig. 28) a Urizenic, triple-crowned ruler (George III as head of church as well as state) is betrayed in his temporal and spiritual ignorance by his bat wings and, in some copies, his bat ears. In *Night Thoughts* he is transformed into a batwinged, papal-tiaraed Lucifer (I, *NT* 91).

This spiritual blindness characterizes Satan himself, for he is, after all, "the limit of Opakeness" (*Jerusalem* 42.30), as stupid as man can become, for he combines the blindness of the Selfhood with his materialistic rationalism. Bat wings almost invariably accompany Satan after his fall;[21] and they characterize many of the devils tormenting victims in the designs for Dante's *Inferno.* Bat wings also help to characterize the horses of the brutal and benighted watchfiends of Satan as on Plate 35 of *Jerusalem* (see Fig. 15) they ride to find and close the Gate of Los — to stifle the divine imagination. The Spectral Satan who appears with bat wings in the late "Epilogue" for *The Gates of Paradise* is a parody of the butterfly Emanations of *Jerusalem,* claiming sun and moon and stars on his wings as the Emanations properly display them. Knowing that for Blake the Emanation controls space, we recognize Satan's claim here as another evidence of his stupidity: "Truly My Satan thou art but a Dunce" (*E*, p. 269).

The bat at his worst is the bat of abstract science and the possessive Selfhood. This bat we see on plates 6 and 33 of *Jerusalem.* On

Plate 6 (see Fig. 29) his Spectre has separated from Los after the Fall of Albion and Man's fragmentation, his loss of vision, and his domination by Urizen:

> His spectre driv'n by the Starry Wheels of Albions sons, black and Opake divided from his back; he labours and he mourns!
>
> For as his Emanation divided, his Spectre also divided
> In terror of those starry wheels: and the Spectre stood over Los
> Howling in pain: a blackning Shadow, blackning dark & opake. . . .
> (6.1-5)

"Panting like a frighted wolf, and howling," the Spectre stands "over the Immortal" (7.1-2). However, we see not the envious, malicious wolf but his alter-ego, probably an adaptation of Goltzius's cruel and voracious batwinged wolves, a batwinged creature of spiritual blindness and selfishness, who by appealing to anger and the Selfhood tempts Los to resign his creative and unselfish task. On Plate 33 (see Fig. 30) Los asks Albion, "Why dost thou thunder with frozen Spectrous wrath against us? / The Spectre is, in Giant Man; insane, and most deform'd" (33.3-4). In the plate we see this most deformed wolf-bat-vulture hiding the sleeping Jerusalem, Albion's Emanation, below, from the rays of Christ's mercy and forgiveness, though above, Christ supports Albion between the oak of weeping and the palm of suffering. For the Spectre persists selfishly and stupidly "to forbid with Laws / Our Emanations, and to attack our secret supreme delights" (33.8-9). He is doubtless in part a vampire bat, but even better equipped, with a vulture neck and beak, to gorge himself upon flesh as well as blood and to rip the Emanation as the eagle-vulture is doing in *Visions of the Daughters of Albion*.

Chapter Six

The Insects

The insect, which the naturalists and Lavater regarded as a lower form of existence than either reptile or marine life, represented for Blake a much higher form than either. Goldsmith noted that "the insect has but one invariable method of operating; no arts can turn it from its instincts; and indeed its life is too short for instruction, as a single season often terminates its existence" (VII, 237-38). Lavater asked, "Do not insects, being almost entirely destitute of brain, differ, more than all other creatures, from man, who is so amply furnished with that organ?" (II, 129).

Others, however, including the naturalist James Barbut, viewed the insect differently, particularly impressed by its metamorphosis. Anna L. Barbauld was ecstatic: "I have seen the insect, being come to its full size, languish, and refuse to eat: it spun itself a tomb, and was shrouded in the silken cone; it lay without feet, or shape, or power to move — I looked again, it had burst its tomb; it was full of life, and sailed on coloured wings through the soft air; it rejoiced in its new being." "Thus shall it be with thee, O man!" she ejaculated, "and so shall thy life be renewed."[1] Swedenborg suggested that caterpillars, or silkworms, and butterflies represent "two States" of reformation and regeneration (*TRC,* Par. 106).[2] Although this transformation had long been a "stale analogy," as Fuseli complained,[3] Blake found the insect metamorphosis peculiarly appropriate for his symbolism. Here there was no need to contrast a noxious insect, like the wasp, with an innocent one, as he did with his animals and birds. All insects pass through states. Similarly man can be just as devouring as the caterpillar or intellectually dead as the chrysalis or as innocent and beautiful as the butterfly. Here in the insect metamorphosis Blake found the most dramatic analogy of his distinction between states and individuals: "Distinguish therefore States from Individuals in those States. / States Change:

but Individual Identities never change nor cease . . ." (*Milton* 32.22-23).

Man's emergence from his spiritual sleep Blake depicted in 1780 in *The Dance of Albion*, or *Albion Rose*. (See Fig. 31.) Here the human butterfly, a nude and handsome youth, greets us with outstretched arms at the break of day. The legend beneath identifies him as Samson-Albion: "Albion rose from where he labourd at the Mill with Slaves / Giving himself for the Nations he danc'd the dance of Eternal Death" (*E*, p. 671). The legend itself may, as Erdman and Bindman contend,[4] derive from the late 90's or even later. But the design, with the abandoned chrysalis at Albion's feet and the batwinged moth flying away back into the darkness, probably should be dated much earlier, though these features do not appear in an early drawing of this design (*B*, Pl. 63). There Blake indicated Albion's present creativity and virility by giving him a small but erect penis.[5] In *Albion Rose* the moth has the single, spike-tipped wings of the bat, but the antennae of the moth, as the batwinged Spectre of *Jerusalem* never has. Probably this insect represents an early concept of the Spectre, here a "night butterfly," as the moth was then frequently called — that aspect of Albion's personality which, like the bat or the moth, prefers darkness to light, or, like Samson, accepts his blindness. At the rising dawn of spiritual awareness it is dispelled along with the outworn chrysalis. Subsequently, when Blake showed the chrysalis, he showed also only the emergent spiritualized and human form.

This metamorphosis Blake exhibited about 1793 on the frontispiece of his emblem book, *The Gates of Paradise*.[6] (See Fig. 32.) Here a caterpillar devouring a leaf hovers over a cocoon which has a child's head and suggests the pattern of metamorphosis: the devouring caterpillar, the dormant cocoon, and the emergent butterfly-human. In 1818 in an added Key, Blake stressed another element, one important in the theme of *Jerusalem* and elsewhere: "The Catterpiller on the Leaf / Reminds thee of thy Mothers Grief" (*E*, p. 268). In 1793, however, Blake had evidently not yet worked out a systematic symbolic pattern, for in Plate 6 an infant cherub emerges from an eggshell over the caption "At length for hatching ripe he breaks the shell" (*E*, p. 32). Perhaps he remembered the "Meditations upon an Egg," in the *Divine Emblems*. There Bunyan compared the soul with a chick:

> The Shell doth crack, the Chick doth chirp and peep;
> ....
> The Shell doth break, the Chick's at liberty;
> The flesh falls off, the Soul mounts up on high.
>
> (p. 7)

In Plate 16 Blake's symbolism is more complex (see Fig. 33), for here he combined the earthworm of mortality with the caterpillar weaving potential butterflies of immortality. In the design a cowled, pensive female looks intently at us, while an earthworm — but is it not also an embryo? — uncoils from behind her back, her loins.[7] The worm seems to be entering the ground to the right, where we see the faces of three buried men, perhaps the father, brother, and son, for the caption tells us, "I have said to the Worm, Thou art my mother & my sister"; and the Key informs us,

> Thou'rt my Mother from the Womb
> Wife, Sister, Daughter to the Tomb
> Weaving to Dreams the Sexual strife
> And weeping over the Web of Life[.] (E, pp. 33, 269)

The "Worm" here is the cowled, silkworm female, but the embryo and the earthworm also. Here the female is spiritualized through both suffering and creativity, not like Tirzah, the embodiment of dominant nature. In 1818 also Blake removed the apparent pessimism of Plate 15, "Death's Door," through which an aged traveller is about to enter. He added as a Key: "The Door of Death I open found / And the Worm Weaving in the Ground" (E, p. 269). For only the silkworm and her sisters weave; the earthworm does not. The door of death remains open, then, for the soul to abandon its tomb or chrysalis, to emerge from, as well as to enter. The paradox reappears in *Visions of the Daughters of Albion,* published about the same time as *The Gates of Paradise.* The enlightened Oothoon asks, "Does not the worm erect a pillar in the mouldering church yard? / And a palace of eternity in the jaws of the hungry grave [?]" (5.41-6.1).

In the central theme of *Jerusalem,* spiritual regeneration, this metamorphosis plays an important part. Los accuses Albion's sons of having "divided themselves by Wrath. they must be united by / Pity":

And the Religion of Generation which was meant for the destruction
Of Jerusalem, become her covering, till the time of the End.
O holy Generation! [*Image*]* of regeneration!
O point of mutual forgiveness between Enemies!
Birthplace of the Lamb of God incomprehensible!

(7.57-58, 63-67)

Subsequently Los exhorts the Daughters of Albion "To the golden Loom of Love! to the moth-labour Woof / A Garment and Cradle weaving for the infantine Terror" (56. 13-14). Later as Gwendolen seeks to impose the Female Will and secure the triumph of nature, she subjects her male counterpart, Hyle, to her dominion by withholding sexual satisfaction and exhausting his energies in war. "Playing in the thunderous Loom in sweet intoxication," she weaves Hyle as she pleases; "drunk with pity" (80.80, 70), she limits his senses and subjects him to moral law and nature, to the mortality of the uncoiled earthworm which extends its length along the right margin of Plate 82. She also expects from her sisters the homage due to a new Virgin Birth: hiding her creation behind her loins, whence in Plate 16 of *The Gates of Paradise* the worm-embryo emerges, she claims, "I have named him Jehovah of Hosts. Humanity is become / A weeping Infant" (81.13-14). When she exhibits her "prophetic falsehood" she reveals "Hyle a winding Worm" "& not a weeping Infant" (82.47, 48). Envious, however, Cambel then attempts "To form the mighty form of Hand according to her will" (82.63); but the worm now becomes an embryo, an emblem of life rather than death. She is trapped by Los into sexual intercourse with Hand, her counterpart; for Los "Shewd her the fibres of her beloved to ameliorate / The envy" (82.61-62). Then indeed "she labour in the Furnace of fire," "in the Wine-press treading day & night,"

Naked among the human clusters: bringing wine of anguish
To feed the afflicted in the Furnaces: she minded not
The raging flames, tho she returnd [*consumd day after day
A redning skeleton in howling woe:*]* instead of beauty
Defo[r]*mity: she gave her beauty to another. . . .

(82.62, 64, 65-69)

The spinsters now begin to weave from their own bowels. (See Fig. 34.) Having experienced a metamorphosis, they begin to create one. This metamorphosis is intimated as early as Plate 28 (see Fig. 35), which provides a chapter title for Chapter II and thus is concerned with the general theme of the poem. In the early state of the plate, a reassuring chrysalis-embryo, deleted in later copies, emerges from behind the woman, apparently, like the embryo-earthworm in *The Gates of Paradise.*

Since all true insects begin as caterpillars or worms, a state of intense devouring for all species, and since Blake seems not to have attempted to discriminate between various types of larvae, we need only look at this state in general for all Blake's insects, with a special glance at the worm of jealousy. From Biblical times the caterpillar has served as an emblem of the devourer or parasite.[8] With beautiful irony Falstaff accuses his merchant victims of being "whoreson caterpillars" (*I Henry IV* II.ii.84). For Goldsmith they were "the most ravenous of all animals whatsoever" (VIII, 10).

In Blake's designs also the caterpillar is the devourer. In *Night Thoughts* Blake pictured a collection of human headed and even venerable looking caterpillars, along with some serpents, to illustrate Young's "steel'd Files of season'd Veterans,/ Train'd to the World, in burnisht Falsehood bright" (II, *NT* 361). The caterpillars on Plates 12 through 15 of *Europe* particularly help us to perceive the discrepancy between Enitharmon's vision of reality and Blake's own perception. Enitharmon perceives a static society dominated by nature and by woman-worship, and Blake has recreated part of her perception. (See Fig. 25.) To Enitharmon her children are like "gay fishes," and the five butterflies swimming onto Plate 14 at top right suggest by their symmetrical rigidity that they are indeed more fish than butterfly: nowhere else in Blake do butterflies observe such a strict conformity. The spiritual bird of paradise Enitharmon degrades into her "lureing bird of Eden" (14.9). The reality of life dominated by nature Blake shows by the spiders, serpents, vulture, and eagles which infest the page and prey upon innocent moths, butterflies, and other insects. Caterpillars appear here also and on Plate 12 (see Fig. 36), supplementing the tigers which "couch upon the prey & suck the ruddy tide" (15.7). Caterpillars and tigers are equally devourers. A special caterpillar-devourer is the parasitic artist:

> the tame high finisher of paltry Blots,
> Indefinite, or paltry Rhymes; or paltry Harmonies.
> Who creeps into State Government like a catterpiller to
>   destroy
>
> (*Milton* 41.9-11)

Another is the priest of organized religion: "As the catterpiller chooses the fairest leaves to lay her eggs on, so the priest lays his curse on the fairest joys" (*MHH* 9.55).

Still another, the cankerworm, which feeds especially upon the rose, had been singled out by Spenser and Shakespeare to suggest jealousy. Phedon laments, "Me liefer were ten thousand deathes priefe, / Than wound of gealous worm, and shame of such repriefe . . ." (*FQ* II.iv.28.8-9). In his "Hymn of Love," speaking of lover's torments, the poet agrees:

> Yet is there one more cursed then they all,
> That cancker worme, that monster Gelosie,
> Which eates the hart, and feeds vpon the gall,
> Turning all loues delight to miserie. . . .
>
> (ll. 266-69)

In *Twelfth Night* Viola tells of a woman who had repressed her love and "let concealment, like a worm i' th' bud / Feed on her damask cheek" (II.iv.111-12). These examples help us to understand the symbolism of "The Sick Rose" (see Fig. 37), where the winged form of the cankerworm is jealousy:

> The invisible worm,
> That flies in the night
> In the howling storm:
>
> Has found out thy bed
> Of crimson joy:
> And his dark secret love
> Does thy life destroy.
>
> (*E*, p. 23)

Here the ravaged maiden-roses show that what is happening to the sick rose has already happened to them: their beauty and joy in life has been blighted by jealousy, suggested by the caterpillars, probably by the parasitic priests who repress, yet feed upon innocent beauty and joy, and by a jealous and devouring society. Several other poems in *Songs of Experience* support this symbolism, particularly "A Little Girl Lost" and "The Garden of Love," where the priests have left only tombstones and briers "where flowers should be" (*E*, p. 26).

Although the chrysalis appears on several of the designs, it rarely appears in the verse, for a state of inactivity does not provide an interesting subject for poetry. In *Night Thoughts* an aged, legless chrysalis admiring himself in a mirror and still enclosed in his cocoon or shell of the Selfhood, is chained round, to illustrate Young's lines

> How, like a Worm, was I wrapt round and round
> In silken thought, which reptile *Fancy* spun,
> Till darken'd *Reason* lay quite clouded o'er. . . .
>
> (I, *NT* 17)

He lacks the imagination needed to break from his enclosed world of the Selfhood. In *The Four Zoas* one of the Eternals uses the chrysalis to characterize man in his dormant, selfish state:

> Man is a Worm wearied with joy he seeks the caves of sleep
> Among the Flowers of Beulah in his Selfish cold repose
> Forsaking Brotherhood & Universal love in selfish clay
> Folding the pure wings of his mind seeking the places dark. . . .
>
> (133.11-14)

In their winged state Blake's butterflies, moths, flies of other types, and bees differ in their symbolism. In the emblem books and even in poets like Shakespeare and Cowper the butterfly and moth frequently appeared as symbols of folly, vanity, or indiscretion.[9] But in art, even more than in poetry, the butterfly had from classical times symbolized the resurrection and immortality. Even the natural scientists appreciated the innocence of the butterfly. As Brookes noted, many moths, without a trunk, "never eat during the short time they have to live" (IV, 109); and Lavater asked, "Who does not perceive inability to hurt imprinted" on the butterfly. Also the moth, "The night-butterfly, slow, peaceful, harmless, is a striking contrast to the active and murderous spider" (II, 132, 130-31).

In his original work Blake used moth and butterfly as emblems of joy, innocence, and grace; and in his most distinctive use, especially in *Jerusalem,* the butterfly and moth symbolize the Emanation no longer dominated by the Selfhood, but desiring a reunion with the Humanity — a secularized resurrection. In his designs Blake evidently did not attempt to discriminate between butterfly and moth, or to reproduce all the shape and color of a particular variety. Unlike Stothard he evidently never hunted butterflies to study their structure;[10] thus he may never have mastered their distinguishing characteristics. Although he had a symbolic purpose in so doing, on Plate 44 of *Jerusalem* he made Enitharmon's antennae emanate from her wings rather than her head; and on an alternative design for the title page for Blair's *Grave,* he gave to the guarding angel at the right only one pair of butterfly wings, each ribbed into five, eyed sections (*B,* Pl. 853).

In his early work Blake seems to have used the butterfly almost exclusively as an emblem of innocence and joy. The symbol is so used by the glib little speaker of "The Fly":

Am not I
A fly like thee?
. . . .
For I dance
And drink & sing;
Till some blind hand
Shall brush my wing.

(*E,* p. 23)

On Plate 7 of *The Gates of Paradise* a heedless youth, hat in hand, has apparently already knocked down one small flying figure and is about to knock down another. Both are more human than butterfly; and the augmented caption reads, "What are these? ALAS the Female Martyr / Is She also the Divine Image?"[11] Perhaps Blake remembered the similar, but hatless youth chasing a butterfly in Wynne's *Choice Emblems* who catches, "but at the same time . . . crushes the insect to pieces." Wynne moralized, "Avoid to take the life we cannot give, / Since all things have an equal right to live" (pp. 82-84). Since the boy in Bunyan's similar design has hat in hand, Blake may, as Judith Wardle has suggested,[12] have owed to Bunyan part of the suggestion, though Bunyan seems not to have been concerned for the butterfly, as was Wynne. In *Night Thoughts* a youth is attempting with his hat to capture a butterfly which has alighted upon a gravestone. Young's line "From a Friend's Grave, how soon we disengage?" (I, *NT* 181) helps to ally this youth with the heedless; and his attempt, with the callous. On Plate 13 of *Jerusalem* still another youth is about to snare a dragonfly. In "Auguries of Innocence" Blake warned, "The wanton Boy that kills the Fly / Shall feel the Spiders enmity." Then a few lines later he humanized the fly:

> The Catterpiller on the Leaf
> Repeats to thee thy Mothers grief
> Kill not the Moth nor Butterfly
> For the Last Judgment draweth nigh[.]
>
> (*E,* pp. 490, 491)

In verse and design the butterfly continues to symbolize beauty and joy. In *Milton* it is part of the beauty created by Los, the divine imagination:

> Thou seest the gorgeous clothed Flies that dance & sport in summer
> Upon the sunny brooks & meadows: every one the dance
> Knows in its intricate mazes of delight artful to weave:
> Each one to sound his instruments of music in the dance,
> To touch each other & recede; to cross & change & return
> These are the Children of Los. . . .
>
> (26. 2-7)

The butterfly of promise and immortality appears also in *The Virgin Hushing the Young Baptist* (*B,* Pl. 491).

More especially, Blake made the butterfly, particularly in *Jerusalem,* the form of the repentant Emanation as she rejects her state of the Shadow and decides to reunite with her Humanity. Even as early as in Design 6 for Gray's "Ode on the Spring," Blake gave his favorite, Io type of butterfly wings to two nursing butterfly mothers. The father butterflies, hovering nearby, are not so distinguished. The butterfly symbolism Blake developed partly in *The Four Zoas.*

There Enion greets the apocalypse: "Into the Sea of Tharmas Soon renewd a Golden Moth / I shall cast off my death clothes & Embrace Tharmas again . . . (132.21-22). In *Milton* Blake associated Leutha, Satan's Emanation, with the moth when she repents and confesses her error: "And Leutha stood glowing with varying colours immortal, heart-piercing / And lovely: & her moth-like elegance shone over the Assembly" (11.32-33).

The butterfly in *Jerusalem* represents this special interim state, a lament often for past separation and Selfhood and the promise of a creative reunion with the Humanity. This is the symbolism of the title page of *Jerusalem*. (See Fig. 38.) Here is apparently a scene of mourning, as four surrounding human butterflies lament the decline of the human butterfly Jerusalem. Jerusalem as she appears on the title page is visualized by Los — only after the Daughters of Albion have renounced their Selfhoods — in terms of an Elizabethan love poem combined with the Song of Solomon and at least one detail from Revelation:

> I see thy Form O lovely mild Jerusalem, Wingd with Six Wings
> In the opacous Bosom of the Sleeper, lovely Three-fold
> In Head & Heart & Reins, three Universes of love & beauty
> Thy forehead bright: Holiness to the Lord, with Gates of pearl
> Reflects Eternity beneath thy azure wings of feathery down
> Ribbd delicate & clothd with featherd gold & azure & purple
> From thy white shoulders shadowing, purity in holiness!
> Thence featherd with soft crimson of the ruby bright as fire
> Spreading into the azure Wings which like a canopy
> Bends over thy immortal Head in which Eternity dwells
> . . . .
> I see the New Jerusalem descending out of Heaven
> Between thy Wings of gold & silver featherd immortal
> Clear as the rainbow, as the cloud of the Suns tabernacle
>
> Thy Reins coverd with Wings translucent sometimes covering
> And sometimes spread abroad reveal the flames of holiness
> Which like a robe covers: & like a Veil of Seraphim. . . .
>
> (86.1-24)

Here Jerusalem is given six wings, gorgeously colored in blue, crimson, and gold, in the tradition of the colors of the Virgin and perhaps patterned upon the Peacock, or Io butterfly, which has the characteristic four eyes which Blake used to incorporate the heavens — the sun, earth, and moon, and a sprinkling of stars. Since the Emanation controls space, this emblematic detail is entirely appropriate. The Io butterfly is also aptly chosen for its own beauty. Donovan believed that there was "not a more beautiful Insect in this country";[13] and it was a favorite of Stothard, though in 1784 in his *Zephirus and Flora,* which Blake engraved, he gave the four eyes to Zephirus and single, Psyche wings to Flora.[14] The three pairs of wings on Jerusalem may actually characterize some moths, though the eighteenth-century English naturalists and Blake evidently knew none. The "many-feathered moth" has twelve pairs of wings.[15] But Blake took his three pairs of wings from Revelation and Isaiah. In Revelation "the four beasts had each of them six wings about him; and *they were* full of eyes within . . . (4.8); and in Isaiah the seraphim "each one had six wings; with twain he covered his face, and with twain he covered his feet, and with twain he did fly" (6.2). Blake may have been influenced here also by Dante, for in his Vision of Beatrice, in Canto XXIX of *The Purgatorio,* Dante gave the zoas six wings.

On Plate 14 (see Fig. 39) Jerusalem appears in an early stage of the separation, but since she is not dominated by her Shadow, she exhibits much of her butterfly form and beauty. Her wings are differently shaped and differently colored, paler than those which she has on the title page, and each separate wing is given an eye. Here she wears a tunic fastened by an ornate girdle. Her appearance may be different because the vision of Los is less certain here than it is later; Los appears to be not fully awake. But since Jerusalem appears in various forms even when she is not being visualized by a particular character, we must attribute most of these differences to changes in the state of Jerusalem herself. Thus as she pleads vainly to her Humanity Albion "like a voice heard from a sepulcher" (23.8), she seems to be assuming form as a chrysalis, though the Golgotha crosses on her angelic,[16] rather than butterfly wings, promise a resurrection.

The other butterfly women on the title page are the Emanations of the Four Zoas, like Jerusalem languishing, but probably lamenting not only the sleep of Jerusalem, but their impending loss of the Selfhood, as Ololon does in *Milton,* and lamenting also their separation from their Humanities. Hovering at the top of the title page is probably Enion, with wings and color somewhat resembling those of the common Pearl Border Fritallary butterfly, or perhaps Ealing's Glory.[17] The form in which she has wanted to appear hovers near her in the small moths in and near the *E* of *Emanation:* the Golden Emperor moth also has four "eyes." The butterfly at the top left must be Ahania, the Emanation of whom we see and hear very little in the poem. The mourning Emanation immediately above Jerusalem at the left is probably Enitharmon. We see her again at a distance on Plate 23, accompanied by her guardian Spectre, who is distinguished from her butterfly form by his single pair of bat wings and by his lack of antennae. We see the pair again on Plate 44 (see Fig. 40); here her wings become diaphanous and float almost free of her body, and her antennae are transferred to her wings so that she may again in virtually human form reunite with her Humanity, Los. Below, the grapevine is beginning to attach itself to the wall at the right — a promise of fruitfulness. Although throughout much of the poem this reunion is unstable, it is necessary for Los to have adequate vision and inspiration to create Golgonooza and to reawaken Albion.

The Emanation-butterfly at the right of Jerusalem is Vala, here not as the Shadow of Albion, but the Emanation of Luvah, and mourning doubtless her own impending renunciation of independence, but lamenting even more the sleep of Jerusalem and Albion and her murder of her own Humanity, Luvah. She reappears in this form on Plate 53, a chapter title (see Fig. 41), her blue wings tipped with vermilion, her eyed wings suggesting her control of earth and moon and heavens, the luminescence behind her probably an effluence of her own. Similar lights on Plate 33 (see Fig. 30) emanate from Christ, who holds in his arms the fainting Albion, and from Christ on the Cross on Plate 76, from whom Los or Albion is receiving the Stigmata, by artistic convention from the right.[18] The wings of Vala here are heart-shaped. Although she wears a triple tiara, here appearing especially in her role as goddess of nature, she holds her head in her hands to support its weight, just as she must to support the weight of her cares and her crown on Plate 51. There she is an emblem of melancholy.[19] The Female Will and the rule of nature have proved of no real satisfaction to Vala; and in the remainder of the poem she plays far less of an active role in the tormenting of man than in the first half, her role being taken over in large part by Rahab and Tirzah and the Daughters of Albion. Although the verses on the chapter title-page are not necessarily related to the design, they seem to be here, for below Vala as mournful butterfly, Los labors

> For the protection of the Twelve Emanations of Albions Sons
> The Mystic Union of the Emanation in the Lord; Because
> Man divided from his Emanation is a dark Spectre
> His Emanation is an ever-weeping melancholy Shadow
> But she is made receptive of Generation thro' mercy. . . .
>
> (53.23-27)

At bottom right we have two vignettes which show this reunion: in the lower vignette the Humanity reaches down with both arms to raise his Emanation, now completely humanized. In the upper one the Emanation has been made "receptive of Generation thro' mercy" and treasures her child upon her lap.

Far less important than butterfly or moth in Blake's work, but still of interest is the ambivalent dragonfly. Goldsmith thought that "Of all the flies which adorn or diversify the face of Nature, these are the most various and the most beautiful." Yet they are "the greatest tyrants of the insect tribe; and, like the hawk among birds, are only hovering up and down to seize their prey" (VII, 312, 320). On Plate 13 of *Jerusalem* a dragonfly is evidently pursuing its dinner, four small flies. Below a boy is catching a butterfly: an unnatural version of the natural scene enacted above. But Blake's other dragonflies seem completely innocent. In Design 5 for Gray's "Ode on the Spring" a human-bodied, green dragonfly is sounding his horn, apparently announcing joy to those above; but the serpent horn which he trumpets is ordinarily a diabolical instrument and here probably suggests the fates which the careless flies will receive (and some have already received) from "Age" and "rough Mischance" (p. 45). On Design 6 a six-winged dragonfly sounds a straight horn as a pair of six-winged dragonflies hover over the solitary and "frolic while 'tis May" (p. 46). As emblems of innocence and beauty they accompany the birds and butterflies on Plate 3 of *The Song of Los* and on Plate 30 of *Milton*. Dragonflies doubtless are the musical flies each one of which sounds "his instruments of music in the dance" (*Milton* 26.5).

In addition to moth, butterfly, and dragonfly, myriads of other flies throng Blake's designs: horseflies, blowflies, gnats, midges, and even tinier insects. Some, like the blowfly, feed on corruption, as it feeds on religious mystery in "The Human Abstract." Most of these small insects, however, like the ant, the beetle, and the glowworm, are emblems of innocence and joy, like the tiny insects noticed by Los in *Milton:*

> Seest thou the little winged fly, smaller than a grain of sand?
> It has a heart like thee; a brain open to heaven & hell,
> Withinside wondrous & expansive; its gates are not clos'd,
> I hope thine are not: hence it clothes itself in rich array;
> Hence thou art cloth'd with human beauty O thou mortal man.
>   (20.27-31)

Many are victims of serpents, vultures, eagles, and spiders of empire, of the church and state.

Known in the Bible primarily as an irritable and vengeful insect, the bee for the emblem writers and the poets sometimes suggested flattery, but more often, industry and prudence, exhibiting preeminently "the art of extracting Good out of Evil."[20] Blake surely knew the song of Isaac Watts:

> How doth the little busy bee
> Improve each shining hour,
> And gather honey all the day
> From ev'ry op'ning flower![21]

Only once, in "Auguries of Innocence," did Blake use the bee, somewhat in Biblical manner, to suggest malicious envy: "The Poison of the Honey Bee / Is the Artists Jealousy" (*E,* p. 491). But in "King Edward the Third" Clarence sees London's merchants "Like summer bees, and all golden cities / In his [father's] land, overflowing with honey" (ii.13-14). In *The Marriage of Heaven and Hell* "The busy bee has no time for sorrow" (*E,* p. 36), but provides an emblem of industry:

Roses are planted where thorns grow.
And on the barren heath
Sing the honey bees.

(2.6-8)

In both *The Four Zoas* and *Jerusalem* the bee with its honey, along with flocks and cattle, provides an emblem of rich and fruitful emotional life.

Along with the true insects we should examine also their debased cousins — their devourer the spider, an arachnid then generally regarded as an insect, and the worm, which lexicographers like Nathan Bailey and natural historians like Oliver Goldsmith viewed as a member of the insect family.

Of no importance as a Biblical symbol, and in emblem literature often an attribute of industry or firmness of touch, the spider was for poets and naturalists alike a symbol of malice.[22] In his *Divine Emblems* Bunyan wrote, "Thy Nature, Venom, and thy fearful Hue, / Both shew what Sinners are, and what they do" (p. 25). In *Richard III* Anne wishes for the murderer of her husband a worse fate than for wolves, "spiders, toads, / Or any creeping venom'd thing that lives" (I.ii. 19-20); and Queen Elizabeth characterizes Richard as "That bottl'd spider, that foul bunch-back'd toad!" (IV.iv.81). Goldsmith thought the spider "Formed for a life of rapacity," "all its habits . . . calculated to deceive and surprise" (VII, 249); and doubtless Blake was fascinated by Stedman's hideous "bush-spider," which kills young birds and sucks their blood (II, 93-94). Boehme included the spider among the "wild venemous and horrible Beasts" (*Mysterium Magnum* 26.30); and in his *Divine Providence* Swedenborg suggested that "infernal Love, with it's . . . Concupiscences . . . may be compared to a Spider and the Web."[23]

Though Blake did not annotate this suggestion in his copy, it may have contributed to the imagery of a "Memorable Fancy" in *The Marriage of Heaven and Hell:*

> By degrees we beheld the infinite Abyss, fiery as the smoke of a burning city; beneath us at an immense distance was the sun, black but shining[;]* round it were fiery tracks on which revolv'd vast spiders, crawling after their prey; which flew or rather swum in the infinite deep, in the most terrific shapes of animals sprung from corruption. & the air was full of them, & seemd composed of

them; these are Devils. and are called Powers of the air, I now asked my companion which was my eternal lot? he said, between the black & white spiders[.] (*E,* p. 41)[24]

Elsewhere in Blake the spider suggests the malign tyranny of empire and the manner in which moral, religious, and legal institutions entrap their victims. In *The French Revolution* an old man in the tower named "Order" is immured in a den "with spiders webs wove, and with slime / Of ancient horrors cover'd, for snakes and scorpions are his companions" (ll.40-41). Oothoon makes vivid the possessiveness of jealous love by visualizing it as a spider, "That clouds with jealousy his nights, with weepings all the day: / To spin a web of age around him. grey and hoary! dark!" (*VDA* 7.18-19). Especially is the spider with its web an emblem of oppression in *Europe.* On the Preludium plate the spider just beneath line 3 awaits the unwary flies and moth to his left and right. Ravens and a bat-winged figure at the bottom of the plate help to underscore the threat in the design and warn the reader of dangers to come. In Plate 12 (see Fig. 36) six spiders have trapped all sorts of flies. At the bottom an entrapped human prays to the spiders above for his release. On the next plate we witness an imprisonment; and above the prisoner another spider with its web awaits its prey. When we reach Plate 14 (see Fig. 25) we are able to disentangle Enitharmon's fancy of butterflies, "gay fishes," and bird of Eden (not represented) from the reality seen by the artist himself: spiders, caterpillar, serpent, vulture, and eagles — emblems of empire and nature, all preying upon the helpless.

In *Urizen* the spider reappears just after Urizen announces his rule of "One King, one God, one Law" (4.40); and the final plate shows Urizen apparently trapped in the web which he has himself woven. In *The Book of Los* he is in the design again a spider, trapping man and woman in his web. In *The Four Zoas* the predatory lion and tiger encourage the desolation of empire: "They cry O Spider spread thy web! Enlarge thy bones & fill'd / With marrow. sinews & flesh Exalt thyself attain a voice" (15.3-4). Later in the poem the web inextricably accompanies the fallen Urizen:

    whereever he traveld a dire Web
Followd behind him as the Web of a Spider dusky & cold

Shivering across from Vortex to Vortex drawn out from his mantle of
 years
A living Mantle adjoind to his life & growing from his Soul. . . .
(73.31-34)

In *Milton* the spiderweb of religion becomes a tree of religion. In *Jerusalem* it becomes a net used by fish-women.

For centuries the earthworm has served as a symbol of fallen man, especially when he is misanthropic or feels, like Bildad, an insect in the sight of an omnipotent God.[25] This earthworm of mortality sometimes appears in Blake in the conventional manner.[26] Thus Tiriel asks why men are "bound beneath the heavens in a reptile form / A worm of sixty winters creeping on the dusky ground" (8.10-11). But often the emblem is invalidated because it is used by a deluded character, like Enitharmon:

Go! tell the human race that Womans love is Sin!
That an Eternal life awaits the worms of sixty winters
In an allegorical abode where existence hath never come. . . .
(*Europe* 5.5-7)

In *Jerusalem* several misanthropic voices proclaim this vermicular abnegation. Thus the Spectre lectures the benighted Albion:

that Human Form
You call Divine, is but a Worm seventy inches long
That creeps forth in a night & is dried in the morning sun. . . .
(29.5-7)

Vala, representative of nature, proclaims, "The Human is but a Worm" (64.12); but on the previous plate (see Fig. 42) Blake showed her encircled by her own blind worm of mortality, her legs crossed to indicate her duplicity, beneath the moon of this Diana of chastity, its blood-red rays suggesting the human sacrifice in which she delights. Even Jerusalem herself desponds, just before the peripety, "I walk in affliction: I am a worm, and no living soul! / A worm going to eternal torment!" (80.3-4).[27]

Yet in the margin, as we are reassured to see, Cambel and Gwendolen are forming the embryo-worms into life. (See Fig. 34.) Here Blake changed the pessimism of the symbol by conflating the earthworm with the caterpillar and the embryo. Despite the mortality which Satan, Albion's Spectre, has brought about, this "worm" retains his potential divinity:

> He witherd up the Human Form,
> By laws of sacrifice for sin:
> Till it became a Mortal Worm:
> But O! translucent all within.
>
> (27.53-56)

The Immortals are confident that Humans can "At will" contract "into Worms" or expand "into Gods" (55.37).

Chapter Seven

The Reptiles

Outside of *The Marriage of Heaven and Hell* the reptiles provide in Blake's world of Experience symbols of fallen, malicious man. These reptile forms include not only snakes and crocodiles, but (in accordance with eighteenth century science as well as popular thought) frogs, toads, and newts.

The toad, or frog, had appeared in Exodus 8.2-14 as one of the plagues of Egypt; and in Revelation 16.13-14, as a form of unclean spirit. For Ovid and the emblem writers it suggested avarice, envy, or hypocrisy.[1] According to Bunyan,

> The Hyppocrite is like unto this Frog;
> As like as is the Puppy to the Dog.
> He is of nature cold, his Mouth is wide,
> To prate, and at true Goodness to deride.
>
> (p. 46)

In *King Lear* Edgar accuses his envious and hypocritical brother, Edmund, of being a "toad-spotted traitor" (V.iii.139). Among the Seven Deadly Sins, Envy "still did chaw / Between his cankred teeth a venemous tode" (*FQ* I.iv.30.2-3). In *Paradise Lost* Satan assumes the disguise of a toad in order to tempt Eve in a dream, and Blake depicted this scene in his *Adam and Eve Asleep* (B, Pl. 649). Mrs. Barbauld refused the toad a place in heaven: "The toad must not spit its venom amongst turtle-doves" (p. 99). Legend had made it poisonous. According to Boehme, the nature of the toad "is so very venemous, that it poisons a tender [or weak] Mind" (*Three Principles* 16.21). For Swedenborg the frog was one of the guises assumed by the Selfhood (*TCR*, Par. 45).

Similarly, in Blake's verse and designs the frog, the toad and their cousin the newt always appear as symbols of envy or selfishness.[2] In *The French Revolution* the "cold newt" and the "damp toad" (ll.297, 298) help to characterize the selfish King. In *Tiriel* Ijim charges that

102

his brother Tiriel "like a toad or like a newt. would whisper in my ears" (4.58). In "The Clod and the Pebble" the frogs at the foot of the plate help to exacerbate the malign selfishness of the pebble. Perhaps Blake owed to Bunyan not only the central symbol of the indurated pebble, but that of the selfish frog as well. In "Auguries of Innocence" the newt is again an emblem of envy: "The poison of the Snake & Newt / Is the sweat of Envys Foot" (*E*, p. 494).

In depicting reptiles, poets and artists did not ordinarily attempt to differentiate between various types of snakes and assign a separate symbolism to each, though the forked-tongued adder or viper was a favorite emblem for fraud or hypocrisy. In his *Inferno* Dante indicated a variety of serpents for his thieves, "strange of shape / And hideous" (XXIV.77-78); and in his illustrations for this canto Blake endeavoured to show some of this variety, without trying to be herpetologically accurate. Similarly in *Paradise Lost* Milton in his final metamorphosis diversified Satan's companions into asp, python, amphisbaena, "cerastes horned," Hydrus, dipsas, scorpion, and "Ellops drear" (X.519-31). But he did not attempt to assign a distinct retile form even to Satan's major companions. According to Boehme, ". . . all evil Spirits appear, in their own Forms, according to their Source [or Quality,] as Serpents, Dragons, horrible Worms, and evil Beasts" (*Three Principles* 17.99). Swedenborg held that "the Serpent signifieth all Evil in general, and Self-Love in particular," but since it consists of "various Genera, and still more various Species, is distinguished in the Word by different Kinds of Serpents, as by Snakes, Cockatrices, Asps, Haemorrhoids, Presters, or fiery Serpents, flying and creeping Serpents, and by Vipers, according to the Differences of the Poison, which is Hatred" (*AC,* Par. 251).

Although in the emblem books the serpent often served as a symbol of health, prudence, foresight, and wisdom, Blake never employed it in any such way. Only in *The Marriage of Heaven and Hell*, moreover, did he paradoxically use reptiles for creative missions. The viper being carried aloft by the eagle on Plate 15 (see Fig. 22) is evidently cooperating with the eagle in creative activity.[3] This viper, or another like it, is in the second chamber of the printing house "folding round the rock & the cave, and others [are] adorning it with gold silver and precious stones." In the first chamber a "Dragon-Man" is "clearing away the rubbish from a caves mouth," and "within, a number of Dragons were hollowing the cave" (*E*, p.

40). Whatever these reptiles may imply in the engraving process,[4] they suggest the emotions and passions necessary in life, though often condemned by the orthodox as sinful, or laid under severe restrictions. Here, no longer are snakes even confined to earth. On Plate 22 an airborne serpent flies above "A Memorable Fancy."

Comparatively unimportant are Blake's serpentine sexual symbols. The sexual connotations in the serpent in the end piece for *Thel* (Pl. 6), and in Plate 11 of *America* (see Fig. 18), seem minor. Blake's three children there are hardly precocious adolescents indulging in erotic play. Although the general context of the design is partly sexual in *Thel,* the serpent there suggests the emotional terrors of Experience, including sex, fled by Thel, but later experienced by Lyca as wild beasts in "The Little Girl Lost" and "The Little Girl Found" and transformed into the Higher Innocence of a fully integrated life — and into three very real children. In designs the use of such putti, especially for decorative frontispieces, headpieces, or end pieces, had long been popular, in zoological plates as well as elsewhere. Blake's particular models for this design were quite possibly the half-plates which serve as headpieces for practically every volume of Buffon's *Histoire Naturelle, Générale et Particulière.* In almost all of these volumes, which Blake had probably seen in the Library of the Royal Academy, headpieces show such children as Blake's playing with or introducing beasts, birds, tame and predatory, and reptiles; and the infants seem not to fear even hissing snakes. Another and more important source was doubtless the prophecy in Isaiah 11.8 — "the sucking child shall play on the hole of the asp, and the weaned child shall put his hand on the cockatrice-den." In Blake's design the weaned child rides between the girl and the suckling child and helps to steady him. The emblem books occasionally used the scorpion, not the phallic serpent, to suggest lust.[5]

However, the snake became a symbol for all kinds of evil. In the *Inferno* Dante employed reptiles to suggest pride, theft, and fraud. The emblem books, the poets, and the naturalists are full of serpents suggesting falsehood, fraud, malice, anger, injury, calumny, and hatred.[6] Lavater observed, "Even the changeableness of their colours, and the whimsical arrangement of their spots, suggest the idea of deceit . . ." (II, 128). The suggestion may have helped to prompt the vivid display of colors Blake used for some of his serpents. Man is often, Boehme maintained, "an Adder and Serpent, subtle, venemous, stinging, poisonous, slanderous in his Words, and mischievous in his Deeds, ill-conditioned and lying, like the Quality of the Devil in the Shape of a Serpent at the Tree of Temptation" (*Three Principles* 16.21). In *The Threefold Life of Man* he suggested that "the Devil's Bodies are figured also in Hell into such Serpents, venemous Worms, and ugly Beasts: for they cannot in their own form be otherwise" (9.56). Swedenborg agreed that the term "serpent" means all evil in general, especially "Reasoning," but that in some cases "Malice, Cunning, and Deceit, are signified by serpents, but by poisonous Serpents, as by Vipers" (*AC*, Par. 6398).

Blake used serpents in conventional manner fairly often, especially to suggest envy or jealousy.[7] For Gray's lines "the fury passions tear, / The vultures of the mind" (p. 58), Blake included in his design not only three grotesque birds, but two serpents. (See Fig. 16.) One entwines the arm of a blue figure, doubtless to suggest "Envy wan" (p. 59), for which the emblematists traditionally used a serpent. The serpent of envy or jealousy appears at the foot of Plate 72 of *Jerusalem,* below the angels who lament a world "Continually Decaying because of . . . Jealousy." More complicated are three serpent symbols of envy or jealousy in *Urizen, Ahania,* and *Milton.* On Plate 25 of *Urizen* (see Fig. 43) Urizen's daughters are human above the waist, reptile below.[8] Born "From monsters, & worms of the pit," the daughters are cursed by their jealous father with serpentine bodies because they could not "keep / His iron laws one moment" (23.21, 25-26). In *Ahania* "an enormous dread Serpent / Scaled and poisonous horned," attacks Urizen: "Great the conflict & great the jealousy / In cold poisons" (3.13-14, 18-19). The monster suggests jealousy specifically, but the Ten Commandments and the code of good and evil of a jealous god as well, for the rock poisoned with the monster's blood "fell upon the Earth, / Mount Sinai" (3.45-46). In *Milton* Leutha, a Miltonic Sin-figure, confesses her jealousy of Elynittria: "O wherefore doth a Dragon-form forth issue from my limbs / To sieze her new born son?" (12.2-3). She admits that her jealousy caused the quarrel between Satan and Palambron: "I form'd the Serpent / Of precious stones & gold turn'd poisons . . ." (12.29-30).

Blake also used the serpent to suggest hypocrisy. In one of the most interesting watercolors for Young's *Night Thoughts* he gave human legs and hips to one of "*Earth*'s subtil Serpents," hypocrites "Which wriggle into Wealth, or climb Renown, / As crooked *Satan* the Forbidden Tree." And representing the hypocrites who surround "The Gay! Rich! Great!" Blake's serpent, entwined around a supine victim, has the torso and head of a man, who has just removed his mask.[9] Within this emblematic convention of the snake of hypocrisy, Tiriel calls his sons "Serpents not sons" and "worms of death" (1.21, 22). He confesses that he is himself "Compelld to pray repugnant & to humble the immortal spirit / Till I am subtil as a serpent in a paradise" (8.23-24). Ijim also uses the emblem for his hypocritical brother: "Then he would creep like a bright serpent till around my neck / While I was Sleeping he would twine I squeezd his poisnous soul" (4.56-57)

Even Sin itself became, in Genesis and *Paradise Lost,* reptilian. Like Satan, Sin had once been seductively beautiful: "Likest to thee," she boasts to Satan, "in shape and count'nance bright, / Then shining heav'nly fair" (II.756-57). After the birth of Death, however, she

> seem'd Woman to the waste, and fair
> But ended foul in many a scaly fould
> Voluminous and vast, a Serpent arm'd
> With mortal sting. . . .
>
> (II.650-53)

In his watercolor versions of *Satan Comes to the Gates of Hell* (B, Pls. 633, 646) Blake preserved Sin's seductive face and torso, but followed the conventional pattern of having each thigh terminate in its separate serpent, in the second version ending with serpent heads.[10] In this tradition on Plate 14 of *America* a viper of hypocrisy emerges from behind the spread thighs of the cowled sybil who, beneath a yew of death, is apparently preaching to a reverent youth concerning man's limitation, if one can judge from her spanning hand.

But the most widely recognized of all the reptile symbols in the Christian tradition, the one reinforced by *Paradise Lost,* is that which represents Satan himself as serpent in his role of tempter, or (less frequently after the Renaissance) as dragon. Blake in depicting Satan almost always suggested his debased nature, dominated by his Spectre, or Selfhood, by using the snake or the dragon to accompany or represent him. Following Milton in allowing Satan early radiance, Blake sometimes represented Satan in the very early stages of his rebellion without an accompanying serpent. Yet even in *Satan in his Original Glory* (B, Pl. 554) he has the serpent draped unobtrusively behind him; and in *Satan's Entry into Paradise* (B, Pl. 635), the serpent entwines him. In the actual temptation scene, whether *The Fall of Eve* (B, Pls. 640, 653), or the tiny scenes on both plates of *The Death of Abel,* Blake followed the Bible and traditional art and represented Satan as the serpent-seducer, rather than seducer accompanied by the serpent. A coiled, crested serpent appears on the Epilogue for *The Gates of Paradise* below the caption "To The Accuser who is The God of This World" and above the line "Truly My Satan thou art but a Dunce" (E, p. 269) to establish Satan as the limit of opacity — of stupidity.

As the dragon of Revelation, Satan makes several appearances in Blake's art.[11] Rather interestingly, in both *The Great Red Dragon and the Beast from the Sea* and *The Number of the Beast is 666* (B, Pls. 582, 583), the earthly dragon is only a parody of the supreme dragon. In *Jerusalem* Blake included several parodies of the dragon of Revelation, in addition to that on Plate 50, where the sons of Albion in their Spectral state provide a seven-headed version of the beast, with four bodies emerging from the triple-headed accuser Hand. On Plate 75 (see Fig. 44) a curious dragon of seven trunks and heads, some with double horns, to provide a total of ten, intertwines with two human forms, probably those of Bath and Rahab in her role of moral law. The seven dragon forms are militant "religious" civilizations (75.16-20). Although it has usually been assumed that the human figures are those of Rahab and Tirzah (*IB,* p. 354), the back of the second is quite muscular, and his short-cut hair also seems to indicate a male. Moreover we are told in the opening lines that "Bath stood upon the Severn with Merlin & Bladud & Arthur / The Cup of Rahab in his hand" (75.2-3). This cup of abominations is usually held by the Whore herself; here, apparently, Bath is Rahab's giant.

Of all the designs in *Jerusalem* the most mystifying has been that on Plate 41 (see Fig. 45), which I would call "The Triumph of Vala." It is a triumphal procession not of victory or even death, but of sleep. Here two bearded animals with ox-like bodies, horned with curving horns somewhat resembling those of Blake's seven-headed

Dragon, pull a chariot, sinisterly. Asleep there are a man whose beard and flowing locks are mocked by those of the oxen (one form of his energies), and a cowled woman, both dressed in black. Each of the two wheels is formed of a serpent; and a third serpent emerges from between them. The heads of the three serpents all point left. Two chicken-headed fowls, or winged gnomes, ride on the backs of the oxen, one of them preparing to write with his left hand. The scene is bathed in flames. It is suggested nowhere in *Jerusalem,* though the lines above it remind us that Albion is still in "the Land of Ulro" (41. 10), or spiritual sleep.

The scene is dominated not by the two sleeping figures but by the oxen and the serpents. The proper animals or energies to plow with, oxen are hardly the proper animals to propel a chariot; but black bulls often draw the chariot of Death (Tervarent, cols. 72-73). The serpents here are those of fallen nature and Spectrous reason. Their assuming the shape of wheels, of the ouroboros, makes them also emblems of repetitious nature, an ironic negation of their own vehicular use here. The sleeping pair are Albion, who is under the domination of his Spectral, Urizenic self, thus spiritually asleep, as he is during most of the poem, and his Shadow Vala, cowled as she appears on Plate 4. She dominates in the state of Ulro, or nature, into which Albion has fallen, for she serves as a nature goddess. Just as in *Europe,* though Enitharmon as the Female Will, or nature, has dominated man for eighteen hundred years, yet she has slept all this time, so does Vala sleep during her triumphal procession, drawn by animals sacred to the nature goddess, oxen and serpents. The chicken-headed fowls atop the oxen doubtless suggest stupid statesmen and stupid artists and writers. When the divine Humanity sleeps, we can expect little vision from these bird-brains, and the one who writes does so sinisterly. The flames which surround the chariot resemble those which surround Hand on Plate 26 and Scofield on Plate 51. They provide heat, but no light.

This interpretation will be reinforced if we look at some watercolor versions of the title page of *Europe,* two of Blake's designs for Dante, some of the material in Jacob Bryant and Hancarville, and a woodcut of Goltzius. Blake anticipated something like this scene, but not so brilliantly ironic, in a watercolor sketch on the Morgan proof copy of the title page for *Europe.* (See Fig. 46.) There Urizen-Satan, or Urizen dominated by his Spectre, is seated upon a shell-shaped chariot drawn by the serpent which dominates the title page; but it is looking the other way and showing no sign of movement. Urizen is holding the tables of the law with his right hand and flourishing a pen with his sinister hand. This scene has many of the elements of the Triumph of Vala. In the Crawford copy of this title proof (*IB*, p. 397) Los is trying vainly to move this serpent emblem of nature condemned to a circular pattern of repetition. Obviously Blake had fairly early in mind the comedy of any attempt to use nature, emblematized by the serpent, particularly the ouroboros, as a vehicle. Yet the serpent is the vehicle of the Satan of Revelation.

Especially helpful for our full understanding of Plate 41 of *Jerusalem* are Blake's Designs 88 and 89 for Dante. There he depicted both the triumphal procession of which this in *Jerusalem* is a free parody, and a more literal parody of that procession. In Dante's triumphal procession (see Fig. 47) the car is drawn by the Gryphon Christ, formed with the body of a lion and the head, wings, and claws of an eagle. Erect upon the chariot (the Church) is Beatrice, symbolizing both Enitharmon — the Emanation of Los — and the spiritual Church; and accompanying her are the symbols of the four Evangelists, or Blake's Four Zoas, now reunited in harmony. The reunion of Dante and Beatrice is a reunion of both Los-Dante, the divine imagination, and Albion-Dante, the divine Humanity, with their Emanation in the Earthly Paradise, a reunion similar to that of Albion with Brittannia and Jerusalem in *Jerusalem*. Beatrice returns from death to unite with Dante just as Milton returns from Heaven to reunite with Ololon.[12] In Blake's design the wheels are not the specialized vortices of *Milton,* but the eyed wheels of spiritual energy which Ezekiel saw and described, to which Dante referred, and which Blake had recreated in his *Ezekiel's Wheels* (B, Pl. 542). Within these wheels are the Emanations of the other three Zoas. In front, to the left and center, are the three Christian Virtues, Charity surrounded by cherubs, her attribute.

Vala's triumph in *Jerusalem* is modelled in part upon a parody of this triumphal procession which is shown Dante at the end of the *Purgatory.* After being subjected to various indignities and depredations, the chariot of the true Church becomes a parody thereof, a gross chariot drawn by a beast with seven heads and guided by the Whore of Babylon, accompanied by her giant. This scene Blake recreated in Design 89. (See Fig. 48.) Here the wheel is, as in the

Morgan watercolor of the title page for *Europe,* provided by the dragon himself. In Blake's design, as in Dante's verse, the giant stands rather than rides; but in the Flaxman illustration of the same scene the giant is riding with the Whore. This design Blake probably knew, for the engraving had been made by Piroli in 1793 and had appeared with Flaxman's other designs for Dante in 1802.[13] Dante also helps us to account for Blake's three serpents, for the chariot

> Did put forth heads, three on the beam, and one
> On every side; the first like oxen horn'd,
> But with a single horn upon their front,
> The four.[14]

The three serpents in *Jerusalem* provide the beam as well as the two wheels. With only two heads furnished by the oxen, Blake needed two more for the full complement of seven for this procession of the Whore of Babylon (Vala) and the giant (the sleeping Albion). Hence the two fowls, one of whom flourishes a sinister pen, like Urizen in the Morgan proof copy of the title page of *Europe.*

Another possible source of inspiration for the *Jerusalem* design was suggested by Sir Geoffrey Keynes as some of the human-headed bulls in Jacob Bryant's *New System, or an Analysis of Antient Mythology* (1774-76), for which Blake himself, as Basire's apprentice, may have worked on some of the engravings.[15] Bryant had called attention to "the author of all generations," the "father of mankind," as "l'Homme-Taureau" and had held that "the Moon, and the sacred Steer were the two principal emblems in the Pagan world" (III, 589, 599). Vala, as nature goddess equivalent to Diana, is in Blake's design appropriately drawn by oxen. But the serpents are apt vehicles for her as goddess of chastity; dragons draw Cynthia in Blake's *Melancholy,* (B, Pl. 678), for Milton's "Il Penseroso"; in both versions of *The Brothers Meet the Attendant Spirit in the Wood* (B, Pls. 619, 627), for *Comus;* and in Plate 14 of *Job.* Still another possible source of Blake's design is the winged bull of Persepolis, a suggestion made by Anthony Blunt, but unfortunately compromised by his statement that Blake borrowed the idea from an engraving which did not appear until 1821, after Blake had already completed the poem.[16] But the winged bull of Persepolis had appeared at least as early as 1711, in the plates of Cornelis de Bruyn's *Reizen over Moskovie, door Persie en Indie* (Amsterdam, 1711), translated into English in 1737 as *Travels into Muscovy,* where Plate 123 of the French edition is retained. The possibility that Blake knew this work is heightened by the fact that some of the plates were adapted for later editions of Jacob Bryant's *New System.* The winged bull also appeared in 1778 in Carsten Niebuhr's *Reisebeschreibung nach Arabien und andern umligegenden Ländern* (Copenhagen, Vol. II, Pl. 20), with face restored as human. Since the latter part of this voyage, and consequently this plate, were not included in the English translations, probably Blake would have been much more likely to meet the winged bull of Persepolis in Pierre François Hughes Hancarville's *Recherches sur l'Origine, l'Esprit, et les Progrès des Arts de la Grece* (1785). It appears there in the Supplement (Plate 9). For this work Thomas Stothard drew and the patron, Charles Townley, engraved a plate dated 1783 and printed, unlike the other, unsigned plates, in wine brown. Blake had apparently studied and made copies of some of the engravings in Hancarville's earlier *Collection.*[17] Since Blake and Stothard were at the time working closely together, Blake probably heard about this work from his friend. The Hancarville engraving of the winged bull of Persepolis brings together several elements in the *Jerusalem* design, not only the bulls with their human faces, but wings suggesting the feathered creatures which ride upon Blake's oxen. Even more influential might have been Hancarville's major thesis, which was conveniently and accurately summarized by Henry Maty in his *New Review* for January, 1785. According to Hancarville, of all the animal symbols

> the ox, and the serpent, which represented the Creator of the material world, and the Author of all sensible beings, were the oldest; these two remained the longest and spread the widest. They are still found in those parts of Asia, in which Mahometanism has not made its way. We find them . . . on great numbers of marbles and monuments of Italy, Egypt, Syria, India, Japan, China, Persia, Tartary, Scandanavia, and all the countries formerly inhabited by the Celtes. . . . in some monuments, we see the ox beginning to take the human head, but still preserving the horns, ears, and bodies of the animal. (VII, 18)

A final possible source may have helped to suggest the two winged gnomes and the sleeping riders. In a woodcut fantasy by Goltzius called *Night,* Night herself rides on the front of her chariot, holding a torch; and a cock rides on a wicker covering overhead. Her owl is perched beside her. Inside the chariot, headed left, like Blake's, the sole occupant, perhaps Persephone, sleeps, crowned with a wreath of poppies. The chariot is drawn by bats (Goltzius, Vol. II, Pl. 420).

Though Plate 41 of *Jerusalem* parodies the dragon of Revelation, the serpents there suggest also the worship of nature. This nature worship characterizes the Spectre and the Shadow, the two sleepers riding in the procession, for the female idea of space separates man from his perceptions and insists upon the reality of the physical, as opposed to the mental and spiritual; and this perversion, man as Spectre is stupid or dormant enough to accept and require others to accept. The serpent, then, sometimes serves as an alternate but virulent form of the earthworm of mortality. Thus on Plate 6 of *Urizen* (see Fig. 49), as Urizen falls, the other three Zoas accompany his fall into materialism, entwined by the uncrested serpent of materialism. Here only Los, as Erdman suggests (*IB,* p. 188), exhibits any sign of hope, throwing out his arms while the others clutch their heads. Later in the poem the inhabitants of the cities shrink together "in reptile forms" (25.37). Blake's symbolism was probably influenced here by Swedenborg: "The Sensual Things in Man," "the most ancient People" called "Serpents, because as Serpents live close to the Earth, so sensual Things are closely connected with the Body; hence Reasonings grounded in Things sensual concerning the Mysteries of Faith, were called by them the Poison of Serpents . . ." (*AC,* Par. 195).

As the ouroboros, the serpent with tail in mouth, the snake suggested for Blake not only the repetitious aspect of nature, with the regular return of constellations and the sun and the seasons, but the circular quality of science, or deductive reason.[18] This emblem appears, for example, on the title page of Night III of *Night Thoughts.* (See Fig. 50.) Though the serpent completes the circle only on the verso design (I, *NT*79), it is already in the act of catching its tail in its mouth. Here Blake contrasted the bound cycle of nature with the aspirations of man, suggested by the heavenward gestures and glance of Narcissa, as she rises superior to the cyclical materialism

The Reptiles 113

of nature and toward the right. Later in *Night Thoughts* the ouroboros provided for Blake an apt base for man, erect upon it, his hands clasped heavenward:

> Emblems just,
> *Nature* revolves, but Man *advances;* Both
> Eternal, *that* a Circle, *this* a Line.
>
> (I, NT257)

These non-venomous snakes are given neither the crests of the viper nor the flames which emanate from some of the more malign serpents.

Many of Blake's snakes of nature, however, are seven-coiled, a symbol of particular virulence. For example, Blake showed, for Young's line "Wit, a true Pagan, deifies the Brute," a worshipper adoring a fork-tongued, crested, and seven-coiled serpent (I, NT163). At the top, bottom, and left-hand margins of Plate 10 of *Europe* (see Fig. 51) a begemmed, seven-coiled, crested, fork-tongued, and fire-breathing serpent represents the vicious aspects of this nature worship, when "Thought chang'd the infinite to a serpent; that which pitieth: / To a devouring flame" (10.16-17). The odd-numbered five horns, or crests on this serpent and others probably suggest its virulence more than Blake's ignorance of herpetological anatomy, although Buffon's successor Lacépède reported that both ancient and modern naturalists had given the horned viper four, or even eight horns.[19] Artists like Aldegrever and the emblematists were fond of the crest for ornamental reasons, in part; for although Aldegrever used it for the Satanic serpent, it appears in the ouroboros of the emblem books. In his "Truth," rather interestingly, Cowper named pride "The subtlest serpent, with the loftiest crest" (l. 476).

A strange double ouroboros in the form of a brazen serpent extruding peacock feathers appears on Plate 62 of *Jerusalem*. (See Fig. 20.) As we have seen in our discussion of the peacock symbol, the giant Albion is here being tormented in part by his own pride, but crushed also by the Spectral body of nature. Earlier the poet lamented, "Reasonings like vast Serpents / Infold around my limbs, bruising my minute articulations" (15.12-13). The more usual form of the Brazen Serpent is that of the vegetated Jesus on the Cross, prefigured by the Brazen Serpent which Moses erected in the Wilderness. This worship of serpentine materialism, of the Brazen Serpent, or the historical Jesus, Blake developed in the "shadowy man," the Spectre:

> Then Rolld the shadowy Man away
> From the Limbs of Jesus to make them his prey
> An Ever devo[u]* ring appetite
> Glittering with festering Venoms bright
> ....
> But when Jesus was Crucified
> Then was perfected his glittring pride
> In three Nights he devourd his prey
> And still he devours the Body of Clay
> For Dust & Clay is the Serpents meat
> Which never was made for Man to Eat[.]
>
> (E, pp. 522-23)

This serpent, as Blake depicted it in *Moses Erecting the Brazen Serpent* (B, Pl. 521), does not cure, but encircles all those who allow it to cast its spell upon them, all those who believe in a physical or magical cure for a spiritual disease.[20]

For Blake the serpentine nature of Satan and the dragon of Revelation suggested not sin against an external God, but the State of Satan — domination of the individual by the Spectre of abstract reason and by the Selfhood. This use of the serpent Blake may have owed to Boehme and Swedenborg. In his *Signatura Rerum* Boehme had held that Christ "will bruise the Head of the Serpent, *viz.* of my Self-hood" (9.65); and in Freher's designs in the Law edition of Boehme, if one unfolds deeply enough, he finds in Volume III, Table 2 a serpent named "SELF LOVE" coiled about the fallen man's heart, a serpent replaced in the regenerated man's heart (Table 3) by a dove. "The Serpent," Swedenborg explained, "signifieth all Evil in general, and Self-Love in particular . . ." (*AC*, Par. 251).

This serpent of the Selfhood appears in Blake as early as *Tiriel*. In his State of Selfhood, Tiriel is inclined to see others there; as we have seen, he curses his sons in Lear's fashion as serpents, and even his faithful daughter: "Laugh serpent youngest venomous reptile of the flesh of Tiriel" (6.32). As Robert Essick has suggested, the snakes which subsequently infest her hair probably represent the curses implanted there by the Selfhood of Tiriel,[21] though they doubtless derive in part from the serpents of Medusa and the Furies. In *Jerusalem* in rejecting her Humanity and asserting her own Selfhood, England resembles "A long Serpent, in the Abyss of the Spectre which augmented / The Night with Dragon wings" (54.29-30). The Abyss suggests the immensity of space which the Shadow, the selfish Emanation, maintains is the final reality; and the night, the spiritual darkness which accompanies and prompts this assertion of the Selfhood.

The serpent of the Selfhood Blake also represented as the Covering Cherub, the angel who guards against our reentering Paradise. The epiphany of the Covering Cherub to Los is one of the final actions of *Jerusalem:*

> Thus was the Covering Cherub reveald majestic image
> Of Selfhood, Body put off, the Antichrist accursed
> Coverd with precious stones, a Human Dragon terrible
> And bright, stretchd over Europe & Asia gorgeous
> In three nights he devourd the rejected corse of death[.]
>
> (89.9-13)

This Covering Cherub of Spectral nature and man's own selfishness is the

> Veil which Satan puts between Eve & Adam
> By which the Princes of the Dead enslave their Votaries
> Teaching them to form the Serpent of precious stones & gold. . . .
> *Jerusalem* 55.11-13)

This same symbol Albion uses at the close of the poem to confess to Christ,

> my Selfhood cruel
> Marches against thee deceitful from Sinai & from Edom
> Into the Wilderness of Judah to meet thee in his pride
> I behold the Visions of my deadly Sleep of Six Thousand Years
> Dazling around thy skirts like a Serpent of precious stones & gold
> I know it is my Self: O my Divine Creator & Redeemer[.]
>
> (96.8-13)

Undoubtedly this serpent of the Selfhood enwraps Satan in the watercolors for *Paradise Lost,* for the entrance of Satan into Paradise heralds the rise of the Selfhood in man.

Not only does the serpent of abstract reason and the Selfhood seduce the individual, but it dominates the law, morality, and religion enforced by the state — the dragon-crocodile Urizen. The dragon Urizen appears at the top of Plate 4 of *America* (see Fig. 52) and, to the left, Urizen in a more human form, clutching his tables of the law and hurling thunderbolts, like an outraged Zeus, at the colonies, enforcing conformity even at the expense of imprisonment, hanging, and war. This dragon in serpent form dominates the title page of *Europe* and, seven-coiled and breathing fire, reappears on Plate 10.

In *Jerusalem* the dragon Urizen reappears with the reptilian Covering Cherub and with "the Serpent, / Orc" (14.2-3), to dominate the fallen Albion. Only at the apocalypse, which we witness in *The Four Zoas,* will Urizen reassume his proper, redeemed form, at the command of the Eternal Man:

> Arise O stony form of death O dragon of the Deeps
> Lie down before my feet O Dragon let Urizen arise
> O how couldst thou deform those beautiful proportions
> Of life & person for as the Person so is his life proportiond[.]
>
> (120.28-31)

On page 70 Urizen the crocodile beast is heavily armored and finned; and the flame which he emits shows his malignancy. Only his feet reveal that his form had once been human. This crocodile form Urizen is anxious to renounce: "Urizen wept in the dark deep anxious his Scaly form / To reassume the human & he wept in the dark deep . . ." (121.1-2). Some aspects of the crocodile appear also in Blake's sea-monster Leviathan.

It was an apt symbol. In the emblem books a symbol for the hypocrite, the crocodile was developed by the naturalists into a terrifying monster. According to Lacépède, in whose plates it stretches to enormous length, "il exerce une domination plus absolue que celle du lion & de l'aigle. . . ." "Cet animal énorme . . .étend sa puissance sur les habitants des mers, & sur ceux que la terre nourit."[22] The alligator of South America, Stedman described as of "violent strength and unequalled ferocity, being particularly fond of human flesh"; and he claimed to have seen the head of a crocodile which "must have measured above sixty feet in length" (I, 145, 147). Lavater suggested, "Thus debased, thus despicable, thus knotty, obstinate, and wicked, thus sunken below the noble horse, terrific, and void of all love and affection, is this fiend incarnate."[23]

The code of religion and morality demanded by the dragon-crocodile Urizen is celebrated by reptile priests in serpentine temples. Here the self-righteous Selfhood protects itself by attributing sin to those who act differently and who therefore commit sin. As Blake asserted in the Keys for *The Gates of Paradise*, "Serpent Reasonings us entice / Of Good & Evil: Virtue & Vice" (E, p. 268). In Plate 11 of *Job* a cloven-footed god pointing to the Ten Commandments is wreathed by the serpent, just below the caption "Satan himself is transformed into an Angel of Light & his Ministers into Ministers of Righteousness." In *Milton* Leutha complains of Satan's becoming "Cloth'd in the Serpents folds, in selfish holiness demanding purity / Being most impure" (12.46-47). On Plate 11 of *Europe* (see Fig. 28) serpent or scorpion tails appear beneath the two angels who flank the Urizenic papal-regal figure to suggest the hypocrisy of those who enforce the legal and moral codes. Both Boudard (II, 33) and Richardson (II, 135) had the tail of a scorpion appear from beneath the figure of Fraud to suggest her deceptive malignity; and Gravelot used a serpent for the same purpose (IV, 91). In "Earth's Answer" and "The Garden of Love" of *Songs of Experience* and in "I Saw a Chapel" and "Infant Sorrow" of the Notebook the serpent again suggests the restrictive and repressive hypocrisy of the priesthood. In "To Nobodaddy" Blake questioned the spirituality of the priest-regulated marriage dominated by Nobodaddy and social and religious codes where "none dare eat the fruit but from / The wily serpents jaws" (E, p. 471). In *America* the priests are terrified when the revolutions in America and France take marriage out of their hands: "The doors of marriage are open, and the Priests in rustling scales / Rush into reptile coverts . . ." (15.19-20).

The serpentine priests officiate particularly in Druidic shrines like Stonehenge. In *Jerusalem* these dragon altars characterize the worship observed by the fallen Albion:

His fires redound from his Dragon Altars in Errors returning.
He drew the Veil of Moral Virtue, woven for Cruel Laws,
And cast it into the Atlantic Deep, to catch the Souls of the Dead.
(23.21-23)

This religion of moral virtue and moral law substitutes vengeance and human sacrifice for forgiveness as "around Jerusalem" "the Druids reard their Rocky Circles to make permanent Remembrance / Of Sin. & the Tree of Good & Evil sprang from the Rocky Circle & Snake" (92.23, 24-25).

As an alternate form of human sacrifice, a reptile priest urges war as divinely sanctioned:

> The Serpent of the woods
> And of the waters & the scorpion of the desert irritate
> With harsh songs every living soul. The Prester Serpent runs
> Along the ranks crying Listen to the Priest of God ye warriors
> This Cowl upon my head he placd in times of Everlasting
> And said Go forth & guide my battles. like the jointed spine
> Of Man I made thee when I blotted Man from life & light
> Take thou the seven Diseases of Man store them for times to
>   come. . . .
>
> (FZ 98.20-27)

The "seven Diseases of Man" are surely the Seven Deadly Sins. The Prester serpent is pictured at the bottom of the page, in cobra form, with hood, looking very like the "Hooded Serpent" of Brookes (opposite III, 265). Its poison, Brookes commented, is "extremely dangerous, and perhaps more strong than that of any other" (III, 378). Charles Owen, a copy of whose *Essay towards a Natural History of Serpents* (London, 1742) was in the Library of the Royal Academy, suggested that its head "looks as if it were cover'd with a large long *Hood,* like a *Monk's Cowl*" (p. 115). Lacépède also noticed the resemblance of the hooded cobra's head to the human face and added that "sa morsure est mortelle."[24] Other serpents, however, are almost as virulent. Thus the Archbishop of Paris, in *The French Revolution,* rises to advise war "In the rushing of scales and hissing of flames and rolling of sulphurous smoke" (l. 127), in an atmosphere recalling some of the hellish councils in *Paradise Lost.*

The serpent also suggests the nature of Orc, the cyclical character who starts out as a revolutionary figure and ends up as its Urizenic opposite. Orc first claims for himself the serpent symbol in *America,* as he becomes the lover of the "nameless female," the "shadowy daughter of Urthona," or nature (1.4, 1). Since he claims the symbol and she accepts it as appropriate for him (2.12), we can hardly

The Reptiles

reject it when Albion's Angel accuses him of being the "Eternal Viper self-renew'd" (9.15), or questions him, "Art thou not Orc, who serpent-form'd / Stands at the gate of Enitharmon to devour her children" (7.3-4). He admits, "I am Orc, wreath'd round the accursed tree" (8.1). We recognize in the serpent symbolism here a reminder of Satan's degeneration in *Paradise Lost*. At first Orc seems to be a heroic rebel battling for humanity against the stifling tyranny of repression. But implicit in the serpent symbolism of the rebel as well as in his name (as we shall see in our next chapter) is his inevitable degeneration. On Plate 5 a human-headed serpent coiled into a downward spiral and clutching a victim (see Fig. 53) probably represents Orc and the punitive tyranny of violent revolution, as it sets up its own retaliatory scales of justice and elevates its sword. It is doubtless also Orc who makes the ironic proclamation of a millenium: "The Spectre glowd his horrid length staining the temple long / With beams of blood; & thus a voice came forth, and shook the temple" (5.6-7). The poet has just remarked that "heat but not light went thro' the murky atmosphere" (4.11).

In *The Book of Urizen*, even though there is an embryonic analogy in the gestation of Orc, the serpent symbolism also seems intended to suggest Orc's reptilian nature:

> The worm lay till it grew to a serpent
> With dolorous hissings & poisons
> Round Enitharmons loins folding. . . .
>
> (19.26-28)

In *The Four Zoas* the serpent imagery for Orc suggests the malevolent and stupid Spectre:

> And Orc began to Organize a Serpent body
> Despising Urizens light & turning it into flaming fire
> Recieving as a poisond Cup Recieves the heavenly wine
> And turning affection into fury & thought into abstraction
> A Self consuming dark devourer rising into the heavens[.]
>
> (80.44-48)

Thus the revolutionary red Orc becomes more and more like the Urizen whom he opposes. When he unites with Vala, he loses human form and becomes a totally destructive force:

> No more remaind of Orc but the Serpent round the tree of Mystery
> The form of Orc was gone he reard his serpent bulk among
> The stars of Urizen in Power rending the form of life
> Into a formless indefinite & strewing her on the Abyss[.]
>
> (93. 24-27)

Perhaps Los makes the clearest statement concerning the serpentine nature of Orc:

> There is a State namd Satan learn distinct to know O Rahab
> The Difference between States & Individuals of those States
> The State namd Satan never can be redeemd in all Eternity
> But when Luvah in Orc became a Serpent he des[c]* ended into
> That State calld Satan[.]
>
> (115.23-27; *E*, p. 380)

Chapter Eight

Marine Life

If all the serpents, outside of *The Marriage of Heaven and Hell*, are to some degree malevolent embodiments of the Selfhood or the Spectre, yet they are capable of being redeemed and reincorporated within the body of Man. However, possibly apart from the dolphin, which Blake never depicted and only once mentioned,[1] all the creatures of the sea seem to be without the prospect of such redemption. Marine life, Blake depicted as life at its lowest possible level, where light penetrates with difficulty or hardly at all, life submerged in the Sea of Space and Time. It is a place of the damned. The fall into the ocean of Time and Space is epitomized by the fall of Tharmas from shepherd to marine god. In *The Four Zoas*, he laments,

> The Body of Man is given to me I seek in vain to destroy
> For still it surges forth in fish & monsters of the deeps
> And in these monstrous forms I Live in an Eternal woe[.]
> (69.11-13)

For in the realms of the sea-god Tharmas all rational and imaginative life has been drowned. At the apocalypse, when Tharmas resumes his role as shepherd, all other forms of life rejoin man, but in Blake's myth the marine creatures apparently do not. In the versions of the apocalypse or near-apocalypse which Blake gave in *The Four Zoas, Jerusalem*, and *America*, there appear all sorts of animal, avian, reptile, insect, and plant life. (See Fig. 1.) The joint worm, the scaly newt, the spider, the grasshopper, the thistle are there. But except for a nonce reference (*FZ* 110.6), fish appear in neither the verse nor the designs. Evidently in the New Jerusalem, when the New Jerusalem, when the sea of materialism is dried up, there will vanish the marine forms which inhabited that sea.

We are prepared for this development by Blake's account of the Flood. In *Jerusalem* not only are the dove and the raven sent out to look for dry land, but the eagle, lion, and serpent also.

> They send the Dove & Raven: & in vain the Serpent over the
>   mountains.
> And in vain the Eagle & Lion over the four-fold wilderness.
> They return not: but generate in rocky places desolate.
> They return not; but build a habitation separate from Man.
>
> (66.70-73)

They do not return because man has sent them out from the ark of his being. There are no amphibians, even, to send; evidently they had previously lived apart from man. Since Blake saw the separation of the animals from man after the Flood as a stage in man's Fall, and since the marine animals are mentioned neither in this separation nor in the apocalypse, they seem to embody an aspect of man's personality not to be reincorporated or redeemed, but rejected. Swedenborg had explicated the death of a third part of the sea creatures, in Revelation 8.9, as "the perishing of every thing scientific that was alive in the natural man" (*AE,* Par. 513). On Plate 37 of *Jerusalem,* in reversed writing are the lines:

> Each Man is in his Spectre's power
> Untill the arrival of that hour,
> When his Humanity awake
> And cast his Spectre into the Lake[.]
>
> (*E,* p. 810)

Blake's marine creatures represent these Spectral qualities.

Within this stultifying sea only the polypus, the orc, and the whale, or Leviathan, exhibit distinctive qualities. Blake's fish are all, indiscriminately, cold-blooded. The Bible makes no distinction among the numerous varieties of Mediterranean and Palestinian fish; and fish appear quite rarely in the emblem books.[2] Even though England was a nation of fishermen and though its poets before as well as after Isaac Walton knew and discriminated among the numerous varieties, Oliver Goldsmith commented that for fish, "Those qualities, singularities or advantages, that render animals worth naming, still remain to be discovered." "Those with the largest mouths pursue almost every thing that has life; and often meet each other in fierce opposition, when the fish with the largest swallow comes off with the victory, and devours its antagonist" (VI, 154, 167). "Compare them with other animals," Lavater commented, "with the lion, for example, and how little meaning do you trace in their physiognomy! Who does not perceive at the first glance, a want of understanding, a total incapacity to reflect and design" (II, 126). Swedenborg reinforced these views. In general he assigned man's will to the beasts; his intellect, to the birds; and "Things scientifical, which have their Birth from Things sensual," to the fish (*AC,* Par. 991). "Fishes and Shell-Fish" are imperfect animals, "forasmuch as they are the lowest of that Degree, are as it were in the Shade when the others are in the Light" (*Angelic Love and Wisdom,* Par. 346). These correspondences are inherent: ". . . the spirits, who are not in spiritual truths, but only in natural truths, which are scientifics, appear in the spiritual world in seas, and when viewed by those who are above, as fishes, their thoughts, which proceed from the scientifics with them, being what thus appear. For . . . the ideas of the thought of those who are natural, and think from scientifics alone, are turned into forms of fishes: hence also there appear in the seas various species of fish . . ." (*AE,* Par. 513). How appropriate that Newton should dominate Blake's Sea of Space and Time, of scientifics.

Blake's fish differ mainly in size and swallow. They are either looking for prey or are potential prey. Goldsmith had commented at length upon the pallid senses of the fish. In his designs and verse Blake's fish suggest man's submerged condition, unable or unwilling to use his senses, as fish are unable to close their eyes. On Plate 13 of *America* (see Fig. 24) four open-mouthed devourers hover about the recumbent figure at the bottom of the sea, ready to amalgamate him; and a sea-serpent entwines one of his legs. Above him swim five closed-mouthed fish, at the moment unmolested. This is Albion, or Man, sunk beneath the Atlantic, or the sea of materialism and hatred, in the internecine struggle between England and America. In *Europe,* in a plate warningly infested with caterpillars, snakes, vulture, and eagles (see Fig. 25), Enitharmon praises her daughter Ethinthus, "queen of waters," "for thy children flock around / Like the gay fishes on the wave, when the cold moon drinks the dew" (14.1,2-3). Like most of her speech, this passage is ironic, though not so intended by Enitharmon, for the cold moon and the fish-women suggest the selfish state of Ethinthus and the placid and cold state of sleep into which man has fallen as a result of the Female Will and the domination of nature and materialism.

In Plate 40 of *Jerusalem* (see Fig. 54) the theme is somewhat varied, for the body of Albion is here trapped in the web or net of Vala rather than submerged beneath the sea. Below the entangled, supine Albion a large, open-mouthed fish is ready to accommodate five closed-mouthed fish headed for his "gently smiling jaws." This particular design of Vala netting her prey has some interesting antecedents and parallels. In Design 4 for Gray's "Ode on the Death of a Favourite Cat" (see Fig. 55) Blake depicted Gray's "Genii of the stream" as two innocent-looking fish-humans, or "angel forms" (p. 50), but both heavily finned. When despite this warning, Selima plunges, they turn at once into their proper selves as spirits of the water, bodies covered with scaly armor (see Fig. 56), as they now flourish their spears. Some twenty years later, in his designs for "Il Penseroso," Blake included the spirits of the water in *The Spirit of Plato* (B, Pl. 680). Here at the lower right a gold-finned fish-woman nets a male victim.

The requisite characteristic of the fish-woman is her scales. She need not display her fins at all in order to exhibit signs of warning. In his Notebook Blake wrote,

> A Woman Scaly & a Man all Hairy
> Is such a Match as he who dares
> Will find the Womans Scales Scrape off the Mans Hairs[.]
>
> (E, p. 517)

Probably Blake was here thinking of Samson and Delilah, who deprived Samson of his virility by cutting off his hair. But scales characterize a number of seductive females, as fish or fish-women, among whom are not only the figures just mentioned, but "the daughters of men," in one of Blake's designs for the book of Enoch, after they have begun to seduce the gods (B, Pl. 1081); and scales are suggested by the fishnet, or linked tunic of one of the three women who are attempting to seduce Christ in *Christ Refusing the Banquet,* a design for *Paradise Regained.*[3]

In *Jerusalem* (see Fig. 19) we again find the fish-woman, without scales but displaying even more vicious fins. The young female swimming sinisterly downstream is Sabrina, whose male counterpart has the region of the Severn (71. 44-45). Offspring of an illicit romance, according to Milton's *History of Britain,* she was thrown into a river by the irate wife, Gwendolen, who then gave the river Sabrina's name — the Severn.[4] Sabrina is thus the genius or the spirit of the Severn. In the lines immediately above her, she and her sister Ignoge (her grandmother in the original account by Geoffrey of Monmouth) are sharpening "their beamy spears" (11.19), as are the genii on the design for Gray's "Ode." Likewise seductive, but fully clothed, the fashionably dressed female on the top of the next plate is Ignoge, her sister or grandmother, betrayed by the fins visible only on her arms. Preening herself, she is evidently sharpening her spear for prey.

Though doubtless Blake got from Milton's *History* the relationship between Sabrina and Ignoge, he got most of his portrait of Sabrina from Drayton's *Polyolbion* and from *Comus*. In *Polyolbion* Drayton presented Sabrina's story at some length, as emanating from female jealousy and causing "the first intestine strife," since "the Britans" were "put a-land upon this promis'd shore."[5] In *The Four Zoas,* similarly, Blake in effect reenacted Cain's murder on the Severn: "The brother & the brother bathe in blood upon the Severn" (25.17); and in *Jerusalem* "As Gwendolen cast the shuttle of war," the borders of Scotland and England and of Wales and England, "The Humber & the Severn: are drunk with the blood of the slain" (66.62, 63). In the maps which accompany *Polyolbion* each stream has its own nude nymph or spirit, but there Sabrina is distinguished by being, apparently, the only nymph who is crowned. Not only does she so appear on several maps (for Songs IV, V, VII, and XIV), but "This noblest *British* Nymph" even holds court: "Now *Sabrine,* as a Queene, miraculouslie faire, / Is absolutelie plac't in her Emperiall Chaire . . ." (IV.23; V.1-2). In the contest which follows, "not the smallest Beck / But with white Pebles makes her Tawdries for her neck" (V.49-50). Although it is not prominent on Plate 11 of *Jerusalem,* Sabrina wears there the coronet which distinguishes her in *Polyolbion*. Her pearled wrists and necklace she owes in part to *Polyolbion*, and in part to *Comus*. In *Comus* Sabrina appears as the genius of the Severn and as a confirmed champion of virginity, Blake's State of the Shadow. As the Attendant Spirit informs the Lady,

> The guiltless damsel flying the mad pursuit
> Of her enraged stepdam *Guendolen,*

> Commended her fair innocence to the flood
> That stay'd her flight with his cross-flowing course,
> The water Nymphs that in the bottom plaid,
> Held up their pearled wrists and took her in. . . .
>
> (ll. 828-34)

In the Huntington copy of *Sabrina Disenchanting the Lady* (B, Pl. 622), the pearls of the nymphs adorn her hair and her wrists. Accompanied by younger nymphs, Sabrina has adequate height for adulthood, but is quite flatbreasted.[6]

Below the fish are the eels, sea-snakes, lampreys, mollusks, and crustaceans which infest the ocean, especially the ocean floor, "imperfect" animals, as Swedenborg called them (*Angelic Wisdom*, Par. 346). These appear almost exclusively in the designs and are sometimes too minute for identification. Water-snakes are often venomous; and on Plate 40 of *Jerusalem* one dives open-mouthed at the line "however fruitful are our fields" (l. 12). On Plate 11 a bloodsucking lamprey, which surges up at the lower right from the black waters surrounding the sinister Sabrina, seems headed for the swan, Shakespeare, the spirit of poetry, above. Drayton, Pennant,[7] and Goldsmith all proclaimed the supremacy of the Severn for its lampreys, but Goldsmith added that the mouth of the lamprey "more resembles the mouth of a leech than an eel" and that the lamprey "has a property resembling that animal of sticking close to and sucking any body it is applied to" (VI, 270). Below even these marine forms, the mollusks and crustaceans represent an almost completely enclosed, trapped form of life, like the oyster, shrimp, starfish, and the murex on Plate 28 of *Jerusalem* (see Fig. 35) or the seashells at the bottom of Plate 15 of *Job* (see Fig. 8), below the predatory eagles and even Behemoth and Leviathan.

But for marine life on its lowest possible terms, Blake developed the symbol of the polypus. It was particularly apt to suggest man's vegetable existence, for the fresh-water polyp was the recently discovered missing link between zoological and botanical forms of life. Moreover, according to Defoe's son-in-law Henry Baker, polypi "are voracious animals: a *Polype* can swallow a Worm, whole, twice or thrice its own length."[8] As a squid or octopus, able to hide itself by its ink, it was a symbol sometimes used for the flatterer and was by Holtzwart linked with Orcus:

Est genus in terris hominium, quos protulit Orcus,
    Assentators lingua Latina uocat.
Hi Polypi mores referunt, mutare colorem[.][9]

The polypus exists in many forms, and Blake seems to have visualized several of them; for he gradually extended both the physical image and the symbol.[10] In his lamentation in *The Four Zoas* Tharmas visualizes himself as a jellyfish: "My skull riven into filaments. my eyes into sea jellies / Floating upon the tide wander bubbling & bubbling" (44.24-25). The Medusa, Blake may have seen in his residence at Felpham, for several types of Medusae were cast ashore on the southeastern coasts of England. "The Medusa, a gelitinous substance," Barbut wrote, "appearing like a lifeless lump of jelly, floating on the surface of the ocean, and plying underneath with its tentacles, embraces the small fry, and devours them. . . ."[11] The polyp evidently first takes this form in Blake's verse, for in *The Book of Los* Blake used it to suggest the yet unorganized body of the fallen Urizen after his lungs have begun to heave: "Dim & glutinous as the white Polypus / Driv'n by waves & englob'd on the tide" (4. 57-58). Later, in *Jerusalem*, after Albion falls, Blake used pretty much the same image: "The Lungs, the Heart, the Liver, shrunk away far distant from Man / And left a little slimy substance floating upon the tides" (49.17-18). Other Medusae, probably, are the pink polypi adjoined to Newton's rock at the bottom of the Sea of Space and Time. (See Fig. 57.) Here the lowest form of animal life and the rock help to characterize Newtonian science.

In *The Four Zoas, Milton,* and *Jerusalem* Blake seems to have visualized a much larger form of the polypus — that of the giant squid or the octopus, the tentacles of which emerge from beneath the fallen Zoas of Plate 92 of *Jerusalem*. (See Fig. 58.) "Pliny," Goldsmith reminded us, "has even described one, the arms of which were no less than thirty feet long" (VIII, 180).[12] The fallen body of Albion now becomes visualized as a polypus. In *The Four Zoas* Los again binds the body of Urizen, now identified as that of Albion; but the body, with its tentacles of nerves and veins, is that of the polyp:

The Corse of Albion lay on the Rock the sea of Time & Space
Beat round the Rock in mighty waves & as a Polypus

> That vegetates beneath the Sea the limbs of Man vegetated
> In monstrous forms of Death a Human polypus of Death[.]
>
> (56. 13-16)

The symbol also, Blake gradually enlarged. In *Milton* it sometimes suggests man's instinctual and emotional nature, devoid of thought and imagination. Thus Los warns his sons against "Eternal Death," "No Human Form but only a Fibrous Vegetation / A Polypus of soft affections without Thought or Vision" (24. 37-38). Here in *Milton* Blake made the symbol more complex by including in the polypus the Five Females, as the senses, and the Shadowy Mother Nature, and by visualizing all the fallen civilizations as a monstrous polypus. The six-fold Ololon

> see the Ulro: a vast Polypus
> Of living fibres down into the Sea of Time & Space growing
> A self-devouring monstrous Human Death Twenty-seven fold
> Within it sit Five Females & the nameless Shadowy Mother
> Spinning it from their bowels with songs of amorous delight
> And melting cadences that lure the Sleepers of Beulah down
> The River Storge (which is Arnon) into the Dead Sea:
> Around this Polypus Los continual builds the Mundane Shell[.]
>
> (34. 24-31)

When Blake accentuated man's fallen emotional, rather than his instinctual nature, he sometimes associated the polypus with Orc:

> In Allamanda & Entuthon Benython where Souls wail:
> Where Orc incessant howls burning in fires of Eternal Youth,
> Within the vegetated mortal Nerves; for every Man born is joined
> Within into One mighty Polypus, and this Polypus is Orc.
>
> (29. 28-31)

Later, now "Woven by Urizen," the polypus encompasses the entire universe with its forty-eight constellations and especially the forty-eight "Cities of the Levites," thus nature and the debased scientific reason and the code of good and evil, rather than man's instincts and emotions: "And the Forty-eight Starry Regions are Cities of the Levites / The Heads of the Great Polypus, Four-fold twelve enormity" (38. 1-2).

In *Jerusalem* the polypus combines hatred and accusation with moral law. Thus Hand, the accuser, absorbs Albion's twelve sons: "Out from his bosom a mighty Polypus, vegetating in darkness" (18.40). The emphasis upon moral law is again suggested in Erin's lament: "O Polypus of Death O Spectre over Europe and Asia / Withering the Human Form by Laws of Sacrifice for Sin . . ." (49. 24-25). Somewhat confusingly for visualization, the daughters of Albion modify the human form into "A mighty Polypus nam'd Albions Tree": "By Invisible Hatreds adjoind, they seem remote and separate / From each other; and yet are a Mighty Polypus in the Deep!" (66.48, 53-54). At times in *Jerusalem* also Blake chose to emphasize the arid rational quality which he gradually associated with the polypus. Thus the Daughters of Albion weave "For Rahab & Tirzah; till the Great Polypus of Generation covered the Earth./ In Verulam the Polypus's Head, winding around his bulk" (67.34-35).

This polypus which combines debased reason with hatred and moral law is perhaps seen most clearly at its latest appearance in *Jerusalem:*

> Then all the Males combined into One Male & every one
> Became a ravening eating Cancer growing in the Female
> A Polypus of Roots of Reasoning Doubt Despair & Death.
> . . . .
> Envying stood the enormous Form at variance with Itself
> In all its Members. . . . (69.1-7)

If the polypus represents man fallen to the lowest form of zoological life, in effect almost a vegetable existence, the whale and Leviathan represent him in his most vicious form. In the Bible the whale was often identified with the terrifying Leviathan. Shakespeare used it several times to suggest inordinate voracity.[13] For Swedenborg it suggested "those who possess the Universals of the Knowledges of Faith, as Scientifics, and apply them to such evil Purposes" (*AC,* Par. 42). "Whales, or large Fish, signify the Generals or Universals of Things scientifical . . ." (*AC,* Par. 991).

Blake's whales are rare, but one of them is particularly important — Orc. In *America* Orc boasts, ". . . sometimes a whale I lash / The raging fathomless abyss" (1.14-15); and the "shadowy daughter" of Urthona sees him as "a Whale in the South-sea, drinking my soul away" (2.14). Orc is obviously asserting his power and importance by identifying himself with the most powerful forces in nature: the lion, king of beasts; the eagle, king of the air; the serpent, king of reptiles; and the whale, monarch of the seas. Orc lists his animal manifestations in approximately the same order as Satan uses them as disguises: as Satan descends from cormorant to lion to toad to serpent, so Orc sees himself successively as eagle, lion, whale, and serpent.

Moreover the very name which Orc gives himself should warn us. The word "Orc" was still in Blake's day used to designate Hades or its keeper; a whale or sea-monster; and specifically the grampus, or killer whale. In his translations of Homer, Pope used the word "Orcus" for Avernus and its master (*Odyssey* 20.428; *Iliad* 5.1037); and Blake must have been familiar with this usage, for in *Tiriel* he had Ijim refer to "vacant Orcus" (4.76). In *The Faerie Queene* Orcus is the fierce keeper of Hades (II.xii.41.7) and a frightening monster (VI.xii.26.9). In *Polyolbion* Drayton referred to "The uglie Orks that for their Lord the Ocean wooe" (II.95) and "the armed Orks of *Neptunes* grieslie Band" (V.97). In his 1783 translation of Ariosto's *Orlando Furioso,* for which Blake furnished an engraving, Thomas Hoole used the term for frightful monsters on both land and sea. Orc is a hideous Polyphemos-like giant in an extended "history" of Norandino and Lucina:

> To paint his bulk misshap'd and giant size,
> Instead of eyes, upon his dreadful face
> Two bones projecting fill'd each eyeless space.
> ....
> Like some wild boar's his spreading tusks appear'd,
> Vast were his jaws, his hairy breast besmear'd
> With filth obscene. . . . (XVII.206-13)

Orc is also a sea dragon (like that guarding Andromeda), that Orlando slays in order to rescue a captive maiden (XI.227-93).[14]

But the most precise use of the word "orc," or "orca," was to designate the grampus, or killer whale. Blake may have read Pliny's description of how in combats with the largest whales, the orcae, "armed with most terrible, sharpe, and cutting teeth," made the seas rough "(with the blasts of their breath, and the blowes giuen by the assailant) so great, as no tempestuous whirle windes whatsoeuer are able to raise" (Bk.IX.ch.vi). George Shaw commented, "The Orc or Grampus . . . is of a fierce and predatory disposition, feeding on the larger fishes, and even on the Dolphin and the Porposse." It is "one of the most ferocious inhabitants of the ocean."[15] Lacépède remarked of "le Dauphin Orc": "Ce nom d'orque nous reppelle plusieurs de ces fictions enchantresses que nous devons au génie de la poésie. Il retrace aux imaginations vives, il reveille dans les coeurs sensibles, les noms fameux et les aventures touchantes, et d' Andromède et de Persée, et d'Angélique et de Roland. . . ."[16] Probably Blake expected his readers to be as alert to the name, for his Orc inhabits the Sea of Space and Time in some of its most degraded manifestations, as killer whale as well as serpent and polypus. Orc is probably the sea-monster described by Pliny, now belching flames toward the left, toward America, at the bottom of Plate 14 of *America,* for not far above the image are the lines:

Fury! rage! madness! in a wind swept through America
And the red flames of Orc that folded roaring fierce around
The angry shores. . . . (14.10-12)

In both verse and design Orc is a destructive, not a constructive force.[17] Orc is firmly tied to such monsters in *The Four Zoas* also. There the fallen Albion sleeps while

    round his limbs the Serpent Orc
Fold without fold encompasses him And his corrupting members
Vomit out the Scaly monsters of the restless deep[.]
(108.25-27)

On Plate 14 of *Job,* finally, the flame-breathing sea monster is probably more orc than serpent.

If the orc was the most ferocious form of actual marine life, the mythical Leviathan was even more terrifying. Just what manner of monster Leviathan was, is open to question, but the enormous sea serpent was in Blake's day more than mythical: natural scientists like Bishop Erik Pontoppidan and even the great Carl von Linné evidently credited stories of the kraken and other monstrous sea serpents. Following Pliny, Owen called Leviathan a *"Marine-Dragon"* or "Marine-Serpent" (p. 143), and atop his Plate 6 exhibited a sea serpent very similar to Blake's Leviathan of *Job.* Blake may have drawn some details of his Leviathan from the South American boa, as described and pictured by Stedman and engraved by himself (Vol. I, Pl. 19). For according to Stedman, this amphibious snake, armed with a double row of teeth and "two strong claws," "will devour . . . a wild boar, a stag, or even a tiger" or a man (I, 175, 176). For Swedenborg Leviathan represented the complete materialist: ". . . by leviathan the oblong serpent, are signified those who reject all things which they do not see with their eyes; thus the merely sensual, who are without faith, because they do not comprehend; by leviathan the crooked serpent, are signified those who therefore do not believe, and yet say that they do believe" (*AE,* Par. 275).

Leviathan, Blake used for one of the most virulent forms of the Spectre — aggressive, self-righteous warfare. In *The Marriage of Heaven and Hell,* Leviathan represents not a real horror, but the terror felt by the Angels of the Establishment at the emergence of unleashed passions of the Revolution in France and their fear of war and invasion thence. As the narrator remarks to the Angel, "All that we saw was owing to your metaphysics" (*E,* p. 42). In *Night Thoughts* (II, *NT*349) another scaled and crested sea-serpent carries a scaled papal rider holding the crosier of religious authority. In *Jerusalem,* however, Leviathan becomes a creation of the Spectre and the embodiment of naval warfare:

> the Spectre reads the Voids
> Between the Stars; among the arches of Albions Tomb sublime
> Rolling the Sea in rocky paths: forming Leviathan
> And Behemoth: the War by Sea enormous & the War
> By Land astounding. . . .
>
> (91.36-40)

Thus in Blake's painting *The Spiritual Form of Nelson Guiding Leviathan* (see Fig. 59), Leviathan suggests England's triumphant but aggressive naval warfare, and the portrayal of its victims shows the oppression and death which it prompts and justifies. In Plate 15 of *Job* (see Fig. 8), finally, Leviathan, "King over all the Children of

Pride," appears as a coiled sea serpent, breathing fire in the colored Butts copy, crested and equipped with six rows of teeth. Like other denizens of the deep, however, Leviathan is doomed to extinction whenever man is ready to renounce the Selfhood which it represents.

Chapter Nine

The Trees

> . . . thou seest the Trees on mountains
> The wind blows heavy, loud they thunder thro' the darksom sky
> Uttering prophecies & speaking instructive words to the sons
> Of men: These are the Sons of Los! These the Visions of Eternity[.]
> *(Milton* 26.7-10)

Just as the zoological forms served Blake as emblems of man's divided personality, so did the botanical forms, particularly in the designs. Man's fall into the materialized life of Experience, Blake sometimes exhibited as an arborization or vegetation. To illustrate Young's line "Half-life, half-death join There," he exhibited a human dendrifying into a laurel, legs enrooted and arms beginning to branch out (I, *NT*258). In *Jerusalem* the Veil of Vala which Albion casts into the Atlantic "To catch the Souls of the Dead" begins "to Vegetate & Petrify / Around the Earth of Albion. among the Roots of his Tree"; and human life becomes an arborized existence "between the Oak / Of Weeping & the Palm of Suffering" (59.3-4, 5-6). Even Jerusalem laments that she is "Encompassd by the frozen Net and by the rooted Tree" (80.1). At the end of *Milton,* however, Ololon, reversing Daphne's metamorphosis, casts off the death clothes of her dendrified existence and reassumes human form.

A particular arboreal symbol which Blake sometimes used for fallen man is the upside-down tree, not the Upanishadic or cosmic Asvatha tree with its roots above in Brahma, but man with his head buried in materialism. Thus in his Design 24 for Dante an arborized suicide is enrooted, head-foremost, in the earth. On Plate 19 of *Milton* when Los opposes the return of Milton, "in fibrous strength / His limbs shot forth like roots of trees" (17.34-35), and his head branches out into roots. In *Europe* the "nameless shadowy female" admits that she is upside down: "My roots are brandish'd in the heavens. my fruits in earth beneath / Surge, foam, and labour into life . . ." (1.8-9).

Like the reversed tree, the forest is also threatening, for it shuts out the light and obscures the way; and it shelters predatory denizens of the dark. It had offered malignant symbolism not only in Spenser's Forest of Error, but in Dante's *selva oscura,* in Canto II of *The Inferno,* and in the "hideous wood" of *Comus.* For Swedenborg the forest was opposed to the "paradise," grove, or garden, and suggested "that the scientific principle has rule" (*AC,* Par. 9642). Blake's forests, especially the "forests of the night," are bewildering fastnesses infested by wild beasts and the owl and the bat — embodiments of the blind, malignant Selfhood. In "To the Evening Star," when the star withdraws its protection, "the wolf rages wide, / And the lion glares thro' the dun forest" (*E,* p. 410). It is the habitat of the Tyger. In *Europe* the misguided Enitharmon urges her "lion Rintrah," now separated from his Emanation and dominated by his Spectre, "raise thy fury from thy forests black!" (8.2). In *The Four Zoas* Urizen's tigers "roam in the redounding smoke / In forests of affliction"; and "Red rage redounds" as Orc rouses "his lions from his forests black" (77.9-10; 91.18). In *Milton* the hero, pushing through a dense forest to find his Emanation, meets his adversary the triple-headed Cerberus. (See Fig. 3.) Just as the dragon Error obstructs the Redcrosse Knight in the "wandering wood," so the Spectrous Negation opposes Milton in the middle of the forest.

In *The French Revolution* the forest suggests also the domination of empire. Burgundy fears lest "the ancient forests of chivalry" be hewn down and urges the nobles to "rouze up the ancient forests of Europe" (ll. 93, 101). Similarly in *Europe* the "nameless shadowy female" laments that she brings forth

> howling terrors, all devouring fiery kings.
> Devouring & devoured roaming on dark and desolate mountains
> In forests of eternal death, shrieking in hollow trees.
>
> (2.4-6)

In *Urizen* Blake developed still another symbolism of the forest — that of separation, a symbolism already adumbrated in the "forests of solitude" of *Visions of the Daughters of Albion* (5.19). Urizen prefers his "vast forests" and his "forsaken wilderness"; and "in his dark solitude / When obscur'd in his forests," he creates monsters of abstraction (*Urizen* 3.23, 15; *Ahania* 3.5-6).

Blake's vegetation is, of course, not always completely symbolic. Some of his trees, boughs, and vines, especially in *Songs of Innocence and of Experience,* were intended partly to furnish a frame or a background for the design. Trees, boughs, or vines overarch the scene or provide at least a partial frame in sixteen plates of *Innocence* and sixteen of *Experience.* If a plate in *Innocence* lacks a foliage frame or a central flower, then at least vegetation decorates the text; and even in *Experience,* where London and interior scenes permitted less vegetation, few plates lack it completely.

But if trees and other vegetation characterize both *Songs of Innocence* and *Songs of Experience,* they do so with a difference. Innocence is characterized by shady, deciduous trees; Experience, by dead or dry ones. Such arboreal symbolism is eminently Biblical. The Psalmist promised that the righteous man "shall be like a tree planted by the rivers of water, that bringeth forth his fruit in his season; his leaf also shall not wither" (1.3). John the Baptist warned that "every tree which bringeth not forth good fruit is hewn down"; and Christ cursed the fig tree for failing to yield fruit in its season.[1] The emblematists used the green tree to suggest virtue and harmony; the dead or dry tree, winter, old age, poverty, melancholy, or apathy.[2] The Renaissance artist used the flourishing tree to suggest life; and the dry tree, death, as did Shakespeare.[3] Such patterns Swedenborg reinforced: "Tree signifies man, and the fruit thereof the good of life." ". . . he produces Leaves, next Blossom, and finally Fruit, for he produces such Things as are of Intelligence, which also in the Word are signified by Leaves, next such Things as are of Wisdom, which are signified by Blossoms, and finally such Things as are of Life, viz. the Goods of Love and Charity in Act, which in the Word are signified by Fruits: Such is the representative Similitude between the Fruit-bearing Tree and the Man who is regenerated . . ." (*Conjugial Love,* Par. 135; *AC,* Par. 5115).

Following these conventions, Blake also distinguished between the flourishing tree of Innocence and the barren tree of Experience. In *Songs of Innocence* the sheltering, leafy trees suggest divine protection, for example in "The Little Black Boy." (See Fig. 60.) Blake doubtless remembered Swedenborg's suggestion in *Divine Love and Wisdom* that the African is spiritually superior (Par. 11). But he was probably drawing also upon the symbolism of the Canticles and the development of this symbolism in the emblem books. The important symbol here is shade. Beneath the willow of his own suffering, as well as Christ's, the Little Black Boy promises for the English boy, "Ill shade him from the heat till he can bear, / To lean in joy upon our fathers knee" (*E,* p.9). Careful to avoid identifying God with an angry Jehovah or with Boehme's principle of Wrath, from whom Christ shields us, Blake had the enlightened mother portray God as a loving sun, giving away his light and heat; and on the second plate he depicted God as Christ the Good Shepherd. But the body of the Little Black Boy, his mother suggests, is "like a shady grove." In the Canticles the sunburnt beloved also is "black," and both unabashed and exculpatory: "I *am* biack, but comely. . . . Looke not upon me, because I *am* black, because the sun hath looked upon me. . . ." This "lily of the valleys," however, is now shaded by her beloved: "As the apple-tree among the trees of the wood, so *is* my beloved among the sons. I sat down under his shadow with great delight. . . ." (1.5-6; 2.1, 3). The conventional interpretation of this passage Blake could have easily seen and read in Quarles: "Jesus, our Saviour, on the Tree, / Yields a delightful Shade. . . ." ". . . that Tree a pleasant Shadow yields / And from the Wrath Divine the Sinner shields" (p. 125). Grateful for his sunburnt face and grove-like body, the black disciple wishes to shade the white boy, seeking his love as the "black" of the Canticles both seeks the love of her beloved and acknowledges his protective shade. This discipleship is suggested not only in the verses but in the virtual sponsorship of the white boy in the design.

Except for the trees in "The School Boy" and "The Little Girl Lost and Found," which were designed for *Innocence,* those in *Experience* are bare, some of them perhaps dead. They afford no protection; and such fruit as they bear is, like that in "A Poison Tree," deadly. Even as early as *There is no Natural Religion* a bare tree on Plate 5 apparently suggests the sterility of the "reasoning power" (*IB,* p. 28). In *The Four Zoas* Los perceives Urizen's envy of Orc to be "like to a blighted tree" (77.27). More dramatically, the blasted human trees on the final plate of *America* suggest present spiritual aridity. (See Fig. 61.) Here a giant, submissive figure dominates the scene, kneeling in prayer, hair or tears (or both) flowing in a Niagara. Behind, human trees, blasted perhaps by the ravages of war, suggest man dendrified, or much rather, spiritually dead, for even the suicides in Canto XIII of Dante's *Inferno,* whom Blake presented on Designs 24 and 25, put forth leaves "of dusky hue" (XIII.4), and so does the arborized Fradubio in *The Faerie Queene* (I.ii.30.6-7). But here in *America* these wooden people give no sign of hope, put forth no leaves. On the giant's thigh a diminutive shepherd pipes to his sheep and dog. However, the serpent hidden among the false roses (lacking hypanthium) and the deadly poppy and the thorns at the bottom threaten more terror and horror to come.

Among Blake's trees the most important and complex is the Tree of Death and Life. Occasionally, in conventional fashion, he presented it as two: in *The Fall of Man* the fatal Tree, at the left of Christ and entwined by the Serpent, bears figs; the Tree of Life, at Christ's right, bears apples. However for many theologians, poets, and artists, and often for Blake, the two trees were but one. Frequently in mediaeval and Renaissance poetry and art the Cross, often along with the fruitful tree of Revelation 22.2, was joined with the Tree of the Fall, so that the Tree of Death becomes the Tree of Life.[4] They become one, for example, in Canto XXX of the *Purgatorio*. For Boehme the two trees were "but *one,* but manifest in two Kingdoms."[5] In Donne's "Hymn to God, my God" the Cross and Adam's tree "stood in one place" (l. 22). Sometimes in Renaissance art "a single tree is bare on one side and green on the other."[6] In the Lucas Cranachs' *Allegory of the Fall and the Redemption* (Nuremburg) that part of the tree to Christ's right is fruited; that to his life, bare; and in *The Fall and Redemption* by Lucas the Younger, the Tree of Life and Death is fruited to our right and withered at our left, for here Christ is not central, but at our right. For Swedenborg, the Tree of Life was "God living in man"; the "tree of the science of good and evil . . . man believing that he lives from himself" (*Conjugial Love,* Par. 135).

Blake also interpreted the traditional arboreal symbolism quite metaphorically. "SCIENCE," he engraved on his *Laocoön,* "is the Tree of DEATH / ART is the Tree of LIFE[.]" In his "Vision of the Last Judgment" he suggested, "The Combats of Good & Evil is Eating of the Tree of Knowledge The Combats of Truth & Error is Eating of the Tree of Life."[7] In his visual designs, however, he frequently combined the trees. In his Design 89 for the *Purgatorio* (see Fig. 48) he adapted the Cranach convention by presenting healthy fruit at the right of Beatrice, Christ's vicegerent, withered fruit at her left. In *Eve Tempted by the Serpent* (B, Pl. 402), he twisted the two trees together as firmly as he did the companion elms in "The Little Girl Found." (See Fig. 6.)

For his Tree of Life and Death Blake used elements of the apple, the fig, and the oak. In both classical and Christian tradition the apple was a fruit of both death and life. Many of the Fathers of the Church identified the fatal Tree as the apple partly because its name, *malum,* meant "evil," also. The apple of Eris which Paris awarded to Venus, in a scene which Blake painted (*B,* Pl. 964), brought war and destruction; and Spenser lamented "that famous golden Apple," "cause of all their wrong" (*FQ* II.vii.55.4; IV.i.22.5). In Renaissance art Adam and Eve are often tempted by an apple. Dürer portrayed an apple tree in his 1510-11 woodcut of the Fall (in the *Small Passion*), and Adam and Eve both hold apples in his engraved *Fall of Man* (1504). Milton made the apple tree that of the Fall; and for Boehme too, the apple was the fatal fruit which Adam ate (*Three Principles* 17.1, 33, 57, 91). Yet in the Canticles the "apple" tree is pictured as beautiful and fragrant; and in the Renassiance the apple tree often represented the grace given man by Christ's Passion (Stewart, pp. 72-73). For example, Quarles's apple tree bears Christ crucified: "Our SAVIOUR's Cross, that cursed Tree! / What gen'rous Fruits it bears for me!" (p. 124).

For Blake the flourishing, fruit-bearing apple tree could be a symbol of Innocence, of creative, fruitful life; the bare or diseased apple tree, of a fruitless or poisoned existence. On the title page of *Songs of Innocence* a protective apple tree bearing varicolored apples and entwined loosely by a young vine shades and doubtless helps to feed the nurse and children. In *Night Thoughts* (II, NT346) a tiny madonna nursing her child is seated upon an apple while an angel spreads his arm in the gesture of joy made by a cherub in "The Blossom." But the apple tree of Experience bears poisonous fruit, if any at all. In *The Four Zoas* Tharmas recalls his separation from Enion almost in terms of the Fall, for Enion turned away, he laments, "Among the apple trees & all the gardens of delight / Swam like a dream before my eyes" (94.2-3). Albion laments, "The Corn is turnd to thistles & the apples into poison . . ." (119.42). The tree of "A Poison Tree" shows only speary twigs, not fruit or even leaves; but beneath is stretched the "foe" who has eaten the "apple bright" (*E,* p. 28). This apple is doubtless the poisonous fruit of the Tree of Mystery growing "in the Human Brain," "the fruit of Deceit, / Ruddy and sweet to eat" (*E,* p. 27). In "To Tirzah" a monstrous branch of an otherwise invisible apple tree bearing seven apples and a few identifying leaves bends over Tirzah as she limits man.[8] An apple appears in the mouth of the serpent in *Eve Tempted by the Serpent* (*B,* Pl. 402) and in the hand of the recumbent Eve in *Satan Exulting over Eve* (*B,* Pls. 384, 389).

Just as the apple tree offered ambivalent symbolism of life or death, so did the fig tree. In the Bible and Roman literature it often suggests peace and prosperity,[9] and so it often served Blake. For Ahania, "My ripe figs and rich pomegranates" are "infant joy" (*Ahania* 5.26, 27). The puritanical Hand and Hyle of course condemn the "sinful delights" "beneath the Vine and Fig-tree" (*Jerusalem* 18.16, 19). With the advent of Job's new spiritual awareness, the fig tree of Plate 19 now flourishes and bears fruit, and Job and his wife sit humbly beneath it upon a grassy mound.

However, since Biblical scholars generally agreed that the fatal Tree could not have been an apple and since the fig tree certainly grew in Eden, furnishing leaves to clothe Adam and Eve, the fatal Tree was frequently represented as a fig tree. In Michelangelo's fresco in the Sistine Chapel, Adam and Eve eat figs from it; and in the Loggia, Raphael's and Giulio Romano's Eve gives Adam a fig from the Tree. For Swedenborg the fig tree usually, though not always, suggested "the natural Good of Man" and "as well the celestial as the spiritual, but external" (*AR,* Par. 334; *AE,* Par. 638); and the fig leaves with which Adam and Eve covered their nakedness, "moral Truths, under which were concealed the Things appertaining to their Love and Pride" (*Divine Providence,* Par. 313).

Blake probably embodied a similar suggestion in the fig leaves which he gave to Adam and Eve in both versions of *The Expulsion* (*B,* Pls. 643, 656) and to their similars on the title page of *Songs of Innocence and of Experience.* Fig leaves also cover the genitals of Adam and Eve in *Night Thoughts,* where "*Sense,* and *Reason,*" show the way to death (I, *NT* 119). Even though Milton had made the apple tree the Tree of the Fall, Blake preferred the fig for this purpose, even in illuminating Milton. He apparently used it, for example, in both versions of *Raphael Warns Adam and Eve* (*B,* Pls. 637, 650) and in both of *The Temptation and Fall of Eve* (*B,* Pls. 640, 653), for even though the fruit is frequently discolored or misshaped (since it is diseased), Blake carefully placed a few fig leaves on the tree to identify it.[10] One cannot, however, always positively identify the fruit of the fatal Tree of Mystery, for on it there grew "shining fruit" "of many colours & of various poisonous qualities / Of Plagues hidden in shining globes that grew on the living tree" (*FZ* 82.20, 21-22).

Invariably malignant, however, is the symbolism of Blake's banyan fig, which sends down suckers to the earth and which Milton described as the source of clothing for Adam and Eve (*PL* IX.1101-4). Possibly Blake made some of his figs of the Fall so round that they look like apples because "Sir" John Hill inaccurately pictured and described the banyan fig (*Ficus benghalensis*) as a "perfect globe."[11] With the labyrinthine banyan, Blake was tempted to conflate the poisonous Upas tree of Java (*Antiaris toxicaria*), which Erasmus Darwin had horrifyingly described in his *Loves of the Plants*.[12] In Blake's Notebook, a pestilence darts from the robe of the French Queen, and she "quite grows to the ground / There is just such a tree at Java found" (*E*, pp. 500, 861).

The banyan image, which is probably suggested in the net entrapping the Urizenic figure in "The Human Abstract," Blake developed in *Ahania* and *The Four Zoas* into his Tree of Mystery. As Urizen writes his "book of iron,"

>   the horrid plant bending its boughs
> Grew to roots when it felt the earth
> And again sprung to many a tree.
> ....
> Enrooting itself all around
> An endless labyrinth of woe!
>
> The corse of his first begotten
> On the accursed Tree of MYSTERY:
> On the topmost stem of this Tree
> Urizen nail'd Fuzons corse.   (*Ahania* 3.65-4.8)

In *The Four Zoas* (78.4-12) Blake related in some detail the formation of the banyan tree of mystery. In *Jerusalem* this tree becomes Albion's, for as Albion is sitting by Tyburn's brook, the scene of executions, "underneath his heel, shot up! / A deadly Tree, he nam'd it Moral Virtue":

> The Tree spread over him its cold shadows, (Albion groand)
> They bent down, they felt the earth and again enrooting
> Shot into many a Tree! an endless labyrinth of woe!
>
> (28.14-15, 17-19)

A third tree which furnished visual and symbolic details for the Tree of Death and Life is the oak. In emblematic tradition it ordinarily suggested utility, prosperity, strength, long life, and courage, and often provided a wreath to honor eminent orators, poets, and musicians.[13] Spenser and Shakespeare several times used the oaken garland for a victor;[14] and in his "Vision of the Last Judgment" Blake crowned Eliakim, who is dragging Satan to judgment, with an oak wreath (*E,* p. 557). The oak wreath which he gave Cicero, however, in his portrait for Hayley (*B,* Pl. 438), he qualified by adding a scene of execution where Cicero presides. In Renaissance art the oak was sometimes the Tree of Life and Salvation.[15] It was the especial favorite of the English. In his *English Garden* William Mason voiced a popular feeling, "for my soul," he avowed, "Holds dear an antient oak, nothing more dear"; and William Gilpin maintained that "The oak of no country has equal beauty."[16] As used by Zoffany and Gainsborough in outdoor portraits of the gentry, the central, protective oak was a symbol of security, longevity, and often aristocracy.[17] Some of the family are usually seated upon an ornamental stone or metal bench; and in his Plate 4 Blake placed Job and his wife, in their early, affluent state, upon a stone bench, beneath an oak.

For Blake the flourishing single oak, especially the village oak, was almost always protective, not threatening. Blake's village oaks shelter happy family groups, some seated below on oaken benches. The singer of one of the songs of *Poetical Sketches* loves the "oaken seat, / Beneath the oaken tree" (*E,* p. 414); and Urizen remembers when "laughter sat beneath the Oaks & innocence sported round" (*FZ* 73.1). A protective oak shelters the villagers seated or playing below in "The Ecchoing Green" (see Fig. 62); and beneath them a lad rolls his hoop much as does a boy who forms part of a similar village group beneath the Selborne oak in Gilbert White's recently published *Natural History of Selborne* (1789).[18] Above Blake's lad flourishes the honeysuckle of plenty; below him is a loaded grapevine of human brotherhood. Beneath a single oak stands the visionary shepherd-prophet in *Moses at the Burning Bush* (B, Pl. 534).

But in the Bible and in Nordic myth the oak was sometimes a symbol of sacrifice.[19] It was also a symbol of English jingoism. A favorite song was, ironically, Thomas Boyce's "Heart of Oak." The oaks of Windsor Forest provided Alexander Pope with symbols of British naval might: they "Bear *Britain's* Thunder, and her Cross display."[20] In "Yardley Oak," however, which Hayley published while Blake was working with him, Cowper lamented the military usage of the oak,

> hewn by the thousands, to supply
> The bottomless demands of contest wag'd
> For senatorial honours. (ll. 101-03)

For Swedenborg the oak represented "the natural man, and by its leaves, the scientifics and knowledges of truth therein," and oak groves suggested "exterior Perceptions, or the Perceptions of Things scientifical, which appertain to the external Man" (*AE*, Par. 504; *AC*, Par. 1443). More specifically, the Biblical Oak of Weeping (Genesis 35.8) suggested "the lowest of the natural Principle, into which, and at last out of which, hereditary Evil is ejected" (*AC*, Par. 4565).

In Experience Blake's single bare oaks, or those flourishing in the forest, represent deadly forces of reaction; the fallen, Spectral reason; and its code of good and evil. In *America* the forces of reaction wish to "bring the stubbed oak to overgrow the hills" (9.8). In *Europe* the Baconian pillars of Verulam are "oak-surrounded" (10.7); and in *Ahania* Urizen sits upon "his dark rooted Oak" (3.16). Here in the oak grove the Spectre dominates, and the Shadow, Nature, becomes "his Tabernacle. / And his Oak Grove" (*Jerusalem* 65.60-61). In Blake's *Adam Naming the Beasts* (B, Pl. 890), an oak, the only tree visible, is presumably the fatal Tree (despite the unattractiveness of mast), for Adam caresses the head of the crested serpent as he points to a prominent acorn.

The oak grove is also the place of human sacrifice. The Druid temples are "Patriarchal Pillars & Oak Groves." The "House of Death" exists "among the rooted Oaks: / Among reared Rocks of

Albions Sons" (*Jerusalem* 27. 38, 80, 81-82). In *Milton* "Jerusalems foundations" are "laid in ruins from every Nation & Oak Groves rooted" (6.15, 16). This religion is also one of military aggression. In *Jerusalem* Albion's sons are "Carried in Arks of Oak before the armies in the spring"; and "blood and wounds and dismal cries" occur under "the shadows of the oak" (21.45; 65.51). "With the iron shuttle of War among the rooted Oaks of Albion," eventually "Albions Forests of Oaks coverd the Earth from Pole to Pole" (71.61; 89.23). Taken all together these characteristics of the oak constitute the "Oak of weeping" which, like the palm, stands upon the "edge of Beulah" (23.24, 25), man's inevitable suffering in arborized Experience.

Though the species of the particular dry deciduous tree is not always symbolically important, the dry oak is especially malign; and Blake occasionally identified his dry or dead oak by the fallen leaves, as in the "Holy Thursday" of *Experience* (see Fig. 68), where at the very bottom of the plate a child lies dead upon a pile of oak leaves. Such leaves, with or without the trunk of the parent tree, frequently imply death or spiritual sleep. At the bottom of Plate 12 of *Europe,* for example (see Fig. 36), a victim of empire prays in vain among fallen oak leaves; and at the very end of the poem, as Los "Call'd all his sons to the strife of blood" (15.11), an oak branch suggests the devastation in prospect. In *And She shall be Called Woman* (B, Pl. 512), as Ms. Piloo Nanavutty has pointed out, the gigantic oak leaf upon which Adam rests may suggest "human misery."[21]

From these trees — the apple, the fig, and the oak — along with the hanging tree, the Cross, the wicker man of Scandanavia, and the net, Blake compounded visual and symbolic details to make up a complex Tree of Death and Life which comprises on the one hand the moral code of good and evil, arid science, the Spectre, human sacrifice, and war, and on the other hand the protective, unselfish, and fruitful pattern of life taught and exemplified by Christ.

The birch, like the apple, the fig, and the oak, can be ominous when bare and benign when flourishing. It provided switches and rods for schoolmasters as early as Pliny and as recently as Cowper and Blake himself, for Modest Dame Lurch, one recalls, does not spare the birch.[22] According to Ms. Raine and Ms. Kaufar, in some of Blake's designs birches may be symbols of death, as they were occasionally in the ballads.²³ Indeed in his designs dead or dry birches, often identifiable by their bark, are ominous, especially that behind the Tyger, where its markings pick up and reinforce those of the beast. The barren tree of "The Human Abstract" may also, from its markings, be a birch; here the spiritual poverty is as shocking as the selfishness of the little apologist of "The Fly," where the tree at our right is again probably a birch. Yet the birch was among "love-animated plants"; according to Aubrey, it was especially sacred, and branches were placed in homes at Easter and St. John's Eve (Wimberly, p. 156, n.). On Plate 2 of *Thel* (see Fig. 76) a flowering silver birch hangs protectively over Thel and the lily of the valley; and in *Night Thoughts* protective flowering birches shelter a lily animated with a humanized family and a mother with her two children (II, *NT*492; I, *NT*63).

Among the other symbolically important deciduous trees, the elm is generally a tree of Innocence; the willow, of Experience. Since the elm most readily accepts the grapevine, this union was used to symbolize marriage from the time of Ovid's *Metamorphoses* (14.661-68); and in the ballads a tree with an entwined vine was a commonplace for enduring love (Wimberly, pp. 38-42). The emblem writers also used the union of elm and vine to suggest friendship;²⁴ and Wynne, the education of youth (pp. 82-88). For Spenser the elm was the "vine-prop Elme" (*FQ* I.i.8.7); and in *The Comedy of Errors* Adriana pleads with the Syracusan Antiphalus, "Thou art an elm, my husband, I a vine" (II.iii.174). In *Paradise Lost* the union symbolizes the wedding of Adam and Eve:

> they led the Vine
> To wed her Elm; she spous'd about him twines
> Her mariageable arms, and with her brings
> Her dowr, th' adopted Clusters, to adorn
> His barren leaves.   (V.215-19)

Except for the dry elm of "A Little Girl Lost," which provides no protection for Ona, Blake's elms follow these conventional symbolic patterns. Many either embrace companion elms or are encircled by vines. At the end of "The Little Girl Found" an entwined pair of elms, a love motif in the ballads (Wimberly, p. 41), suggests the enduring and fruitful marriage which Lyca has found by traversing

Experience and entering a Higher Innocence. In an interesting variant in *Night Thoughts* two pairs of entwined trees, probably elms, comment ironically upon the ephemeral grief and unions of the mourning Ephesian widow, as Cupid shows her the way to assuage her grief for her dead husband in the arms of a lover (I, *NT* 189). The entwined elms of education appear as early as Plate 3 of *There is No Natural Religion:* there a mother or nurse is teaching a child near a vine-twined tree, and a similar scene occurs beneath the apple tree, again with its symbolic vine, on the title page of *Songs of Innocence*.

Although in the Bible the willow occasionally suggests rejoicing, there and elsewhere it has been more traditionally associated with lamentation, for example, in Blake's *By the Waters of Babylon* (*B,* Pl. 541). For the Greeks it was a symbol of mourning and death; and "because it was 'fruit-destroying,' was a symbol of sexual continence."[25] The emblem writers developed it as an attribute of sterility; and for the Renaissance artists it suggested sterility, famine, and mourning (D'Ancona, pp. 408-09). In *The Faerie Queene* the willow is worn by "forlorne Paramours" (I.i.9.3). In the "ballad" "The Willow-Tree" the deserted Cuddy wears a branch of willow in his hat; and in the lyric "Willow, Willow, Willow" the abandoned lover laments, "O the greene willow shall be my garland."[26] This song Desdemona takes, she says, from her mother's forsaken maid Barbary:

> She had a song of "Willow,"
> An old thing 'twas, but it express'd her fortune,
> And she died singing it.   (*Othello* V.iii.28-30)

So does Emilia subsequently sing it, as she is slain by her husband.[27]

For Blake also the willow suggested sorrow or sterility. The willow of present sorrow or future suffering is quite common in the designs, especially the weeping willow. Blake associated it particularly with the suffering of Christ. It appears, for example, above John the Baptist in *Our Lady with the Infant Jesus Riding on a Lamb* (*B,* Pl. 505) and, as Ms. Kostelanetz points out (p. 249), faces the sleeping child in the Goyder *The Christ Child Asleep on a Cross* (*B,* Pl. 495). As an omen of future suffering an isolated, emblematic branch of weeping willow appears above the happy children in "Nurse's Song" of *Innocence*.[28] In *The Gates of Paradise* the weeping willow under which a woman finds mandrake children may suggest the spiritual sterility of such vegetable births as well as foreshadow the inevitable future suffering. In *Jerusalem*, Plate 11 (see Fig. 19), the weeping willow at the top right suggests not only the suffering of Experience, but the spiritual sterility of man when he is dominated by the fish-woman, the siren Nature, below. In "The Clod and the Pebble," finally, the willow suggests both the suffering which characterizes the unselfish group above and the sterility of the selfish group below.

Among Blake's important evergreens — the yew, the laurel, and the palm — the yew, like the willow, is a tree of Experience. Although it was associated with immortality, it became in classical times an emblem of death, the Furies, and Hades, in the *Metamorphoses* 4.432-33 shading the path thereto. In England it was traditionally planted in churchyards;[29] and sprigs were used in funerals. According to Gilbert White, ". . . we seldom see any other very large or ancient tree in a church-yard but yews. . . ." "In the south of *England* every church-yard almost has it's yew, and some two . . ." (p. 326). In Gray's "Elegy" and in Blake's Design 4 for the poem, such a funereal yew is shaded "Beneath those rugged elms" (p. 150). In *Macbeth* slips of yew provide a poisonous ingredient for the witches' brew;[30] and in *Twelfth Night* Feste requests a shroud "stuck all with yew" for a lover "slain by a fair cruel maid" (II.iv.55, 54).

The melancholy and poisonous yew appears in Blake as early as *Poetical Sketches*, where a deserted woman laments that Despair "Brings me yew to deck my grave" (*E*, p. 413). Thereafter the yew appears mainly in the designs, where it cannot always be easily distinguished from the other evergreens, like the cypress. Since their symbolism is similar, precise identification of the particular evergreen is not always imperative. But Blake's yews can be distinguished from the weeping willows by their relatively horizontal twigs and from the other evergreens by the hollow which is eventually created in the center of the trunk by the decay and disappearance of the heartwood. Such yews, fairly frequent in Blake's designs, seem always to be associated with the fall into a poisoned Experience or death.

For example, in the Preludium plate of *America* (see Fig. 63), the foetus Orc, below, has been generated by the coupling roots of the yew tree above him.[31] Above, he has managed to struggle up the birth canal of the hollow and is now manacled by his jealous father, Los, as we understand clearly from *Urizen,* Plates 19 and 20. This sort of simultaneous presentation of two or more episodes characterizes not only much mediaeval art, but Plates 4, 5, and 15 of *America.* To help his readers to perceive this simultaneity, Blake placed at Orc's left, above, a miniature version of the six-coiled, headless earthworm which he portrayed at Orc's left below, where Orc takes the foetal position. Vegetative or vermicular, Orc is doomed from the outset to a cyclical existence. Some elements of the design can be seen and understood most clearly if we juxtapose this design with the vision of the Eternals in *Urizen,* published only a few months later. In the embracing tree roots we may well have the spectacle witnessed by the Eternals who

> shudder'd when they saw,
> Man begetting his likeness,
> On his own divided image.   (19.13-15)

On Plate 14 a yew with the same central opening and with similarly deeply embedded roots suggests an avenue to the cave beneath, or to Hades. On Plate 12 the yews afford to the aged pilgrim, perhaps Orc himself, now grown old, a return to the earth from which he originally emerged.[32]

Though the laurel is not mentioned or depicted in the illustrated canon, it appears fairly often elsewhere in Blake's work. Associated especially with Apollo, it suggested victory and honor, Apollo and poetry, or health and virtue.[33] Against the laurel as a wreath for the military aggressor, Blake protested, "The Strongest Poison ever known / Came from Caesars Laurel Crown" (*E,* p. 492). In a "Song" the poet proclaims his own gifts: "Round my young brows the laurel wreathes a shade" (*E,* p. 416). It encircles the heads of several poets in the portraits which Blake painted for Hayley; it characterizes the vision of the poet-prophet in Designs 1, 2, and 8 for Dante, graces the way to the Earthly Paradise, and helps to characterize it in Designs 85-87. In "A Vision of the Last Judgment" a prophetic

"Demon crownd with Laurel" drags down Time and Death (*E,* p. 556).

In the illuminated canon Blake preferred the more spiritualized palm. From primitive times date and coconut palms have emblematized peace and magnificence. Palm fronds strewed Christ's triumphal entry into Jerusalem and grace the white-robed multitude in Revelation 7.9. Emblem writers and poets used the palm to suggest peace, honor, magnificence, victory, temperance, joy, liberty, virtue, fortitude, truth, and eternal felicity.[34] Renaissance painters like Fra Angelico, Botticelli, and Raphael used it also to suggest the Passion (D'Ancona, pp. 279-87). In Freher's designs for Boehme the palm tree is the Tree of the Soul and the Tree of Paradise, emerging from the roots where the will and the spirit unite (Vol. I, Fig. 2). For Swedenborg, finally, the palm suggested "the divine wisdom of the Lord" and "the goods of the Spiritual Church, which are the goods of truth" (*AE,* Par. 458; *AC,* Par. 8369).

Blake's date palms and coconut palms carry the traditional felicitous implications. In "Edward III" Dagworth anticipates "palms of victory" in Heaven (v.29); and in *The Marriage of Heaven and Hell* a coconut palm as an emblem of magnificence follows the words "the fountain overflows" (8.35). Most of all, however, Blake associated the palm with Christ the divine imagination and the immortal spirit. Palms, usually date palms, promise his advent in *The Angel of the Divine Presence Clothing Adam and Eve* and appear in *The Repose, The Virgin and Child in Egypt, Christ's Entry into Jerusalem, The Hymn of Christ and the Apostles,* and *Judas Betrays Him* (*B,* Pls. 513, 543, 962, 515, 546, and 570). At the top of Plate 3 of *Europe,* on the serifs of the "A" in "A Prophecy," are a tiny flowering palm and a tiny willow, probably to suggest the advent, triumph, and subsequent suffering of the "secret child" (3.2), Jesus. In *The Four Zoas* and *Jerusalem* the palm of suffering, particularly that on Plate 33 (see Fig. 30), suggests not only Christ's Passion and the pain which the imaginative and unselfish must experience, but the ultimate victory of the immortal, imaginative spirit. The palm is, again, a tree of death and life.

Chapter Ten

The Plants

I had not taught thee then, the Alphabet
Of flowers, how devisefully being set
And bound up, might with speechlesse secrecie
Deliver arrands mutely. . . .¹

Man arborized is only a special form of man vegetated. Man rooted in the earth in plant form — as herb, weed, grain, vine, or flower — is also man limited by nature.² In *Jerusalem* as Reuben, Blake's embodiment of the sensual man, "enroots his brethren" (15.25), his father, Isaac, enroots and begins to assume the shape of the brier which has trapped the sacrificial ram. In Plate 40 (see Fig. 54) Albion himself, netted by Vala, has begun to vegetate: branches extrude upwards from his torso; and roots extend from below his thigh. Even though man is thus limited, however, he can be a malicious thorn or an insidious nettle or an aspiring sunflower or an unselfish lily.

The basic human plant is the mandrake. Although in Genesis 30.14-16 this herb is an aphrodisiac, the ancients usually regarded it as the herb of Circe which bestialized man (Rahner, p. 224). For Richardson, it was a "dangerous narcotic," which "causes stupifaction, forgetfulness and sleep" (I, 89). For Blake it was an apt symbol of man vegetated. In Plate 1 of *The Gates of Paradise* a woman, probably the malign nature goddess Vala, pulls her mandrake children from the earth. The "Keys" tell us, in verses which recall the mandrake of John Donne's "Progress of the Soul," of man's vegetation:

My Eternal Man set in Repose
The Female from his darkness rose
And She found me beneath a Tree
A Mandrake & in her Veil hid me[.]³

150

Later, in *Jerusalem*, Albion's degenerate son Schofield "is like a mandrake in the earth"(11.22).

To the contrary of the mandrake, the wild thyme, "Los's Messenger to Eden," Pliny had assigned all sorts of beneficial effects (XXI.xxi). According to Oberon, it characterizes Titania's favorite haunt: "I know a bank where the wild thyme blows" (*MND* II.ii.249). In "Lycidas" the death of the hero is lamented by woods and caves "With wilde Thyme and the gadding Vine o'ergrown" (l. 40); and in his *Fables of Flowers* Wynne celebrated the herb: "Thy purple dye, thy fragrant smell, / Sure no sweet blossom can excel."[4] Perhaps following Philip Miller's derivation in his popular *Gardener's Dictionary*,[5] or using his own knowledge of Greek, Blake associated wild thyme with the Passion, and with both Luvah and Los:

> The Wild Thyme is Los's Messenger to Eden, a mighty Demon
> Terrible deadly & poisonous his presence in Ulro dark
> Therefore he appears only a small Root creeping in grass
> Covering over the Rock of Odours his bright purple mantle
> Beside the Fount above the Larks nest in Golgonooza
> Luvah slept here in death & here is Luvahs empty Tomb[.]
> (*Milton* 35.54-59)

Thyme is deadly to Ulro because like Christ, the living Luvah, it threatens Ulro existence. Like the lark, it is a spiritual messenger of Los, a messenger of imaginative unselfishness.

Alternate forms of the mandrake are the weeds, especially the insidious brier, or spiny runner. In the Bible the brier is a symbol of sin: "that which beareth thorns and briers *is* rejected, and *is* nigh unto cursing; whose end *is* to be burned" (Hebrews 6.8) Some Renaissance artists used this symbolism; but Gravelot and the poets externalized it.[6] Swedenborg, however, again internalized the symbol: "the pricking briar denotes the false of the concupiscencies of self-love" (*AC,* Par. 9144). Blake used briers sometimes in conventional fashion as external dangers, sometimes as the binding forces of restrictive society, and sometimes as Biblical and Swedenborgian exhibits of selfishness. In *The Four Zoas* the fallen land is for Ahania a "land of briars & thorns / Where once the Olive flourishd" (109.14-15). Briers are underfoot as Virgil and Dante begin their journey in Design 1 and for Adam and Eve in *The Expulsion* (*B,* Pls.

643, 656), where doubtless they suggest Miltonic sin as well as their subsequent suffering. In "The Garden of Love" societal and religious restraint and restriction are "binding with briars, my joys & desires" (*E,* p. 26). In Plates 5 and 8 of *Job,* however, they suggest the nadir of Job's spiritual strength, especially in Plate 5, where their serpentine tails are a legacy of the Fall and an indication of the Selfhood. The briers at the feet of the Harlot and her giant on Design 89 of Dante (see Fig. 48) also suggest the Selfhood, as they do on Plates 15 and 40 of *Jerusalem.*

In the Bible thorns, part of man's curse for original sin, symbolize suffering (especially on the brow of Christ crucified), sin, and sloth; and in the emblem books and the poets, suffering, ignorance, jealousy, vice, and sloth.[7] Swedenborg suggested that "by Thorns and Thistles, which the Earth shall bring forth, is signified mere Falsehood and Evil," or "evil and the false vastating the goods and truths of worship" (*Divine Providence,* Par. 313; *AC,* Par. 9144). Blake also used thorns to indicate man's sufferings, especially from his own jealousy, from restrictive society, and from nature. Heavily rooted, they encrust the Tree in *The Temptation and Fall of Eve* (*B,* Pl. 653). Not only are the wife's jealous thorns in "My Pretty Rose Tree" the lamenter's only reward for his constancy, but thorns characterize also the envy which Enitharmon attributes to her parents: "They will withhold sweet love, whose food is thorns & bitter roots" (*FZ* 10.6). In "Holy Thursday" of *Experience* the paths of the children are "fill'd with thorns," inflicted by a callous society (*E,* p. 19). In "The Mental Traveller" nature "binds iron thorns around his head / She pierces both his hands & feet" (*E,* p. 484); and in *Jerusalem* the Daughters of Albion bind their victims with "thorns of iron."[8]

Thistles also are a part of man's fallen heritage, the equivalent of the Biblical tares.[9] Milton recorded them in *Paradise Lost* X.203-04; and Blake duly placed them underfoot in *The Expulsion*. In Renaissance art they became an emblem of envy, sin, and sorrow.[10] In Freher's designs for Boehme, for whom thistles are *"poisonful,"* they characterize fallen man and appear with thorns for "The Mystery of Iniquity" and beneath *"Reprobation."*[11] "These Thistle-Children," Boehme remarked in *The Election of Grace,* receive the "hot *Ens* of the sun," but not love, "according to the *Kind* of a Thistle." "For the Thistle can receive it no otherwise but in the *Likeness* of its Essence; as a Toad sucks nothing but Poison out of a good *Ens*"

(11.77-79). For Blake also the thistle suggested pride and envy. In *Night Thoughts* (II, *NT* 381) Satan sows tares, or thistles, by night in a wheatfield, as he does in a dramatic illustration for Hertel, Plate 49. Enion laments that she is "made to sow the thistle for wheat; the nettle for a flourishing dainty"; and the Eternal Man, that "The Corn is turnd to thistles & the apples into poison" — a line repeated in *Jerusalem*.[12] The thistle, "whose bitterness is bred in his milk / . . . lives on the contempt of his neighbour" (*FZ* 136.36-37). In a letter which Blake wrote to Butts the thistle was the envious tempter: to the outward eye a thistle, it was to the inward eye "an old Man grey," who warned him to remain in contented subjection to Hayley.[13]

The contrary of the thistle, grain suggested peace and prosperity, those who are to be gathered to Christ, and sometimes Christ himself, for not only is the bread his body in the communion, but in Renaissance art the Christ child is often portrayed upon a sheaf or stack of wheat.[14] In *The Four Zoas* and *Milton* as the Last Harvest is gathered, the corn of the fruitful is thrashed for the Last Supper.[15] On Plate 49 of *Milton* we see the "Human Harvest" of grain; and on the last plate the humanoid sheaves are ready for the harvest. On Plate 18 of *Job* the ripe stalks in the borders and the wheat field on Plate 19 indicate newly found peace and prosperity. In Experience, however, the grain is almost invariably blighted or denied. The "fat fed hireling with hollow drum; / Who buys whole corn fields into wastes, and sings upon the heath" (*VDA* 5.14-15) probably glances at George III and the military policies which were depleting England's grain fields. Again in *Jerusalem* "the Corn fields thunder along / The Soldiers fife" (16.5-6). Enion laments, "There is no City nor Corn-field nor Orchard! all is Rock & Sand" where once sparrow and robin "Gave songs of gratitude to waving corn fields round their nest" (*FZ* 16.5; 17.7). Although in *America* Orc boasts that the forces of reaction "cannot smite the wheat, nor quench the fatness of the earth" (9.5), yet plagues fall upon it "As a blight cuts the tender corn when it begins to appear" (14.6). On Plate 9 in the lodged wheat we see a child, prone as in "Holy Thursday" of *Songs of Experience*, and likewise apparently dead from the famine or the poison of war. The poppies growing nearby (perhaps common red field poppies), long a symbol of death, were by emblematists used to suggest sleep and ignorance.[16] Spenser's Cave of Mammon breeds the "Dead sleeping *Poppy*" (*FQ* II.vii.52.3); and Pope used it as an emblem of ignorance in *The Dunciad*. Darwin warned, "The plants of this class are almost all of them poisonous . . ." (p. 69, n.); and J. E. Smith agreed, "The whole plant is foetid, and of a poisonous quality. It is said to occasion madness."[17]

Prominent in the designs and complex in their symbolism are Blake's vines. Two analogues to the upside-down tree are particularly interesting: the falling vine and the independent vine. A vine which falls when it should naturally rise is either denying its own nature to aspire or exhibiting helplessness. On Plate 9 of *Jerusalem* the vine which coils around a tree (see Fig. 64), instead of rising, snakes downward into the Serpent, which tempts Eve below. On Plate 1 of *Europe* the falling vine at the right, unable to climb the rock above, probably suggests the destruction wrought by empire. On Plate 6 of *America* (see Fig. 65), for the "Slave Delivered," who optimistically looks up and to our right, the design conflicts with the promise which the verses and his gesture seem to extend. The blooming convolvulus on his left, possibly the morning glory, has nothing to support it in its beauty and can only fall. The falling grapevine on his right, some of its leaves already scattered, will never bear grapes. Below, the malignant toad, along with its cousin the eft, threatens a poisoned future, as does the central burdock or smooth-stemmed thistle. Moreover the vine which refuses to entwine a nearby support and, instead, even before a leaf appears, begins to twist around itself, exhibits an independence which is both selfish and sterile. The exuberant end spirals on Plate 36 of *Jerusalem,* where Los and Enitharmon create harmoniously, carry no such suggestions; nor does the Tree of Jesse motif in "The Ecchoing Green," Plate 2. But in "The Angel" (see Fig. 66) such a vine of the Selfhood characterizes the Maiden Queen, who reclines beneath the willow of sterility, for above her an independent vine stretches and waves both its free hands mockingly.

Just as the bread suggests the body of Christ, so does the wine, his blood. Comparatively easy to identify by its leaves, but quite varied in its implications is the grapevine, for like the fig and the apple, the grape can be a symbol of death as well as of life. The promise of the grapevine can also be deceptive. Swedenborg warned that "No grapes on the Vine denotes that there was no interior or rational Good" (*AC,* Par. 5117). Through no fault of its own, the vine which entwines the tree in "A Little Girl Lost" is denied protection from a parent elm whose head shows no leaves, let alone blossoms. In "The Angel" neither the perverse vine above the perverse Maiden Queen nor the grapevine below her will ever blossom.

Attributes of Bacchus, grapes and wine in the emblem books often suggest drunkenness, debauchery, and lust.[18] Indeed the grape was sometimes regarded as the fruit of the fatal Tree (D'Ancona, p. 164), and Blake probably presented as Earth's indictment, the quite unsupported cluster which hangs above the serpent and follows Earth's accusation of the jealous "Father of the ancient men" (E, p. 18). Sometimes Blake's grapes are intoxicating or poisonous, suggesting, particularly, war or the dominion of nature. In *The French Revolution* when Burgundy rises to speak, "red as wines / From his mountains, an odor of war, like a ripe vineyard, rose from his garments" (ll. 83-84). When in *Europe* Orc awakens, "in the vineyards of red France appear'd the light of his fury," and Los calls his sons "to the strife of blood" (15.2, 11), to corporeal warfare evoking the lions and tigers of destruction. In *Milton* and *Jerusalem* this intoxication becomes mental and spiritual. In fallen Albion

> the existence of friendship & benevolence is denied:
> The wine of the Spirit & the vineyards of the Holy-One.
> Here: turn into the poisonous stupor & deadly intoxication[.]
> *(Jerusalem* 38.27-29)

Yet from at least as early as The Song of Solomon the beloved's breasts are as "clusters of the vine" (7.8); and grapes and the vine have frequently served as symbols of sexuality, love, and marriage, especially when the vine entwines the elm, as in *Paradise Lost* V.215-19 and in Blake's *And She Shall Be Called Woman* (B, Pl. 512). In Blake's own canon the sexual suggestions of the grape are generally healthy. On Plate 8 of *The Marriage of Heaven and Hell* Blake placed a cluster of grapes after his proverb "The lust of the goat is the bounty of God" (E, p. 36). Often grapes suggest the onset of adolescence, the approaching of a full emotional life, as in "The Ecchoing Green," where a youth hands down to a girl a bunch of grapes, or in "Nurse's Song" of *Experience,* where grapevines and grapes surround an open doorway and two juveniles.[19] For the nude, repressed females at the bottom of Plate 15 of *America* (see Fig. 67), the cluster of grapes overhead promises a full life: "They feel the nerves of youth renew, and desires of ancient times, / Over their pale limbs as a vine when the tender grape appears" (15.25-26). Apparently after she has partaken, one flies up toward the light. Like Daphne, she arborizes, but into full Experience, for she is accompanied by her child. In a tiny scene above that, she fondles him; but above even that scene she is abandoned and disconsolate, a victim of Experience. In "Infant Sorrow" it is the possessive, matrimonial myrtle which is entrapping, not the healthy "Clusters of the wandring vine" (*E*, p. 797). Only the sterile, like Hand and Hyle, reject this rich emotional life: they vow to permit "No more the sinful delights" "beneath the Vine and Fig-tree" (*Jerusalem* 18.16, 19). The "wine of lovers in the Wine-press of Luvah" (80.82) is an unselfish, redemptive force. Because of this love, we see Cambel and Gwendolen

> In the Furnaces of Los & in the Wine-press treading day & night
> Naked among the human clusters: bringing wine of anguish
> To feed the afflicted in the Furnaces. . . . (82.64-66)

The grapevine as symbol of universal brotherhood and love, Christ himself established: "I am the vine, ye *are* the branches . . . (John 15.5). In the Last Supper the wine becomes "my blood of the new testament which is shed for many for the remission of sins" (Matthew 26.28). In his *Descriptive Catalogue* Blake recognized Christ as "the vine of eternity"; and in "A Vision of the Last Judgment" he acknowledged, "He is the Bread & the Wine" (*E*, pp. 536, 561). The grapevine became in art occasionally the cross or the Tree of Life, the latter sometimes in the form of the Tree of Jesse,[20] as it is, in a modified form, in the "Introduction" to *Songs of Innocence* and even in the entwined vines of "The School Boy." Swedenborg had remarked that when wine "is read in the Word, and also is received in the Sacred Supper; on such Occasions the Angels" think "of Charity towards their Neighbor" (*AC*, Par. 4217). In his *Night Thoughts* Young praised, citing John 15.1, "Great VINE! on THEE: on THEE the Cluster hangs; / The filial Cluster! infinitely spread" (II, *NT*512). In Blake's design Christ dominates, surrounded by grapevines and clusters of grapes. But to universalize the scene, Blake placed lovers in the foreground; and at the right a mother nurses one of her two children.[21]

One of the most easily distinguishable of the vines of Innocence is the honeysuckle, with which, in 1775, William Curtis identified Shakespeare's woodbine and Milton's eglantine and which he praised for its "beauty, singularity, and exquisite fragrance of its flowers."[22] Its long tube was for Erasmus Darwin an emblem of fertility: "With artless grace and native ease she charms / And bears the Horn of Plenty in her arms" (I.215-16). In Blake's symphony of flowers in *Milton* the honeysuckle is early awakened by the odors of the herbs and flowers as it is "sleeping on the Oak": "the flaunting beauty / Revels along upon the wind" (31.54-55). In Design 3 for Gray's "Ode to Spring" the humanized flowers bring to birth and suckle the infants of this early-blooming vine of the "honied spring" (p. 44). Blossoming honeysuckle appears above the boy rolling his hoop in "The Ecchoing Green," almost as an alternate form of the grapevine below. (See Fig. 62.) In a number of designs Blake seems to have depicted the scarlet trumpet honeysuckle (*Lonicera sempervirens*) long cultivated in English gardens because of its beauty, its evergreen leaves, and the longevity of the flowers.[23] Perhaps Blake was attracted to it also because its color suggested the Passion and its name seemed to suggest a floral voice. At any rate in *Our Lady With the Infant Jesus Riding on a Lamb* (B, Pl. 505), the red-tubed trumpet honeysuckle is beginning to entwine the tree near the boy John the Baptist; and in "The Shepherd" it is in Copy *B* encircling the tree beside another whose tongue is "filled with praise" (*E*, p. 7).

One of the most decorative features of *Songs of Innocence* is the presence of high climbing vines which loosely entwine the trees in "serpentine" loops and festoon the pages, as in "The Lamb." (See Fig. 10.) Since most of these suggest an early state of unorganized Innocence, they are not usually given blossoms (here again Blake was following Swedenborg's symbolism); and their tiny, stylized leaves make identification difficult and often impossible. But most of them appear to be of the morning glory family (*Convolvulaceae*), high climbing vines then quite popular in England. One of them sometimes used by Renaissance artists as an emblem of perfect love (D'Ancona, pp. 109-11), the morning glory was an apt symbol of

Innocence, needing protection, yet not harming the protective tree. It blossoms for Lyca (see Fig. 5); and for her the bird of paradise and promise flies up and to the right. But where, before it blossoms, the vine is cut off from its root, it frequently suggests Innocence doomed. So we see it in "A Little Boy Lost," somewhat resembling the Sweet William (*Impomoea quamoclit*),[24] and in "Holy Thursday" of *Experience*. (See Fig. 68). The morning glory loosely wreathes the head of Thomas Alphonso Hayley in a portrait which Blake painted for the grieved father (*B*, Pl. 453); and in Plate 9 of *Europe*, as it loosely entwines the wheat, both are destined to destruction by the mildew which is being spread by the trumpeting demons.[25]

Easily distinguishable from the vines of Innocence by its relatively straight lines and by its tight adherence, the ivy is a vine of Experience. It was a symbol of death in Pliny and for the emblematists usually suggested selfish ambition, envy, stubbornness, ingratitude, or lust.[26] Wynne's Eglantine characterizes the Ivy as selfish and ungrateful: "'Like a false friend, too sure, her will / Is her supporter to destroy. . . .'"[27] In the procession of the Seven Deadly Sins, Gluttony "on his head an yuie girland had."[28] In *The Tempest* Prospero explains to Miranda that his brother became "The ivy which had hid my princely Trunk / And suck'd the verdure out on't" (I.ii.86-87). In his usage of ivy Blake followed this emblematic tradition. In "The Angel" the ivy below the Maiden Queen helps to characterize her parasitic, stubborn nature. The flourish of ivy surrounding the lines which announce the bloodletting of empire provides, on Plate 15 of *Europe,* a sinister omen, as does the ivy which is beginning to ascend the tree to our right on the frontispiece of *Songs of Experience,* to suggest the constraints imposed by mind-forged manacles. On Plate 34 of *Jerusalem,* indeed, the ivy, perhaps the Virginia creeper (*Hedera quinquefolia*), ascends an invisible wall in the left margin to form an equivalent of the chain on Plate 65.[29]

For Blake the important flowers were the sunflower and the marigold, the lotus, the rose, the lily, the lily of the valley, and the anemone. Though in Ovid's myth Clytie was punished by being rooted as a sunflower, yet that flower was a symbol of aspiration, gratitude, and constancy; and in 1771 in his *Fables of Flora,* later illustrated by Stothard, John Langhorne also made the sunflower an emblem of devotion.[30] In "Ah, Sunflower" a tiny female figure holds up her hands to the rising sun. Remembering Darwin's charge of the sunflower's barrenness, the poet here may lament the rootedness of vegetated man and his unrealized desires, or unrequited love, in Experience. Yet all flora are rooted in Experience, and the sunflower, more than most others, exhibits an aspiration which denies and transcends this rootedness. In *Night Thoughts* a ten-petalled sunflower nymph opens her arms to Apollo, somewhat in Stothard fashion, to "drink the Sun" as he rides overhead (I, *NT*89). In Design 4 for Gray's "Ode for Music" the sunflower, along with the lily, springs almost from Milton's foot as he strikes "the deep-ton'd shell" (p. 136), suggesting Milton's devotion to Apollo and to Christ. Finally, on page 124 of *The Four Zoas* a nude woman, probably Ahania, on a thirteen-petalled sunflower rehumanizes, casting off her "death clothes" (125.26) to rejoin her Humanity, Urizen.

Opening its petals with the sun rather than turning towards it, the marigold had a similar emblematic meaning — that of love, devotion, and constancy. It was especially associated with the Virgin Mary.[31] Blake's marigolds are of several types and meanings, but none is dedicated to virginity, unless it is the English cowslip (marigold) held by the Attendant Spirit in the Huntington *Comus Disguised as a Rustic* (B, Pl. 617).[32] On the other hand, two tiny six-petalled flowers, probably English cowslips, on Plate 12 of *Milton* precede Leutha's confession of tragic sexuality. Oothoon's plucking of a different variety of marigold on the "Argument" of *Visions of the Daughters of Albion,* where the nymph emerges from her flower, suggests not only Oothoon's devotion to Theotormon, but her free acceptance of sex.[33] On Plate 23 of *Jerusalem* a similar marigold suggests Jerusalem's constancy and adoration, as she laments, "Why hast thou hidden me, / Remote from the divine Vision: my Lord and Saviour" (23.11-12).

Like the marigold, the water lily or lotus opens its petals with the sun. The oriental lotus, or tamara, symbolized the universe and served as the seat of the god. In Jacob Bryant, two engravings signed by Blake's master, Basire, place Isis upon a stylized lotus bell.[34] According to Captain F. Wilford, the Hindus "often represent the physiological mysteries of their religion, by emblem of the *Lotos;* where the whole flower signifies both the Earth, and the two principles of its fecundation. . . ." The lotus is described, Wilford added, "as the cradle of BRAHMÁ, or mankind."[35] Robert John

Thornton, an acquaintance of Blake whose lotus designs differ considerably from Blake's, printed a poem by Sir William Jones telling how Brahma, on his lotus leaf, created the goddess Maya and then "this gorgeous universe." Another poem, by Thomas Maurice, recalled:

> Within thy fair corolla's full-bloom bell
> Long since th' immortals fix'd their fond abode;
> There day's bright source, *Osiris,* lov'd to dwell,
> While by his side enamour'd *Isis* glow'd.[36]

For Blake's Thel, the lotus symbolizes evanescent beauty, especially her own: "O life of this our spring! why fades the lotus of the water? / Why fade these children of the spring?" (1.6-7). Similarly, in *The Four Zoas,* the Spectral Tharmas laments that he fades "even like a water lilly / In the suns heat" (131.3-4). On Plate 53 of *Jerusalem* (see Fig. 41) the flower upon which Vala is seated incorporates features of both the marigold and the lotus, for here Vala is a nature goddess like Isis, separated from her Humanity, but she is lamenting the separation, as both the marigold and the butterfly symbols suggest. The lotus element also is prominent in the design, and the triple tiara resembles somewhat the triform lotus which Isis sometimes wears upon her head, as she does in the final plate of the learned *Illustrations of the Lotus of Antiquity* (1813), by Richard Duppa, biographer of Michelangelo and Raphael.

It is upon a water lily, as Lily of Havilah, that Vala appears in the embraces of Albion on Plate 28, a chapter title of *Jerusalem.* (See Fig. 35.) Here is depicted a scene visualized earlier in the poem, when "Albion lov'd thee!" Jerusalem recalls, "he rent thy Veil! he embrac'd thee! he lov'd thee!" (20.36). In its original state the plate showed Albion, at the right, and Vala, like Osiris and Isis, copulating upon a lotus.[37] Albion has triumphed over Vala, has "rent her Veil," but the net or veil remains obtrusively draped over her shoulders, not as a trophy of his conquest, but as an augury of his own entrapment by Vala, or nature. For with her sinister hand she seems to be transferring her net to the shoulders of Albion. (On Plate 40 she has succeeded.) The division into sexes represented for Blake a step in man's fall, and that fall is suggested not only in the net, but by the presence below of sea shells, the lowest form of zoological life. Yet the embryo-chrysalis emerging from behind Vala provided an emblem of hope. If man falls into further division because of the sexes, yet the sexes rise to work and weep — to "holy Generation! [Image]* of regeneration!" (7.65).

Traditionally the rose had suggested beauty and love, as it does in the great *Roman de la Rose*. Botticelli's Venus is born from the sea in a shower of roses; and the Three Graces often appear with them. In the emblem books and the poets, roses usually suggest mercy, grace, beauty, cheerfulness, pleasure, love and marriage, and lyric poetry.[38] In Paradise Dante placed the Madonna, with her multitude, upon the petals of a white, thornless rose; and recreating this vision, Blake in his Design 99 also placed her there, holding, as Christ's vicegerent, his scepter, the red lily of the Passion, and holding up the looking glass of divine contemplation.[39] Yet roses were also reminders of the brevity and uncertainty of life.[40] At the Bower of Bliss, Guyon hears a song urging him to "Gather the Rose of loue, whilest yet is time" (*FQ* II.xii.75.8) even more eloquently than Herrick's "Gather ye rosebuds"; and in *Twelfth Night* the Duke comments to Viola, ". . . women are as roses, whose fair flow'r / Being once display'd, doth fall that very hour" (II.iv.38-39).

Blake's roses share this ambivalent symbolic heritage. He often used the rose as a symbol of love and beauty. In *Satan Watching the Endearments of Adam and Eve* in the Boston Museum version (*B*, Pl. 648), Adam holds a lily; Eve, a rose. Roses and lilies are marital flowers also in *Job, Jerusalem*, and apparently also in *Bathsheba at the Bath* (*B*, Pl. 498), where the honeysuckle of fertility climbing the column at our left may be intended to remind us of David's line. On Plate 19 of *Job* wingless female figures characterized by the lilies and roses below almost touch as they comment upon the now fully integrated life of Job and his wife and perhaps also upon the implied marriages of Job's daughters, whom we see gathered around him in the next plate. On Plate 18 of *Jerusalem* Vala the Lily of Havilah at the left (the conventional side for the physical) and Jerusalem, decorated with roses at the spiritual right, celebrate the nuptials, look on approvingly and touch toe to toe — Shadow and Emanation in concert here, as on the next plate — while, above, a maiden at the left embraces a youth at the right. These are doubtless the "sinful delights" of "boy and girl" (18.16, 17) as they appear to Hand and Hyle. Moreover, just as in *Purgatory* a concert of birds and a flower description precede the reunion of Dante with Beatrice, and a similar passage precedes the nuptials of Adam and Eve in *Paradise Lost,* so in *Milton* a flower description, in which the rose is singled out for special attention, preludes the reunion of Milton with his Emanation, Ololon:

> listening the Rose still sleeps
> None dare to wake her. soon she bursts her crimson curtaind bed
> And comes forth in the majesty of beauty[.]   (31.56-58)

But the rose is also sometimes an emblem of the brevity of life or of selfish love. In "Mary" the cankerworm of jealousy blights the rose, just as it does in "The Sick Rose." In *Night Thoughts* Blake used a rose garland to crown a "Phantom of an Hour" and to adorn the head of Death (II, *NT*440; I, *NT*205). So superior was the lily in Blake's symbolism that to the effeminate men whom Young called "Lilies *Male*! who neither toil nor spin," Blake gave roses instead of lilies (I, *NT*51). In the rifted marriage of Los and Enitharmon in *The Four Zoas* the roses with which they are crowned are tainted by jealousy.[41]

"My Pretty Rose Tree" is complicated by several symbolic conflations.[42] (See Fig. 69.) The rose tree is both the reclining woman and the gnarled shrub on which she leans. She is partly an exotic which demands special care, "To tend her by day and by night" (*E,* p. 25). Her thorns, implied in "The Lilly" below, by way of contrast to the nature of the lily, provide the lamenter's only delight — none at all. She is also a hawthorn. The bare shrub at the right is too large for a rose bush; it is probably one of the rosetree family (*Rosaceae*), evidently a white thorn, or hawthorn, entwined loosely by a flowering vine, possibly the jessamine, which blossoms sometimes as early as January and as late as November. When the speaker is offered "such a flower as May never bore," he is offered a flower which blossoms earlier or later, and which is lovelier than the hawthorn blossom, for "May" is an alternate name for the hawthorn, and twice Blake so used it.[43] The hawthorn is continuously associated with marriage. The Romans used the hawthorn branch for wedding torches, and its bushes or berries decorated the maypole or the kissing bush. Occasionally the hawthorn was for Blake an image of sheer beauty,[44] but in "The Golden Net," just as here, it symbolizes marital entrapment: the Notebook version opens, "Beneath the white thorn lovely May" (*E,* p. 859).

Often paired with the rose was the lily, a flower of Paradise. Associated with the bride in The Song of Solomon and praised for its beauty by Christ himself (Luke 12.27), the lily had for centuries symbolized beauty, purity, and divine grace. So the emblematists and the poets had used it.[45] Renaissance artists frequently assigned it to Mary as an attribute; and the lily or its symbolic equivalent almost invariably appeared in the Annunciation.[46]

As an emblem of beauty and purity the lily appears several times in *Poetical Sketches;* and doubtless it suggests innocence and purity also in "Mary" and "The Land of Dreams." The "fairy lilies," or Zephyr lilies (*Zephyranthes atamasco*) on which Titania sleeps while Oberon watches, in *Oberon and Titania on a Lily* (*B,* Pl. 294) and on Plate 5 of *The Song of Los,* remind one of their alienation throughout almost all *A Midsummer Night's Dream* and may here ironically suggest the code of chastity imposed upon Oberon and Europe by the Female Will, asleep, like Enitharmon in much of *Europe.* But for Blake the lily, like the marigold, was not ordinarily an emblem of chastity, but of unselfish love. In "The Lilly" it is contrasted with the protective rose almost in the manner of the flower debates in Langhorne's and Wynne's respective *Fables of Flowers* and is the emblem of unselfish, unprotected love: "the Lilly white, shall in Love delight, / Nor a thorn a threat strain her beauty bright" (*E,* p. 25). As a vision of divine grace a lily, resembling a Meadow Lily, appears reassuringly by the head of Jerusalem as she begins to vegetate on Plate 23 of *Jerusalem.* Lilies appear on Plate 19 of *Job* to suggest the new humility and unselfishness of Job and his wife.

Moreover Renaissance artists often used the lily as an emblem of Christ himself; and so did Boehme: ". . . the Noble Lily Twig or Branch *grows* in *Patience and Meekness,* and *takes* its essence, power and smell out of the soil of God, as also out of Christ's Incarnation; for Christ's Spirit is its Essence; God's Substance is its Body."[47] Doubtless led by Boehme and the artists, Blake adopted the lily as the particular flower to emblematize the unselfish nature of Christ. Thus in the Goyder *The Christ Child Asleep on a Cross* (*B,* Pl. 495), a lily entwined with roses faces the sleeping child; and one appears below him in *The Holy Family* (*B,* Pl. 556). In "The Little Black Boy" (see Fig. 60) a tall, stylized lily rises behind Christ to suggest his unselfishness; and another stylized lily represents Christ in "To the Jews," on Plate 27 of *Jerusalem*. More particularly, a scarlet lily was a symbol of the Passion;[48] and thus in his *Allegory of the Redemption, Baptism, and Ascension* (Weimar), Lucas Cranach the Younger placed by the side of Christ the Turk's Cap Lily (*Lilium martagon*).

Since the sexual interpretation of "The Blossom" became popular, the central plant (see Fig. 70), here and in "The Divine Image," has been loosely identified as a "flame plant," whatever that may mean. In an attempt to be precise, Ms. Kauvar suggested Jacob's Ladder (*Polemonium caeruleum*) (pp. 164-65). But Blake's plant resembles neither it nor the Red Hot Poker (*Kniphofia*), the flame flower, or at least the one most often so designated. But here there is no floral blossom depicted, even though Blake called his poem "The Blossom" and "flame" plants are always so designated because of their vivid scarlet or crimson blossoms, not their stalks. Moreover in these two poems the stalk is colored red or magenta in only ten copies. In the early copies it is usually green; in the later ones, yellow — in a total of fifty-three.[49]

As we can see from the offsets and the interior lines, the plant looks not like a flame, but like the stalk of a lily, especially the Turk's Cap Lily, and particularly that drawn and engraved by Blake's acquaintance James Sowerby for the first volume of William Curtis's new *Botanical Magazine* (1787).[50] (See Fig. 71.) There it is pictured with numerous green shoots, issuing from the stalk much as in Blake's design. The flower itself, which Sowerby colored scarlet, with its six protruding stamens, Blake suggested partly by the long, delicate offsets bent left, but even more by his Madonna and child — the blossom — and six surrounding putti. For Sowerby's companion flower at the top right, colored scarlet, orange, and yellow, Blake substituted another flowerless offset at the bottom left, as a balance, for he had to move the stalk to one side to gain space for his verses. To the stalk itself, Blake in some copies gave some of the colors of the second flower, with symbolic appropriateness and with confusing results only if we fail to perceive here that the "flame" is not sexual appetite, but the love of the Divine Humanity. Here is clearly a Madonna with her infant at her breast; and she has wings and, in copies *X* and *Z*, a halo. In a Madonna, surrounding, admiring or even inattentive putti were of course conventional. Although the floral design includes the Madonna and the putti, the "blossom" is surely the child. In his *Dictionary* Samuel Johnson defined "blossom" as "The flower that grows on any plant, previous to the seed or fruit. We generally call those flowers *blossoms,* which are not much regarded in themselves, but as a token of some following production" (4th ed., 1773). Johnson's definition should be supplemented by another in use in Blake's day: "one lovely and full of promise" (*OED,* 1, 2b). These identifications are strengthened by those in the parallel "Infant Joy," where the Madonna and child are again central in a floral design.

In this *Mater Dolorosa* the Madonna participates in the robin's sorrow, for all the birds' emotions occur, as she says, "near my bosom." Both child and birds are literally near her bosom, the birds in some sort of arbor suggested by the lily stalk and the verses. In the design we cannot see the anticipated pain in the mother's eyes; but Blake knew the Madonna's sorrow both in the Bible and in iconographic tradition. The sensitive artist in the Middle Ages and the early Renaissance, like Giotto, Duccio, Simoni Martini, or Hugo van der Goes, depicted the inevitable suffering, both child's and mother's, of which Mary is aware. With the *Mater Dolorosa* and the Madonna of the birds, Blake was familiar. In his *Virgin and Child* (B, Pl. 963) her tears are unmistakable; and in his *Virgin Hushing the Young Baptist* (B, Pl. 491) John is bringing as a present to Christ a butterfly, an obvious borrowing from Raphael's *Madonna of the Goldfinch,* substituting butterfly for the traditional bird.

In "The Divine Image" (see Fig. 72), in which again Blake used the lily stalk as the central emblem of the Divine Humanity, it surges from the feet of Christ himself as he raises man and woman from their prone positions; and in copy G some of the lavender of Christ's gown appears on the lily stalk just above and opposite him, to enforce the identification. In his very next plate after the Turk's Cap Lily, oddly enough, Sowerby pictured the jessamine, which is very similar to the vine which in "The Divine Image" entwines the lily stalk and helps to suggest the efflorescence of six divine-human figures. Jessamine and morning glory both emblematize grace and divine love (D'Ancona, pp. 194-96). Similarly in *Our Lady with the Infant Jesus Riding on a Lamb* (B, Pl. 505), honeysuckle apparently entwines the lily which John carries before the Christ child, in lieu of John's conventional sceptre-like cross. Here the lily is Christ's sceptre;[51] the honeysuckle, again the emblem of the disciple. Earlier, in "The Little Black Boy," Blake had essayed something like this floral symbolism, for at the front left (see Fig. 60) he engraved a vine-encircled lily, as an emblem of Christ and the discipleship of the Little Black Boy.

Among the lilies, the lily of the valley (*Convallaria majalis*) was particularly the emblem of humility. Renaissance artists often used it as an attribute of Mary and of humility, and of Christ. In Dürer's *Madonna of the Siskin*, for example, the Baptist presents it to the Christ child. In Freher's designs for Boehme it appears at the end of Volume I as an attribute of "The Mystery of Godliness" and of "Repentance." In Blake's own day it still grew on Hampstead Heath; and William Curtis believed that "few are the flowers which can boast such delicacy with such fragrance."[52] Although Blake used the lily of the valley somewhat infrequently, he added it to Milton's other flowers in some of his designs for the prelapsarian scenes in *Paradise Lost*, for example, below Eve in *Satan Watching the Endearments of Adam and Eve* (B, Pl. 648). But he used it with special effectiveness in *Thel*. Indeed the "language of flowers" distinctly helps the reader to understand the nature of the heroine and the theme of the poem.

In his *Fables of Flowers* Wynne had in his "The Lily and Narcissus" contrasted the two flowers, the first selfless, the other a symbol of self-love (pp. 53-55). In *Thel* the narcissus, Thel, is trying to imagine herself at first, an anemone, then a lily of the valley.[53] The title page (see Fig. 73) shows the heroine under a graceful, arching willow, a tree which, as we have seen, threatens both sorrow and sterility. Both threats are apt for Thel: throughout the poem she laments her fate; and she apparently elects a sterile life by fleeing from Experience. Here she is fancying herself a maiden wooed by a lover, visioning herself at the moment as an *aenome pulsatilla* wooed by a wind-lover. Still to be seen on Newmarket Heath, it had been recommended by Pliny for fertility: "All the sort of Anemone or Windfloure, bee . . . comfortable to the matrice of women, and increaseth their milk" (XXXI.xxiii). In *Emblems for Youth* the anemone symbolizes, as it did traditionally, "Beauty, its transient Glories, and frail State"; and it is also associated with Shakespeare's Adonis flower.[54] As Ms. Kauvar has suggested (pp. 168-69), Blake probably had in mind especially Darwin's "sad ANEMONE," who prays,

The Plants

"Breathe, gentle AIR! from cherub-lips impart
Thy balmy influence to my anguish'd heart";
....
So shines the Nymph in beauty's blushing pride,
When Zephyr wafts her deep calash aside;
Tears with rude kiss her bosoms gauzy veil,
And flings the fluttering kerchief to the gale.

(I.264-68)

The feminine spirit of the *anemone pulsatilla* which she sees before her is a miniature of herself as she imagines herself being courted by the wind-lover, the wafter of seed. Fully clothed, however, she holds up her hands in shocked modesty at her lover's nudity and audacity. In contrast, in front of the *anemone pulsatilla* which Lyca partly obscures (see Fig. 5), she embraces her nude lover in "The Little Girl Lost," rejecting the sterile life which the willow above her threatens and accepting the fertile life which frightens Thel.

After using Darwin's pasqueflower in *Thel* as an emblem of sexuality, in "Infant Joy" Blake used it in a madonna scene. (See Fig. 74.) On a stylized anemone are madonna, child, and one angel. Blake may well have recalled that in Wynne's *Fables of Flowers,* when the anemone is addressed as the passion flower of Venus and Adonis, it replies in Christian terms,

Then here let all their rev'rence pay,
   And bow as at an holy shrine
Where Angel hosts themselves might pray
   And humbly offer rites divine. (p. 51)

In his symbolism Wynne was perfectly traditional, for the anemone was a symbol of the Passion.[55] Blake so used it in both *Our Lady with the Infant Jesus Riding on a Lamb* (B, Pl. 505), in *The Holy Family, or Christ in the Lap of Truth* (B, Pl. 556), and in *The Repose* (B, Pl. 543). In "Infant Joy" Blake's angel is secularized with psyche wings, for every mother is a madonna, and every child, a potential Christ child.

After her brief imagined sexual encounter as anemone, Thel imagines herself in the role of mother; and her floral image here is that of the humble and selfless lily of the valley. (See Figs. 75 and

76.) In these plates Thel remains beneath a flowering silver birch looking at a lily of the valley whose leaves become more and more like those of a monstrous narcissus. Our focus gradually shifts around to perceive the scene from different angles; and Thel's imagined roles gradually shift, as does our perception of her. But the lily of the valley, with its narcissus leaves, remains central, almost erect as it bows to her in Plate 2, accompanied by the highly decorative spirit of the flower in which Thel sees herself, wearing lilies of the valley as a fringe for her dress! In Plate 4, near the infant, it leans heavily toward our left; in Plate 5, after we have come around in front of Thel it has the same elevation, but toward our right. In these plates Thel interviews the lily of the valley, the unselfish Clod of Clay, and the worm-embryo — her own imagined child. All counsel unselfishness, remaining faithful to their own symbolic natures. They are all, however, creations also of Thel's fantasy world, wherein she sees mainly herself. She is a narcissus, playing fantasy roles as lover and as mother and finally rejecting both roles because they demand unselfishness. As she says of her narcissistic self, she is "Like a reflection in a glass. like shadows in the water" (1.9). Never does she exhibit the humility which characterizes the lily of the valley. When she consults the lily, it "bowd her modest head" (2.17), just as Wynne had his lily "bowing from her place" (p. 54). But Thel imagines the lily of the valley addressing her as "Queen of the vales." Later she is the "virgin of the skies" for the Cloud and the "beauty of the vales of Har" for the Clod of Clay. She is an humble lily of distinction! Moreover, on Plates 2 and 4 the honeysuckle, emblem of fruitfulness, at first entwines the silver birch beside Thel, for she seems ready perhaps to embrace Experience. But as she rejects the babe she is unwilling to bear, the honeysuckle begins to untwine from the tree and to spiral upward in a fruitless, independent rejection.

Then, finally, on Plate 5 (see Fig. 77), Blake associated Thel with some gross form of monocarp, here possibly with what William Curtis, in 1788, called "Virgins-Bower," the Entire-leaved clematis (*Clematis intergifolia*), an unusual form quite different from the Virginia climber. Curtis commended it only for its "singularity."[56] The extruded stamens of Blake's plant, as Erdman has aptly remarked (*IB*, p. 33), suggest the fuchsia (*Fuchsia coccinea*), a recent expensive importation which Curtis illustrated and praised in October 1789.

On Plate 14 of *Europe* (see Fig. 25) the hot-house fuchsia, however, is not Blake's vision of beauty, but that of the deluded Enitharmon. The "corpse-plant" (*IB,* p. 39) which Erdman has identified as the plant on our left is also symbolically fitting for the whole group: all three plants are of the same species, the one at the left quite dead. But Thel's botanical enormity — probably Blake's own conflation — is the development of the lily-narcissus which we saw on Plate 2, merely grown increasingly narcissistic. "Lilies that fester," Shakespeare remarked, "smell far worse than weeds" (Sonnet 94.14). The gross products of her festering, of her narcissism, Thel herself does not see: she has turned her back to the final exhibit. But in the language of flowers we can see clearly what is happening to her.

The more one studies Blake's biological symbolism in the light of the conventional iconography which he inherited and knew — especially in graphic art, poetry, and the Bible and Biblical commentary — the more clearly one sees that virtually all his biological symbolism is traditional. Blake originated and subverted, or perverted, few biological symbols. His Newtonian sparrows of abstract science, probably prompted by Vincent Bourne, are evidently Blake's own creation. But they are Blake's private joke, never incorporated into the illuminated canon. Inspired perhaps by the recently discovered freshwater polyp which linked botanical life with zoological, Blake developed the polypus into a useful symbol of vegetated man, a symbol varying in meaning but clear from its contexts. Even here, however, he was using a popular "missing link."

Only in obviously paradoxical or ironic contexts — once in *Poetical Sketches,* especially in *The Marriage of Heaven and Hell,* but rarely thereafter — did he invert or subvert his biological symbols. But through some perversity of fate, some of his emblems, like the tiger, are widely misinterpreted because of their vivid paradoxical usage there. This paradoxical usage of emblems in *The Marriage of Heaven and Hell* has in fact been a major stumbling block to the systematic interpretation of Blake's symbolism. Too many critics have applied to the rest of his work what is virtually unique there. Nowhere else is a plant like the Venus fly trap associated with discipleship.[57] Nowhere else do bat wings symbolize intellectual or spiritual perception. There the "Tygers of wrath are wiser than the horses of instruction" (*E,* p. 37), but nowhere in Blake are they creative or redemptive. Angry with contemporary codes of morality and religion, Blake in *The Marriage of Heaven and Hell* praised "the lust of the goat," "the pride of the peacock," and "the wrath of the lion" (*E,* p. 36). But he was attacking conventional morality, not attempting to subvert traditional symbolism. The former he continued to attack, and he continued to employ irony and paradox; but his perversion of biological symbolism is confined almost solely to *The Marriage of Heaven and Hell.* Subsequently we do not meet in Blake heroic or creative goats or satyrs, nor does the peacock become an emblem of justifiable or proper pride. The wrathful lions and tigers subsequently embody crippling rage and malevolence; and the eagle of genius becomes a scavenger, a symbol of militant empire.

As we have seen, Blake attempted to make clear the implications of symbols which were traditionally ambivalent. Even Biblical writers used the lion to suggest sometimes Satan, sometimes Christ; but the context there prevents ambiguity. In his verse and designs Blake tried to guard against ambiguity not only by creating clear contexts, but by adding to an ambivalent symbol, like the lion or the eagle, an unmistakably malevolent companion, like the wolf or the vulture.

Blake certainly created his own system, rather than be enslaved by another man's. He created his own myth, or myths, and his own characters. He utilized his biological symbols — the horse, for example — in various ways. His symbols, moreover, are not limited to their traditional associations, but are enriched by their contexts in Blake's own myth. But as Leopold Damrosch, Jr., has suggested, Blake "reshaped traditional symbols so that they could, as it were, recover their symbolic value" (pp. 78-79). Needing to give clarity to his myths and characters, he gained some of it by using familiar biological symbols whose traditional implications he could expect his readers and viewers to understand.

If Blake scholarship is to proceed upon firm ground, rather than wander in private worlds of impressionistic conjecture, we must study to understand more fully his traditional use of symbols. Already, from our inquiry into the biological symbolism, we can be surer about some of the most controversial poems and designs. The Tyger, as we can now perceive, is neither Christ militant nor creative energy, but an ugly and malevolent manifestation of the Selfhood. "The Clod and the Pebble," as the symbols help us to perceive, does not suggest that a conflation of selfish and unselfish love is necessary; rather it rejects the inferior, selfish view for the superior, unselfish one. Her finny nature helps now to identify the swimming Sabrina, on Plate 11 of *Jerusalem,* as the sinister spearer of men. The "serpentine" vine, loosely entwining a tree, no longer appears a threat; ironically enough, the relatively straight, parasitic ivy is the malignant vine. These are merely a few of the poems and designs which a study of the traditional biological symbols assists us to understand. More detailed study of Blake's symbolism should help to reveal Blake's poetry and visual art with far greater precision and depth.

Notes

Notes for Chapter One

[1] *The Complete Poetry and Prose of William Blake,* ed. David V. Erdman (Garden City: Doubleday, 1982), p. 124, subsequently cited in the text as *E* with page numbers or, more frequently, by plate and line numbers.

[2] See Blanche Henrey, *British Botanical and Horticultural Literature before 1800* (London: Oxford Univ. Press, 1975).

[3] Blake to Hayley, 27 April 1804, in *The Letters of William Blake,* ed. Geoffrey Keynes, 3rd ed. (Oxford: Clarendon Press, 1980), p. 88. Evidently Miss Henrietta Poole, of Lavant, gave or lent Bruno to Blake on his preliminary trip to Felpham in the summer of 1800, for on 16 September 1800 he evidently declined the offer to ride Bruno from London to his new home in Felpham.

[4] See Richard D. Altick, *The Shows of London* (Cambridge: Harvard Univ. Press, 1978), p. 29, and "A Description of the Holophusicon, or, Sir Ashton Lever's Museum," in *The European Magazine,* 1 (January 1782), 17-21.

[5] See our "Blake's Inflammable Gass," *Blake Newsletter,* 10 (1976), 51-52. An entomologist himself, Fuseli translated his brother Caspar's *Archives of Entomology* (1795) and reviewed for *The Analytical Review* a number of books on entomology, especially on lepidoptery.

[6] See Martin Butlin, *The Paintings and Drawings of William Blake* (New Haven: Yale Univ. Press, 1981), Pl. 182. Subsequent references cite this work as *B*.

[7] Since Keynes, Erdman, and Bentley all date this poem in the period 1809-1811, it seems quite possible that Blake was reminded of these two performing animals by a perusal of the second edition of Strutt, which appeared in 1810. Since Strutt (d. 1802) was an engraver, Blake doubtless knew him. See G. E. Bentley, Jr., "The Freaks of Learning: Learned Pigs, Musical Hares, and the Romantics," *Colby Library Quarterly,* 18 (1982), 87-104.

[8] The Royal Academy of Arts, London, *A Catalogue of the Library in the Royal Academy, London* (London, 1802), p. 19. I have edited this catalog for publication.

[9] See the discussion in Chapter X.

[10] Ronald Paulson, *Emblem and Expression: Meaning in English Art of the Eighteenth Century* (Cambridge: Cambridge Univ. Press, 1975), p. 10. See also Leopold Damrosch, Jr., *Symbol and Truth in Blake's Myth* (Princeton: Princeton Univ. Press, 1980), p. 116.

[11] *The High and Deep Searching of the Threefold Life of Man* 6.47, in *The Works of*

Jacob Behmen, The Teutonic Philosopher, trans. John Sparrow, Humphrey Blunden, and John Ellistone (London, 1764-81), II, 63, first pagination. Since most works are separately paginated, all subsequent quotations of Boehme cite chapter and verse of this edition, reproducing the brackets there.

[12] Emanuel Swedenborg, *A Treatise concerning Heaven and Hell,* trans. William Cookworthy and Thomas Hartley, 2nd ed. (London, 1784), p. 34, Par. 59, All other quotations from Swedenborg cite paragraph numbers rather than volume and page numbers, for eighteenth-century editions are sometimes difficult to locate.

[13] Johann Caspar Lavater, *Essays on Physiognomy, designed to Promote the Knowledge and the Love of Mankind,* trans. Henry Hunter (London, 1792-98), I, Sig. A[2], recto. Parenthetical documentation always cites this edition. The Advertisement is not part of the original Volume I, but was written before Hunter's Preface, which is dated 24 December 1798.

[14] *Animals in Art and Thought to the End of the Middle Ages,* ed. Evelyn Antal and John Hartham (Cambridge: M.I.T. Press, 1971), p. 87.

[15] Blake could have read Pliny as a student: *A Catalogue of the Library in the Royal Academy,* p. 26, lists Philemon Holland's translation, *The Historie of the World* (London, 1635). All quotations follow this edition.

[16] Ernest Hans Josef Gombrich, *Symbolic Images: Studies in the Art of the Renaissance* (London: Phaidon, 1972), p. 146; Mario Praz, *Studies in Seventeenth-Century Imagery,* 2nd ed. (Rome: Edizioni di Storia e Letteratura, 1964), p. 201, hereafter cited as "Praz."

[17] *Meaning in the Visual Arts* (Garden City: Doubleday, 1957), p. 163.

[18] *Iconologia, or Moral Emblems* (London: P. Tempest, 1709; rpt. New York: Garland, 1976), subsequently cited as "Tempest." Concerning Richardson, see Ann Hope, "Caesare Ripa's Iconology and the Neoclassical Movement," *Apollo,* 86 (October 1967), Supplement, pp. 1, 3.

[19] There Blake could have consulted the editions published at Padua in 1625, at Amsterdam in 1644, at Perugia in 1764-66, and the new edition of Richardson. In her "Blake and Emblem Literature," *JWCI,* 15 (1952), 258-61, Ms. Piloo Nanavutty suggested that in his designs Blake was indebted to the emblem books of Andrea Alciati, Claude Paradin, Francis Quarles, Achille Bocchi, and perhaps Henry Hawkins. Few of these alleged borrowings are at all convincing. Although Blake probably knew Quarles from one of the reprints frequently published in the century and may have seen George Cumberland's copy of Bocchi, he is unlikely to have been familiar with the others. The Library of the Royal Academy did not have any of them. The same defect characterizes Joseph S. Salemi's "Emblematic Tradition in Blake's *The Gates of Paradise,*" *Blake: an Illustrated Quarterly,* 15 (1981-82), 108-24.

[20] Hubert-François Bourguignon (called Gravelot) and Charles-Nicolas Cochin, *Iconologie par Figures, ou Traité Complet des Allégories, Emblèms, &c.* (Paris, 1764-80; rpt. Geneva: Minkoff, 1972), subsequently cited as "Gravelot." The Royal Academy's "A Series of 36 Allegorical Figures" (Paris, n.d.) may have been a part of this work. Blake reproduced a fragment of a conversation between Basire and Gravelot, with the Frenchman's broken English (*E,* p. 574). The Boudard

Iconologie (Parma, 1759) also has its charm; and the Hertel edition of Ripa (Augsburg, c. 1758-60) featured the *fatti,* or dramatic illustrations of Gottfried Eichler.

[21] Bunyan's *Divine Emblems* had eighteenth-century English "editions" in 1701, 1707, 1724, 1757, 1770, and 1793; Wynne's *Choice Emblems,* sometimes entitled *Riley's Emblems,* in 1772, 1775, 1778, 1779, 1781, 1784, 1788, and 1793. The influence of Quarles was suggested by David V. Erdman in his *Notebook of William Blake* ed. David V. Erdman, rev. ed. (Readex Microprint Co., 1977), p. 9, n. 2. The influence of several designs in Bunyan's *Divine Emblems* and Wynne's *Choice Emblems* was briefly discussed by Judith Wardle in "The Influence of Wynne's *Emblems* in Blake," *Blake Newsletter,* 9 (Fall 1975), 46-47.

[22] Frye, "Introduction," *Blake: a Collection of Critical Essays,* ed. Frye (Englewood Cliffs, N. J.: Prentice-Hall, 1966), p. 3; "Poetry and Design in William Blake," *Journal of Aesthetics and Art Criticism,* 10 (Sept. 1951), 36.

[23] Blake's continued indebtedness to Swedenborg is recognized by, *inter alios,* Northrop Frye, *Fearful Symmetry: A Study of William Blake* (Princeton: Princeton Univ. Press, 1947), p. 52, hereafter cited as "Frye"; Peter Fisher, *The Valley of Vision: Blake as Prophet and Revolutionary,* ed. Frye (Toronto: Univ. of Toronto Press, 1961) pp. 128-35; Kathleen Raine, *Blake and Tradition,* Bollingen Series XXXV.11 (Princeton: Princeton Univ. Press, 1968), I, 3-7; David Bindman, *Blake as an Artist* (Oxford: Phaidon, 1977), pp. 51, 52; Raymond Henry Deck, Jr., "Blake and Swedenborg" (Brandeis diss., 1978); and Morton D. Paley, "'A New Heaven is Begun': William Blake and Swedenborgianism," *Blake: an Illustrated Quarterly,* 13 (1979), 64-90.

[24] Swedenborg, *Arcana Coelestia: or Heavenly Mysteries contained in the Sacred Scripture,* trans. John Clowes (London, 1783-1806), Pars. 3218, 143, subsequently cited as *AC.*

Notes for Chapter Two

[1] Caesare Ripa, *Iconologie, ou la Science des Emblemes, Devises, &c., Moraliseé par Jean Boudoin,* trans. Boudoin (Amsterdam, 1698), I, 485, hereafter designated "Boudoin"; Tempest, p. 31; Jean Baptiste Boudard, *Iconologie tireé de Divers Auteurs* (Vienna, 1776; rpt. New York: Garland, 1976), II, 9, 54; Ripa, *Sinnbilden und Gedancken,* ed. Georg Hertel (Augsburg, c. 1758-60), rpt. as *Baroque and Rococo Pictorial Imagery,* trans. and ed. Edward A. Maser (New York: Dover, 1971), Pls. 77, 168, hereafter cited as "Hertel"; Gravelot, I, 90-92; Ripa, *Iconology, or a Collection of Emblematical Figures,* ed. George Richardson (London, 1777-79), I, iv; II, 59, hereafter designated "Richardson." Richardson was obviously borrowing from the natural historians when he wrote that the tiger "levels all with indiscriminate fury, and seems to prefer preying on the human race, rather than on any other animal." "The tyger is the only animal," he continued, "whose spirit seems untameable; neither force nor flattery has the least effect on his stubborn nature; and with . . . malignity, he snaps at the hand that feeds him" (II, 59).

[2] *Coriolanus* V.iv.27-28; *3 Henry VI* I.iv.111, 137, 154-55, *The Riverside Shakespeare,* ed. G. Blakemore Evans (Boston: Houghton Mifflin, 1972), pp. 1434, 677. All subsequent references quote this edition, giving play and act, scene, and line numbers.

[3] Marotti, "Animal Symbolism in *The Faerie Queene:* Tradition and the Poetic Context," *Studies in English Literature, 1500-1900,* 5 (1965), 80.

[4] See *Paradise Lost* IV.403-408, in *The Works of John Milton,* ed. Frank Allen Patterson (New York: Columbia Univ. Press, 1931-38) I, pt.i, 120-21, subsequently cited as *PL* and quoted from this edition.

[5] "Autumn," l. 90, in *The Twickenham Edition of the Poems of Alexander Pope,* ed. John Butt et al. (London: Methuen, 1939-69), I, 86. All subsequent quotations of Pope cite this edition by poem, book, and line. *The Complete Poetical Works of William Cowper,* ed. H. S. Milford and Norma Russell (London: Oxford Univ. Press, 1934; revised rpt., 1967), p. 1, subsequently cited in this edition, usually by poem, book, and line.

[6] *Collected Works of Oliver Goldsmith,* ed. Arthur Friedman (Oxford: Clarendon Press, 1966), IV, 300.

[7] George Louis Leclerc, comte de Buffon, and L. J. M. Daubenton, *Natural History, General and Particular,* trans. George Smellie, 2nd. ed. (London, 1785), V, 155, 153-54, 156, subsequently cited as *NH.*

[8] Goldsmith, *An History of the Earth, and Animated Nature* (London, 1774), III, 235, 238, subsequently cited in all quotations of Goldsmith.

[9] John Gabriel Stedman, *Narrative of a Five Year's Expedition against the Revolted Negroes of Surinam* (London, 1796), II, 49-50.

[10] Lavater, *Essays on Physiognomy, for the Promotion of the Knowledge and the Love of Mankind,* trans. Thomas Holcroft (London, 1798), facing II, 171.

[11] Swedenborg, *The Wisdom of Angels concerning Divine Love and Divine Wisdom,* trans. N. Tucker (London, 1788), Par. 254.

[12] See David V. Erdman, *Blake: Prophet against Empire, a Poet's Interpretation of the History of his own Times,* 3rd ed. (Princeton: Princeton Univ. Press, 1977), pp. 312-15, subsequently cited as "Erdman."

[13] William Wordsworth, *The Prelude, or Growth of a Poet's Mind,* ed. Ernest de Selincourt, rev. Helen Darbyshire (Oxford: Clarendon Press, 1959, rpt. 1965), p. 371, n. The John Carter transcription of c. 1817-19 here cited is even more interesting than the standard version quoted in Erdman, p. 65.

[14] Swedenborg, *True Christian Religion, containing the Universal Theology of the New Church,* trans. John Clowes, 2nd ed. (London, 1786), Par. 45, hereafter cited as *TCR.*

[15] John Beer, *Blake's Visionary Universe* (Manchester: Manchester Univ. Press, 1969), p. 65.

[16] For differing interpretations of "The Tyger" see *The Tyger,* ed. Winston Weathers (Columbus, Ohio: C. E. Merrill, 1969).

[17] Erwin Panofsky, *Early Netherlandish Painting: Its Origins and Character* (Cambridge: Harvard Univ. Press, 1953, I, 147.

[18] See Coleman O. Parsons, "Blake's 'Tyger' and Eighteenth-Century Animal Pictures," *Art Quarterly,* 31 (1968), 297-312. Also useful is his "Tygers before Blake," *Studies in English Literature, 1500-1900,* 8 (1968), 573-92.

[19] Swedenborg, *The Apocalypse Revealed, wherein Are Disclosed the Arcana there Foretold,* trans. Nathaniel Tucker (London, 1791), Par. 566, hereafter cited as *AR.*

[20] *Notebook*, ed. Erdman, p. N109 transcript.

[21] *A Philosophical Inquiry into the Origin of our Ideas of the Sublime and Beautiful*, 3rd ed. (London, 1761), p. 114.

[22] Lavater, I, Sig. A[2], recto.

[23] Algernon Charles Swinburne, *William Blake, a Critical Essay* (London, 1868), p. 120, n.

[24] For a discussion of Blake's subsequent tigers, see "Blake's Other Tigers, and 'The Tyger,'" *Studies in English Literature*, 15 (1975), 563-78, by Mary R. and Rodney M. Baine.

[25] Carl G. Jung, *Symbols of Transformation*, trans. R. F. C. Hull (New York: Pantheon, 1956), p. 438, n. 87.

[26] See Hendrik Goltzius, *The Complete Engravings and Woodcuts*, ed. Walter L. Strauss (New York: Abaris, 1977), I, 173; II, 643, 647, 653; Ripa, *Iconologia of Uytbeeldinghe des Verstands*, trans. Dirck Pers (Amsterdam, 1644; rpt. Soest: Davaco, 1971), p. 169, hereafter cited as "Pers"; Boudoin, I, 31; Boudard, I, 47. Richardson characterized the animal in terms which Goldsmith had used for the tiger: "The disposition of the wolf is as mischievous as his form is beautiful — he is fierce and savage beyond measure; correction cannot terrify him, nor indulgence tame him" (II, 49).

[27] *The Works of Edmund Spenser, a Variorum Edition*, ed. Edwin Greenlaw, Charles Grosvenor Osgood, Frederick Morgan Padelford, et al. (Baltimore: Johns Hopkins Press, 1932-49), I, 30, cited subsequently by poem, divisions, and line, *The Faerie Queene* as *FQ*.

[28] "Lycidas," l. 128; *PL* IV.183.

[29] *Poems by Mr. Gray, a New Edition* (London, 1790), p. 99. This is the edition which Blake illustrated for Ms. Flaxman. James Thomson painted a horrifying picture of wolves, "Cruel as death," tearing a screaming infant from its mother's breast. See *The Complete Poetry*, ed. J. Logie Robertson (London: Oxford Univ. Press, 1908; rpt. 1965), p. 200.

[30] "Charity," ll. 286-87; *The Task* IV. 102-103.

[31] *NH*, IV, 209; Goldsmith, III, 323.

[32] For some of Blake's earlier uses of the wolf, see *The French Revolution*, l. 26; "King Edward III" ii.66; iii.113, 119; "Gwin, King of Norway," l. 27; "Samson," *E*, p. 445.

[33] Boudard, II, 12; Richardson, I, 86, 88, 97; II, 6, 30, 80; John Huddlestone Wynne, *Riley's Emblems, Natural, Historical, Fabulous, Moral, and Divine, for the Improvement and Pastime of Youth*, 4th ed. (London, 1781), p. 11, subsequently cited as "Wynne"; Gravelot, III, 63; Guy de Tervarent, *Attributs et Symboles dans l'Art Profane, 1450-1600, Dictionnaire d'un Langage Perdu* (Geneva: Droz, 1958-59), cols. 93-96.

[34] William Hayley, *Ballads, founded on Anecdotes relating to Animals, with Prints, designed and engraved by William Blake* (London, 1805), p. 129. The designs are conveniently available in *CGW*, Pls. 396-98, 403, and 406. Blake also depicted several loyal dogs in his watercolors for *Night Thoughts*.

[35] See "On Another's Sorrow," *America*, Pl. 16, and *Jerusalem*, Pl. 9.

[36] Goltzius, I, 173, 175; Samuel C. Chew, *The Pilgrimage of Life* (New Haven: Yale Univ. Press, 1962), p. 109; Gravelot, III, 43; Richardson, II, 37; Hertel, Pl. 57.

[37] Beryl Rowland, *Blind Beasts: Chaucer's Animal World* (Kent, Ohio: Kent State Univ. Press, 1971), pp. 155, 161.

[38] Isaac Watts, *Poetical Works* (Edinburgh, 1782), VII, 60, 77. In Gray's "Descent of Odin" "Foam and human gore distill'd" from the jaws of the "dog of darkness," Fenris (p. 119), which Blake depicted on Designs 3 and 10. See Irene Tayler, *Blake's Illustrations to the Poems of Gray* (Princeton: Princeton Univ. Press, 1971). I refer to Blake's designs as he numbered them for the individual poems.

[39] For Blake's *Dante*, I cite the design numbers in Albert S. Roe, *Blake's Illustrations to the Divine Comedy* (Princeton: Princeton Univ. Press, 1953). See also Milton Klonsky, *Blake's Dante* (New York: Harmony House, 1980).

[40] Could Blake have recalled here, in Samuel Butler's *Hudibras*, Agrippa's *"Stygian Pug"* "That was his *Tutor*"? Agrippa was no *"Paracelsus,* no nor *Behmen"* (II.iii.635, 636, 643), *Hudibras,* ed. Zachary Grey, 2nd ed. (London, 1764), II, 60, 61.

[41] Displaced, he flees atop *The Overthrow of Apollo and the Pagan Gods* (B, Pl. 663).

[42] *William Blake's Designs for Edward Young's* Night Thoughts, ed. John E. Grant et al. (Oxford: Clarendon Press, 1980), I, *NT*234. See also II, *NT*342 and Design 25 for Dante.

[43] G. E. Post, in Hastings' *Dictionary of the Bible*, III, 126-127.

[44] *The Holy Bible* (Cambridge: Cambridge University, 1762), Sig. Uuu2, verso. All subsequent Biblical quotations cite this edition, by book, chapter, and verse.

[45] Richardson II, 53. See also I, iv; II, 103, 104; Goltzius, I, 161, 171, 175; Max Geisberg, *Heinrich Aldegrever* (Dortmund: Rehfus, 1939), p. 81; Boudard, I, 93, 99; Hertel, Pls. 47, 64, 169; Gravelot, I, 66-67; Wynne, pp. 103-104; Pers, p. 74.

[46] *The Works of Geoffrey Chaucer,* ed. F. N. Robinson, 2nd ed. (Boston: Houghton Mifflin, 1957), pp. 32, 33, 34, 42. All subsequent quotations cite line numbers only.

[47] Marotti, "Animal Symbolism," p. 70.

[48] *3 Henry VI*, II.v.74-75. Cf. *Troilus and Cressida* I.iii.37-38. In Gray's "Bard" Queen Elizabeth is given "lyon-port" (p. 103).

[49] Richard Brookes, *A New and Accurate System of Natural History* (London, 1763-64), I, 177.

[50] Swedenborg, *The Apocalypse, or Book of Revelations, Explained according to the Spiritual Sense,* trans. W. Hill and John Clowes (London, 1811-15), Par. 782, subsequently cited as *AE.*

[51] T. H. Gaster, in *The Interpreter's Dictionary of the Bible,* I, 376; G. E. Post, in *Hastings' Dictionary*, I, 266.

[52] Richardson, II, 42; cf. Hertel, Pl. 91; Tervarent, col. 214.

[53] So held Mark Schorer, *William Blake: The Politics of Vision* (New York: Holt, 1946), p. 174; Anthony Blunt, *The Art of William Blake* (New York: Columbia

Univ. Press, 1959), pp. 97-100; Erdman, pp. 446-55; and Morton D. Paley, *Energy and Imagination: A Study in the Development of Blake's Thought* (Oxford: Clarendon Press, 1970), pp. 180-181.

[54] Taken from Casa 1020 of the Herculaneum-Pompeii excavations, the scene was engraved for the Accademia Ercolanese di Archelogia, Naples, *Le Antichità di Ercolano*, Vol. IV (Naples, 1765), Pl. 62.

Notes for Chapter Three

[1] See I Kings 22.17; Isaiah 40.11; Psalms 100.3; John 1.29; and Revelation, passim.

[2] Richardson, I, v. See also I, 85; II, 127; Boudard, III, 201; Gravelot, III, 13; Tervarent, cols. 2-3; Chew, pp. 119, 201; Chaucer, B.1771; *FQ* I.i.5.1; I.x.57.6-7; "Lycidas," l.125; *Essay on Man* I.81-84; Charles and John Wesley, *Hymns and Sacred Poems* (Bristol, 1742), p. 48; Christopher Smart, *Rejoice in the Lamb;* and Raphael's *Holy Family with the Lamb*.

[3] Sheep and lambs make comparatively unimportant appearances in *Poetical Sketches* (*E*, pp. 417, 445). For the pastoral elements in the *Songs* see especially Martha Winburn England and John Sparrow, *Hymns Unbidden: Donne, Herbert, Blake, Emily Dickinson, and the Hymnographers* (New York: New York Public Library, 1966), p. 47; Anne Kostelanetz, *Blake's Human Form Divine* (Berkeley: Univ. of California Press, 1974), p. 4; and David Wagenknecht, *Blake's Night: William Blake and the Idea of Pastoral* (Cambridge: Harvard Univ. Press, 1973).

[4] The grass in the design resembles the *Anthoxanthum odoratum*, the "Sweet-scented or Vernal Grass," or "*Spring Grass*" as depicted in William Curtis's *Flora Londinensis* (London, 1777-98), Fascicle 1, Pl. 4.

[5] Discussion of the symbolism in *Thel* is found at the end of Chapter Ten. In his designs for *Night Thoughts* Blake sometimes pictured the shepherd's life as an ideal, even when Young had not suggested it; and in two of these scenes Christ appears with children and lambs when Young addresses the "Great Legislator" or the "DREAD SIRE," instead. See I, *NT*63 and II, *NT*340, and with Christ, II, *NT*378 and 513.

[6] *FZ* 113.34, 38-39; *E*, p. 843. See also *The Ghost of Abel* 2.18. The human-handed sheep looking left in *The Number of the Beast is 666* (*B*, Pl. 583) is obviously "another beast coming out of the earth; and he had two horns like a lamb, and he spake as a dragon" (*B*, Cat. 522, citing Revelation 13.11-12, 18) — a sinister perversion of Christ the Lamb, the dead body worshipped by the world.

[7] Boudard, II, 166; Pers, p. 594; Tempest, pp. 50, 73, Hertel, Pls. 70, 132; Goltzius, I, 177; Geisberg, p. 70; Goldsmith, III, 55; *AC*, Par. 4769.

[8] See especially III.iii.180-82 and IV.i.263.

[9] Psalms 42.1; Boudoin, II, 58-59; Praz, pp. 95-96, 229-30. See also Blake's *Jacques and the Wounded Stag* (*B*, Pl. 590).

[10] See Spenser's "Hymn of Heavenly Love," l. 227; Gay's *Fables, with a Life of the Author* (London: Stockdale, 1793), II, 137-44; Cowper's *Task* VI.420; V.31-32; Goldsmith, III, 25, 110-11.

[11] *A Book for Boys and Girls* (London, 1686), pp. 9-10, hereafter cited as "Bunyan."

[12] See also *Urizen* 25.1 and *Tiriel* 8.9.

[13] *FQ* II.viii.42.1; VI.v.19.1; VI.vii.27.2.

[14] Erwin Panofsky, *Albrecht Dürer* (Princeton: Princeton Univ. Press, 1945), I, 177.

[15] Goltzius, I. 125. See also Geisberg, p. 81.

[16] Rowland, p. 140; *Troilus and Cressida* II.i.17-18; III.iii.126, 306-307.

[17] For a watercolor version, see *B*, Pl. 595.

[18] See, for example, "To Summer" and "Contemplation," in *Poetical Sketches* (*E*, pp. 409, 442).

[19] See also Jung, pp. 275-79.

[20] M. Oldfield Howey, *The Horse in Magic and Myth* (London: Rider, 1923), p. 166.

[21] For other warhorses, see the "Prologue to King John" (*E*, p. 439); *The French Revolution*, ll. 80, 81, and 102; and *The Marriage of Heaven and Hell*, Pl. 5 and 25.15.

[22] Boudard, I, 169; II, 55, 93; Hertel, Pls. 149, 151; Richardson, II, 6, 24-25, 41, 127; Tempest, pp. 65, 73; Thomson's "Summer," l. 719; Lavater, II, 104, 116; Goldsmith, IV, 253.

[23] [Ralph Beilby], *A General History of Quadrupeds* (Newcastle, 1790), pp. 151, 157. Because of the woodcuts, the book is usually credited to Thomas Bewick.

[24] Pers, p. 64; Tempest, p. 12.

[25] See John Locke, *An Essay concerning Human Understanding* IV.iii.23, ed. Peter H. Nidditch (Oxford: Clarendon Press, 1975), p. 554.

[26] Johannes Sambucus, *Emblemata* (Antwerp, 1566), p. 214.

[27] Thomas Pennant, *British Zoology*, 4th ed. (London, 1776), I, 130-31 and n. In the first edition (1766) Pennant had called Buffon's suggestion "gross." (p. 53).

[28] See A. Pigler, *Barokthemen, eine Auswahl von Verzeichnissen zur Ikonographie des 17 and 18 Jahrhunderts*, 2d ed. (Budapest: Akadémiai Kaidó, 1974), II, 308-309.

[29] See Goltzius, I, 125, 177; Geisberg, p. 82; Tempest, p. 37; Boudard, III, 36; Gravelot, I, 5; Wynne, p. 92.

[30] *NH*, III, 511. Cf. Goldsmith, III, 176, 178; Lavater, II, 113.

[31] See also *Mysterium Magnum* 66.39 and *Threefold Life* 9.22.

Notes for Chapter Four

[1] Richardson, II, 56; Gravelot, III, 30-31. See also Judith Wardle, "William Blake's Iconography of Joy: Angels, Birds, Butterflies and Related Motifs from *Poetical Sketches* to the Pickering Manuscript," *Blake Studies*, 9 (1980), 5-44.

[2] See Pigler, II, 156-60; Spenser's *Prothalamium*, l. 42; *The Merry Wives of Windsor* V.v.7; and Pope's "Epistle II. To a Lady," l. 10.

[3] See Louis Réau, *Iconographie de l'Art Chrétien* (Paris: Presses Universitaire de France, 1955-59), I, 103; Tervarent, cols. 140-41; Boudoin, I, 42, Tempest, p. 9; Boudard, I, 52; Hertel, Pls. 82, 183; *Emblems, for the Improvement and Entertainment of Youth* (London, 1769), p. 37; *Romeo and Juliet* I.ii.87; *Prothalamium*, l. 37.

[4] George Louis Leclerc, comte de Buffon, et al., *Historie Naturelle des Oiseaux* (Paris, 1770-83), IX, 1-3. Cf. Goldsmith, VI, 113; Pennant, III, 564.

[5] Ben Jonson, *Poems*, ed. Ian Donaldson (London: Oxford Univ. Press, 1975), p. 310. See also Robert F. Gleckner, "Blake's Swans," *Blake: an Illustrated Quarterly*, 15 (1982), 164-69.

[6] "Buffon," *Natural History of Birds, Fish, Insects, and Reptiles* (London, 1798), I, 180, subsequently cited as BFIR.

[7] Richardson, I, 80, 81; II, 107, 122, 149.

[8] Chew, pp. 84, 105; Pers, p. 215; Boudard, II, 141; Tempest, p. 34; Gravelot, I, 82, 91; Hertel, Pl. 74.

[9] Swedenborg, *The Delights of Wisdom concerning Conjugial Love*, trans. John Clowes (London, 1794), Par. 378.

[10] Praz, p. 225. See also Tervarent, col. 248.

[11] *Troilus* III.iii.25; *1 Henry VI* III.iii.6-7; *Comedy of Errors* IV.iii.80. See also Goltzius, I, 143, 145, 173; Geisberg, p. 81; Tempest, pp. 3, 7, 55; Hertel, Pls. 29, 92, 126, 129; Boudard, I, 151; Gravelot, I, 8; II, 101-102; Richardson, I, iv; II, 48, 63, 86, 91, 142.

[12] The peacock appears in Vol. III, Table 2, with tail feathers displayed, in the right breast of "Fallen Man Awakening," opposite the dove in his left breast. In Table 3 it appears as a proper emblem of unselfconscious beauty, head bowed and tail feathers retracted. For Freher's authorship, see Charles A. Muses, *Illumination on Jacob Boehme: The Work of Dionysius Andreas Freher* (New York: King's Crown Press, 1951), p. 70.

[13] In *Emblems for Youth* it finally becomes a symbol of those who pay "their chief Regard to heavenly Things" (p. 111).

[14] George Edwards, *Natural History of Uncommon Birds* (London, 1743-64), III, 110, and Pl. 110.

[15] See Brookes, II, 258-63; Goldsmith, V, 299; BFIR, II, 1.

[16] *Hamlet* V.ii.219-20; *Troilus* II.i.71-72; *As You Like It* II.iii.43-44.

[17] Richardson, I, 90, 102; II, 46-47.

[18] Tervarent, col. 299; *Canterbury Tales* A.626; *Measure for Measure* III.ii.175-76; Pope's "Epistle to Cobham," ll. 228, 233; Brookes, II, 259; Pennant, I, 338.

[19] William Hayley, *The Life and Posthumous Writings of William Cowper, Esq.*, 2nd ed. (London, 1803), II, 354-56.

[20] Gravelot, II, 47; III, 59; Boudoin, I, 71.

[21] Herbert Friedmann, *The Symbolic Goldfinch: Its History and Significance in European Devotional Art*, Bollingen Series VII (New York: Pantheon, 1946), pp. 8, 75. For Gilbert White the swallow was a "pattern of unwearied industry and affection." See *The Natural History of Selborne* (London, 1789), p. 169.

[22] See those in "The Ecchoing Green," "Laughing Song," MHH, Pl. 8, and

America, Pls. 3 and 11. Some of these birds look like birds of paradise to Erdman, and sometimes he may be right; but the optimistic symbolism would be quite similar.

[23] Francis Quarles, *Emblems and Hieroglyphics of the Life of Man,* modernized (London, 1766), p. 146; *The Notebook of William Blake,* pp. 18, 27, 33; Fig. 40.

[24] Goldsmith, V, 332; James Bolton, *Harmonia Ruralis* (Stannary and London, 1794-96), II, 55-56; Cowper, p. 554.

[25] Ernest Ingersoll, *Birds in Legend, Fable and Folklore* (New York: Longmans, Green, 1923), pp. 114-15.

[26] *The Works of Michael Drayton,* ed. J. William Hebel, Kathleen Tillotson, and Bernard Newdigate (Oxford: Shakespeare Head Press, 1931-41), II, 482.

[27] *The Poems of William Collins,* ed. Edmund Blunden (London: Etchells and Macdonald, 1929), p. 138. Some additional material on the robin is included in our "Blake's 'Blossom,'" *Colby Library Quarterly,* 14 (March 1978), 22-27.

[28] Thomas Percy, ed., *Reliques of Ancient English Poetry* (London, 1765), III, 176. Wynne's *"Redbreast* mild" performs the same service (p. 100).

[29] *Fabulous Histories,* 4th ed. (London, 1791), pp. x-xi.

[30] The poem had been popular in England from at least the middle of the century. See David Lambert Lack, *Robin Redbreast* (Oxford: Clarendon Press, 1950), pp. 29-57.

[31] Edward A. Armstrong, *The Folklore of Birds: An Enquiry into the Origins and Distribution of some Magico-Religious Traditions,* 2nd ed. (New York: Dover, 1970), p. 167.

[32] Armstrong, p. 168. See also Ingersoll, p. 115.

[33] Armstrong, pp. 141-43; Pers, p. 561; Tempest, p. 62.

[34] Boudoin, I, 235; Boudard, I, 75; Richardson, I, 106; II, 100; Wynne, p. 20; *FQ* IV.viii.3-12; "Epithalamium," ll. 357-59; *Midsummer Night's Dream* I.i.171; Gay's "Introduction" to the *Fables;* Cowper, pp. 303-304; Goldsmith, V, 294.

[35] See "Song," of *Poetical Sketches* (*E,* p. 414).

[36] Matthew 10.16; Boudard, III, 135; Richardson, I, v; II, 106-107; *2 Henry VI* III.i.71; *NT,* I, *NT*101; Lavater, II, 121.

[37] See also *2 Henry IV* IV.i.46; *PL* I.21; *PR* I.30-32, 83-85, 281-86; *Windsor Forest,* ll. 429-30; Pope's "Messiah," l. 12.

[38] See *Jerusalem,* Pl. 61; "The Everlasting Gospel," *E,* p. 522; and *An Allegory of the Spiritual Condition of Man* (*B,* Pl. 894). See also Nicholas O. Warner, "Blake's Moon-Ark Symbolism," *Blake,* 14 (1980-81), 44-59.

[39] Like Enion, Ololon is casting her "death clothes" into "the Sea of Tharmas" (*FZ* 132.22, 21). See also Peter Butter in *"Milton:* the Final Plates," *Interpreting Blake,* ed. Michael Phillips (Cambridge: Cambridge Univ. Press, 1978), pp. 158-60.

[40] See also Design 2 for Gray's "Progress of Poetry"; Tayler, p. 83; and Richardson, I, 110.

[41] *Shepherd's Calendar,* "Nov.," l. 25; *FQ,* sonnet to Raleigh; Cowper, p. 414, "Table Talk," l. 576; Goldsmith, V, 327; Pennant, I, 366.

42 "Il Penseroso," l. 62; *Comus*, ll. 233-34; *PL* III.39-40; *The Poems of Samuel Taylor Coleridge*, ed. Ernest Hartley Coleridge (London: Oxford Univ. Press, 1912; rpt. 1949), p. 94.

43 Spenser's *Astrophel*, ll. 31-35; *FQ* I.i.44.7; *Love's Labor Lost* V.ii.904; *Romeo and Juliet* III.v.6, 27-28; *PR* II.279-81.

44 See Wynne, pp. 19-20; *Venus and Adonis*, ll. 853-56; Pennant, I, 354; Beilby, I, 176; and Goldsmith, V, 333-34.

45 Nathaniel Cotton, *Various Pieces in Verse and Prose* (London, 1791), I, 69.

46 "Spring," ll. 580, 590-93. Thomson's and Blake's songs of spring are compared by Michael J. Tolley in his "Blake's Songs of Spring," *William Blake: Essays in Honour of Sir Geoffrey Keynes*, ed. Morton D. Paley and Michael Phillips (Oxford: Clarendon Press, 1973), pp. 122-28.

Notes for Chapter Five

1 Thomas Bewick, *History of British Birds* (Newcastle, 1797-1804), I, xi-xii. The letterpress is by Ralph Beilby in Vol. I and by Henry Cotes in Vol. II.

2 See G. E. Post, in Hastings' *Dictionary*, I, 632.

3 Tervarent, col. 8; Boudard, II, 133; III, 123; Hertel, Pl. 182; Richardson, I, 55, 58, 87, 92; II, 98, 107-108.

4 See *Timon of Athens* I.i.49; *Cymbeline* I.i.139-40; *3 Henry VI* II.i.91-92; *Samson Agonistes*, ll. 95-96; Pope's "Temple of Fame," l. 140; Gray, p. 91.

5 See "King Edward the Third," iii.116-17; vi. 59-60.

6 See Rudolph Wittkower, "Eagle and Serpent," *JWCI*, 2 (1939), 325.

7 This identification was proposed by Judith Ott in "The Bird-Man of William Blake's *Jerusalem*," *Blake Newsletter*, 10 (Summer 1976), 48-51; it was developed by William J. T. Mitchell, *Blake's Composite Art: A Study of the Illuminated Poetry* (Princeton Univ. Press, 1978), pp. 27, 211-12.

8 Samuel Palmer to Alexander Gilchrist, 23 August 1855, in Bentley, *Blake Records*, p. 565, n. 3.

9 Geisberg, p. 81; Wynne, pp. 85-87, 126.

10 Gravelot, IV, 33; Boudoin, II, 410; *Merry Wives of Windsor* I.iii.84; *Rape of Lucrece*, l. 556; *NT*, II, *NT*367; *BFIR*, I, 10.

11 Anne T. Kostelanetz, "Blake's 1795 Color Prints: An Interpretation," in *William Blake: Essays for S. Foster Damon*, ed. Alvin Rosenfeld (Providence: Brown Univ. Press, 1969), p. 122.

12 *FQ* II.xii.36.2-6; *Macbeth* I.v.38-39; *King John* IV.iii.153; *Julius Caesar* V.i.84; *Othello* IV.i.21; *Midsummer Night's Dream* II.ii.114, *Twelfth Night* V.i.131; and *Romeo and Juliet* III.ii.19.

13 Boudard, I, 53; Tempest, p. 81; Richardson, II, 78, 138.

14 *Pericles* IV.Introduction.32-33; *Winter's Tale* IV.iv.218-19; *Romeo and Juliet* I.v.48; see also *All's Well* IV.iii.286-88.

15 John Latham, *A General Synopsis of Birds* (London, 1781), I, 370; Pennant, I, 224.

[16] Walter L. Strauss, ed., *The Book of Hours of the Emperor Maximilian the First, decorated by Albrecht Dürer* (New York: Abaris, 1974), p. 71; Geisberg, p. 82; *FQ* I.ix.33.6-9; *Richard II* III.iii.183; *Rape of Lucrece*, l. 359.

[17] Stedman, II, 142-44, and Pl. 37; "Blake's Spectre," *The Book Collector*, 28 (Spring 1979), 60-66. See also Alice Mills, "The Spectral Bat in Blake's Illustrations to *Jerusalem*," *Blake Studies*, 9 (1980), 87-99; and Nelson Hilton, *Literal Imagination: Blake's Vision of Words* (Berkeley: Univ. of California Press, 1983), pp. 156-65.

[18] *NT*, II, NT383, NT365, NT295, NT484.

[19] John E. Grant, "The Meaning of Mirth and her Companions in Blake's Designs for *L'Allegro* and *Il Penseroso*," *Blake Newsletter*, 5 (1971-72), 195.

[20] See Sir Geoffrey Keynes, *Blake Studies: Essays on his Life and Work*, 2nd ed. (Oxford: Clarendon Press, 1971), Pl. 32.

[21] They help to characterize him, for example, in *Satan in Council* (B, Pl. 688); in both versions of *Christ Offering to Redeem Man* (B, Pls. 634, 647); in both of *Satan Watching the Endearments of Adam and Eve* (B, Pls. 636, 648); in *Satan Exulting over Adam and Eve* (CGW, Pl. 325); in *The Devil Rebuked, or the Burial of Moses* (B, Pl. 536); in both versions of *The Great Dragon and the Woman Clothed with the Sun* (B, Pls. 580, 581); the tempera *Satan Smiting Job with Boils* (B, Pl. 972); and in Pls. 3, 4, 6 and 10 of *Job*.

Notes for Chapter Six

[1] *Hymns in Prose for Children*, 6th ed. (London, 1794), pp. 91, 92; Barbut, *Les Genres des Insects de Linné* (London, 1781), p. 165. This work is in French and English.

[2] See also *Heaven and Hell*, Par. 108.

[3] Prospectus for Blake's designs for Blair's *Grave*, in *Blake Records*, p. 170.

[4] David V. Erdman, "The Dating of William Blake's Engravings," *PQ*, 31 (1952), 337-43; *CGW*, p. 479.

[5] B, Pl. 63. Much clearer is Pl. 1 in *Pencil Drawings by William Blake*, ed. Geoffrey Keynes (London: Nonesuch, 1927).

[6] A detailed discussion is Frank M. Parisi, "Emblems of Melancholy, *For Children: The Gates of Paradise*," *Interpreting Blake*, pp. 70-110. Far more general is Edward J. Rose, "Blake's Human Insect: Symbol, Theory, and Design," *Texas Studies in Literature and Language*, 10 (Summer 1968), 215-32.

[7] Bo Lindberg argued earnestly that the cowled figure is male. See his *William Blake's Illustrations to the Book of Job* (Abo: Abo Akademi, 1973), pp. 259-61. But see also B, Pls. 149, 150.

[8] Joel 1. 4; 2.25; *Richard II* II.iii.166; Cowper, "Tirocinium," ll. 597-98, 591-94.

[9] Gravelot, II, 100, 102; IV, 70-71; Wynne, pp. 53-55; *Lear* V.iii.13-14; *Task* VI.211-12. To illustrate *Night Thoughts* Blake used butterflies to suggest effeminacy, sloth, and "a mere froth of joy" (I, NT51; II, NT478, NT409).

Notes

[10] Mrs. Anna Eliza (Kempe) Stothard Bray, *Life of Thomas Stothard* (London, 1851), p. 32.

[11] *E,* p. 263. I have omitted Erdman's editorial brackets and added the question mark.

[12] Wardle, "The Influence of Wynne's Emblems on Blake," *Blake Newsletter,* 9 (1975), 46-47; "William Blake's Iconography of Joy," *Blake Studies,* 9 (1980), 15-19.

[13] Edward Donovan, *The Natural History of British Insects* (London, 1792-1801), VI, 66.

[14] *Engravings by William Blake: The Separate Plates,* comp. Geoffrey Keynes (Dublin: Walker, 1956), Pl. 40.

[15] Donovan, a reliable lepidopterist, showed five pair on his "white-feathered moth" (IV, 5-6) and twelve pair on his "many-feathered," and attested that "every part, though separate, acts in perfect unison with the rest" (IV, 75-76).

[16] In his *William Blake's Jerusalem* (London: Trianon Press, 1954), p. 154, Joseph Wicksteed called attention to these crosses.

[17] Donovan, IX, 51 and Pl. 312; V, 76 and Pl. 165.

[18] "The ray of divine illumination must strike the person blessed with this illumination from his or her right" (Panofsky, *Netherlandish Painting,* I, 147); and the ray of natural illumination, from his left (I, 148). On Plates 32 and 37 of *Milton,* Blake followed this convention, lovingly suggesting, with the ray at his own left foot and his left foot advanced, an inferior revelation to that granted his brother Robert, where Robert, his right foot advanced, receives divine illumination from his right.

[19] Janet Warner surveyed these Shadows in "Blake's Figures of Despair: Man in his Spectre's Power," *William Blake: Essays in Honour of Sir Geoffrey Keynes,* pp. 208-224.

[20] Wynne, p. 48. See also Chew, pp. 99, 251; Tervarent, col. 2; Pers, p. 556; Gravelot, III, 11; Richardson, II, 45, 72-73; Cowper, pp. 386, 389; *The Task* IV.107-112; Goldsmith, VII, 81.

[21] *Poetical Works,* VII, 64. Swedenborg's attitude was ambivalent. See *Heaven and Hell,* Par. 108, and *AE,* Par. 410.

[22] See *Richard III* I.iii.241-42; *Richard II* III.ii.14-16; *Winter's Tale* II.i.45; *2 Henry VI* III.i.339-40; *Henry VIII* I.i.62-63; *Cymbeline* IV.ii.89-91; *Midsummer Night's Dream,* II.ii.20-23; Thomson's "Summer," ll. 266, 277; Richardson, II, 80.

[23] Swedenborg, *The Wisdom of the Angels concerning the Divine Providence,* tran. Nathaniel Tucker (London, 1790), Par. 107.

[24] See Morris Eaves, "A Reading of Blake's *Marriage of Heaven and Hell,* Plates 17-20, on and under the Estate of the West," *Blake Studies,* 4 (Spring 1972), 81-116; and Hilton, pp. 102-07.

[25] Job 25.6. See also *Tempest* III.i.31; *Samson Agonistes,* ll. 73-74; Cowper, "Expostulation," ll. 89-90; "Truth," l. 142; and "Hope," l. 711.

[26] See also *NT,* I, *NT*29; II, *NT*442, and I, *NT*112.

[27] See also *The Song of Los* 7.7-8; *FZ* 132.18-19; and *Jerusalem* 30.57.

Notes for Chapter Seven

[1] See *Metamorphoses* 2.959, and 6.348-81.

[2] See also *Job*, Pl. 6, and *Poetical Sketches*, E, p. 446.

[3] See Rudolf Wittkower, "Eagle and Serpent," *JWCI*, 2 (1939), 293-325.

[4] See David V. Erdman, "A Temporary Report on Texts of Blake," *William Blake: Essays for S. Foster Damon*, ed. Alvin Rosenfield (Providence: Brown Univ. Press, 1954), pp. 410-13; and *IB*, p. 112.

[5] For example, see Hertel, Pl. 48.

[6] Wynne, p. 73; *Midsummer Night's Dream* III.ii.72-73; *Lear* II.iv. 160-161; *Hamlet* I.v.38-39; Goldsmith, VII, 167.

[7] See, for example, "An Imitation of Spenser," E, p. 421; and "Then She Bore Pale Desire," E, p. 446.

[8] These may be the same as the three female heads which emerge from one serpent body at the bottom of *FZ*, p. 14.

[9] II, NT368, NT358. See also I, NT25; II, NT296, NT361, NT366, NT368; *Job*, Pl. 10; and Design 3 for Gray's "Ode for Music."

[10] The design (B, Pl. 646), with Sin extending her arms to oppose the confrontation of Satan with Death, may owe something to the gesture of an ornament of Aldegrever. See Geisberg, p. 43.

[11] As single-headed dragon he appears, for example, in the watercolor "He Cast Him Into The Bottomless Pitt" (B, Pl. 585). He has his seven heads in *The Great Red Dragon and the Beast From the Sea* (B, Pl. 582), *The Number of the Beast is 666* (B, Pl. 583), *The Whore of Babylon* (B, Pl. 584), and in both versions of *The Great Dragon and the Woman Clothed with the Sun* (B, Pls. 580, 581). With the Whore of Babylon and her cup of abominations he also appears in *Night Thoughts* (II, NT345); and he coils up threateningly in the Whitworth and Huntington versions of the Nativity for Milton's "On the Morning of Christ's Nativity" (B, Pls. 662, 668), minus one of his heads in the Whitworth version (that of Luther?). He appears also in *The Last Judgment* (B, Pl. 871) and *The Vision of the Last Judgment* (B, Pls. 868, 870); and in the "Vision of the Last Judgment" "in the Caverns of the Earth is the Dragon with Seven heads & ten Horns . . . & above . . . is the Harlot siezed & bound" (E, p. 552).

[12] For the current, disruptive interpretation, see Roe, pp. 166-71; see also David Sten Herrstrom, "Blake's Transformations of Ezekiel's Cherubim Vision in *Jerusalem*," *Blake: an Illustrated Quarterly*, 15 (1981-82), 74 and n. 19. In his *William Blake* (London: Tate Gallery, 1978), Martin Butlin perceptively noted that Plate 41 "recalls both the Whore of Babylon and the various dragons of the Apocalypse . . . and the later vision of the Whore of Babylon in the Dante illustrations" (p. 130).

[13] John Flaxman, *La Divina Comedia di Dante Aligheri, Composto da Giovanni Flaxman, Scultore Inglese* (Rome, 1802), Vol. II, Pl. 37.

[14] Dante, *The Vision, or Hell, Purgatory, and Paradise*, trans. Henry F. Cary (London, 1814), II, 152.

Notes

¹⁵ Ruthven Todd, *Tracks in the Snow: Studies in English Science and Art* (London: Grey Walls Press, 1946), pp. 31-38.

¹⁶ Blunt was noncommital about the exact source earlier in "Blake's Pictorial Imagination," *JWCI*, 6 (1943), 205. He erred in *The Art of William Blake*, p. 38. The winged bull he cited there is a small detail on Pl. 41 in Vol. II of Sir William Ouseley's *Travels into Various Countries of the East, more particularly Persia* (London, 1819-23). Blake's friend Linnell engraved three designs for this work; but H. Mutlow, the plate in question.

¹⁷ *Collection of Etruscan, Greek, and Roman Antiquities from the Cabinet of the Hon. W. Hamilton* (Naples, 1766-67). Anne Kostelanetz recorded Blake's copying, in *Blake's Human Form*, p. 112 and n. 17.

¹⁸ See H. B. De Groot's well-illustrated article "The Ouroboros and the Romantic Poets: A Renaissance Emblem in Blake, Coleridge and Shelley," *English Studies: A Journal of English Letters and Philology*, 50 (1969), 553-64.

¹⁹ Bernard Germain Étienne de la Ville sur Illon, comte de Lacépède, *Histoire Naturelle des Quadrupèdes Ovipares et des Serpens* (Paris, 1788-89), II, 74.

²⁰ See Anthony Blunt, "Blake's Brazen Serpent," *JWCI*, 6 (1943), 225-27.

²¹ Robert N. Essick, "The Altering Eye: Blake's Vision in the *Tiriel* Designs," *William Blake: Essays in Honour of Sir Geoffrey Keynes*, p. 59.

²² Lacépède, *Histoire des Serpens*, I, 190, 189. See also Goldsmith, VII, 132; Richardson, II, 104, 125; Charles Owen, *An Essay toward a Natural History of Serpents* (London, 1742), p. 118; *BFIR*, IV, 279-80.

²³ Lavater, Holcroft trans., II, 175. This passage does not appear in the Hunter translation.

²⁴ Lacépède, *Histoire des Serpens*, II, 90.

Notes for Chapter Eight

¹ For my "Bromion's 'Jealous Dolphins,'" see *Blake*, 14 (1981), 206-207.

² Pers used the torpedo fish as an emblem of sloth (pp. 518-19); in Hertel's design of Incredulity, her cloak is covered with fish scales (Pl. 125); and Tervarent, col. 310, recorded the use of fish to suggest hate.

³ *B*, Pl. 689. In the engraving *Lucifer and the Pope in Hell* (*CGW*, Pl. 323) Lucifer himself is scaled.

⁴ Milton, *Works*, X, 15-16.

⁵ Drayton, IV, 115; Song VI. 158-59.

⁶ She is more fully developed in the Boston Museum version and wears no ornaments there. Concerning her sea shells, see also Pamela Dunbar, *William Blake's Illustrations to the Poetry of Milton* (Oxford: Clarendon Press, 1980), p. 29, and Irene Tayler, "Say First! What Mov'd Blake? Blake's *Comus* Designs and *Milton*," in *Blake's Sublime Allegory*, ed. Stuart Curran and Joseph Wittreich, Jr. (Madison: Univ. of Wisconsin Press, 1973), p. 247.

⁷ Drayton, Song XXVI.262; Pennant, III, 76.

[8] Henry Baker, *The Microscope Made Easy*, 4th ed. (London, 1754), Sig. H3, recto; cf. Goldsmith, VIII, 184; Brookes, III, 230.

[9] Mathias Holtzwart, *Emblematum Tyrocinia* (Strassburg, 1581; rpt. Stuttgart: Reclam, 1968), p. 146.

[10] How Blake developed this symbol is studied by Paul Miner in "The Polyp as a Symbol in the Poetry of William Blake," *Texas Studies in Language and Literature,* 2 (1960), 198-205. See also Aram Vartanian, "Trembly's Polyp, La Mettrie, and Eighteenth-Century French Materialism," *Journal of the History of Ideas,* 11 (1950), 259-86; and Hilton, pp. 85-95.

[11] James Barbut, *The Genera Vermium, exemplified by Various Specimens of Animals* (London, 1783-88), I, 77, 78, 79-80, xii. A copy was in the Library of the Royal Academy.

[12] Pliny, Bk. IX, ch. xxx.

[13] *All's Well* IV.iii.220-21; *Pericles* II.i.30-34; *Troilus* V.v.22-23.

[14] Lodovico Ariosto, *Orlando Furioso,* trans. Thomas Hoole (London, 1783), II, 16, 254.

[15] George Shaw, *General Zoology* (London, 1800-26), II, pt. ii, 53; cf. Pennant, III, 72.

[16] Lacépède, *Historie Naturelle des Cétachées* (Paris, 1803), p. 298.

[17] See Edward J. Rose, "Goodbye to Orc and All That," *Blake Studies,* 4 (1972), 135-51.

Notes for Chapter Nine

[1] Matthew 3.10; 21.19-21. See also Daniel 4.20-22; and Ezekiel 31.3-13.

[2] Tempest, p. 11; Hertel, Pls. 17, 108; Boudard, I, 176; II, 180; III, 198; Richardson, I, 77; II, 110; Bunyan, p. 43.

[3] Mirella Levi D'Ancona, *The Garden of the Renaissance: Botanical Symbolism in Italian Painting* (Florence: Olschki, 1977), pp. 381-82, subsequently cited as "D'Ancona"; Sonnet 73.

[4] Stanley Stewart, *The Enclosed Garden: The Tradition and the Image in Seventeenth-Century Poetry* (Madison: Univ. of Wisconsin Press, 1966), pp. 75-86.

[5] *Mysterium Magnum* 17.11. See also 24.18 and *The Election of Grace* 7.126.

[6] Gertrud Schiller, *Iconography of Christian Art,* trans. Janet Seligman (Greenwich, Conn.: N. Y. Graphic Society, 1971-72), II, 136.

[7] *E,* pp. 274, 563. I have omitted Erdman's angle brackets.

[8] See also Blake's portrait of Milton done for Hayley (*B,* Pl. 446).

[9] Harold N. and Alma L. Moldenke, *Plants of the Bible* (Waltham, Mass.: Chronica Botanica, 1952), pp. 103-106; *Fasti* 2.411-12.

[10] See also Pl. 1 of *The Ghost of Abel.*

[11] *Exotic Botany,* 2nd ed. (London, 1772), p. 34.

[12] Erasmus Darwin, *The Botanic Garden,* Part II, *The Loves of the Plants* (London, 1789), pp. 106-108 and n., 167-73.

¹³ Tempest, pp. 20, 32, 63; Boudard, III, 177; Hertel, Pls. 56, 140, 167; Gravelot, IV, 53; Richardson, II, 53, 142-43, 149; Tervarent, col. 91.

¹⁴ *FQ* VII.vii.11.5; VI.ix.44.6; *Coriolanus* I.iii.14-15; II.ii.98; II.i.124-25.

¹⁵ It so appears, for example, in Giulio Romano's *Madonna of the Lizard,* in the Uffizi, and in Raphael's *Holy Family under an Oak Tree,* in the Prado. See also D'Ancona, pp. 250-54.

¹⁶ Lacépède, *Historie Naturelle des Cétachées* (Paris, 1803), p. 298.

¹⁷ Mario Praz, *Conversation Pieces: A Survey of the Informal Group Portrait in Europe and America* (University Park: Pennsylvania State Univ. Press, 1971), pp. 125-35.

¹⁸ "This venerable tree," White commented, "was the delight of old and young, and a place of much resort in summer evenings; where the former sat in grave debate, while the latter frolicked and danced before them" (p. 5). Flourishing village oaks protect groups also in "Laughing Song," Design 10 for Gray's "Elegy," *The Sunshine Holiday,* for "L'Allegro" (*B,* Pl. 675), in *Christ Blessing the Little Children* (*B,* Pl. 507), and in a similar scene in *NT,* II, *NT*378. In "Spring" mother and child are apparently seated upon the bole of an oak, or perhaps on a large root.

¹⁹ Elaine M. Kauvar, "Blake's Botanical Imagery" (Northwestern Diss., 1971), p. 70, n. 19.

²⁰ *Windsor Forest,* l. 386. The same attitude appears, e.g., in Mason's *English Garden* and in James Wheeler's *Modern Druid* (1747).

²¹ Piloo Nanavutty, "She Shall Be Called Woman," *The Divine Vision: Studies in the Poetry and Art of William Blake,* ed. Vivian de Sola Pinto (London: Gollancz, 1957), p. 186. In the other versions of *The Creation of Eve* (*B,* Pls. 639, 652, and 658), however, the leaf seems to be shaped somewhat like that of an anemone.

²² Pliny, XVI, xviii; D'Ancona, p. 64; *Measure for Measure* I.iii.24; Cowper's "Valediction," l. 36.

²³ Raine, I, 135; Kauvar, pp. 108, 112; Lowery Charles Wimberly, *Folklore in the English and Scottish Ballads* (Chicago: Univ. of Chicago Press, 1928), pp. 156-58.

²⁴ Tempest, p. 3; Hertel, Pl. 52; Boudard, I, 29; Gravelot, I, 23.

²⁵ Hugo Rahner, *Greek Myths and Christian Mystery,* trans. Brian Battershaw (London: Burns and Oates, 1963), pp. 289, 291.

²⁶ Percy, *Reliques,* III, 136; I, 176.

²⁷ See also *Merchant of Venice* V.i.10 and *Much Ado* II.i.187, 191-92. Even Evelyn's eighteenth-century editor accepted the traditional symbolism of the willow. See John Evelyn, *Silva,* ed. Alexander Hunter, new ed. (York, 1786), I, 242, n.

²⁸ See also *NT,* I, *NT*244, and Design 10 for Gray's "Ode on a Distant Prospect."

²⁹ See Vaughan Cornish, *The Churchyard Yew & Immortality* (London: Muller, 1946).

³⁰ *Macbeth* IV.i.27. Though Evelyn distrusted the reports of the poisonous quality of the English yew leaves, Hunter supplied an account demonstrating

their toxicity (II, 260, n.); and in his *Treatise of Forest-Trees* (Edinburgh, 1775), William Boutcher, an Edinburgh nurseryman and perhaps a relative of Blake's wife, agreed that the English yew was "noxious to cattle" (p. 191). For details about the Edinburgh Boutchers, see Henrey, II, 403-406.

[31] G. E. Bentley noted "what may be a naked old man clasped between the legs of a nude woman" — *William Blake's Writings*, ed. Bentley (Oxford: Clarendon Press, 1978), I, 137.

[32] *See also NT*, I, NT90, NT177, NT247, NT248; II, NT424, NT442.

[33] See, for example, *Metamorphoses* 1.558-67; D'Ancona, pp. 201-203; Tervarent, cols. 231-34; Hertel, Pl. 193; "Knight's Tale," A 1027, 2875, 2175-76; *Antony and Cleopatra* I.iii.100; "Lycidas," l. 1; *TCR*, Par. 815.

[34] Tervarent, cols. 293-97; Tempest, pp. 51, 62; Hertel, Pls. 42, 56, 62, 79, 140, 155; Gravelot, II, 37-38, 69; IV, 119, 121; Richardson, I, 81, 98; II, 21, 24, 94.

Notes for Chapter Ten

[1] *The Poems of John Donne*, ed. H. J. C. Grierson (London: Oxford Univ. Press, 1929), p. 80.

[2] See Edward J. Rose, "Blake's Human Root," *Studies in English Literature*, 20 (1980), 575-90.

[3] *E*, p. 268. For Blake's knowledge of Donne's "Progress of the Soul," see the *Notebook*, pp. 28, N85.

[4] John Huddlestone Wynne, *Fables of Flowers* (London, 1781), p. 161. See also *FQ* I.ii.40.7.

[5] Philip Miller, *The Gardener's Dictionary*, 8th ed. (London, 1768), Sig. 13F [2], recto.

[6] D'Ancona, pp. 69-70; Gravelot, II, 7; *FQ* I.x.35.3; *As You Like It* I.iii.12; *The Task* VI.1013.

[7] Ezekiel 28.24; Hosea 2.6; Proverbs 22.5, 24.30-31; Bunyan, p. 41; Tempest, pp. 19, 34; Hertel, Pls. 87, 88, 142; Boudard, II, 141; Gravelot, IV, 5, 10, 61; *FQ* IV.v.31.3; *Hamlet* I.v.87-88.

[8] *Jerusalem* 66.23. See also *The Ghost of Abel* 2.16, and *Night Thoughts*, II, NT350, NT444.

[9] Genesis 3.18; Hosea 10.8.

[10] D'Ancona, pp. 375-76. See also *The Task* IV.335.

[11] *Mysterium Magnum* 24.1. See Vol. I, Fig. 1, Parts 4 and 12, and Vol. II, Tables I and II.

[12] *FZ* 35.1; 119.42; *Jerusalem* 19.10. See also *The Expulsion* (B, Pl. 643), *Hecate* (B, Pls. 396, 415, 416), and Plate 8 of *Job*.

[13] Blake to Thomas Butts, 22 November 1802, in *Letters*, p. 44.

[14] Matthew 13.27-30; 37-42; *Metamorphoses* 5.341-45; Richardson, II, 32, 35, 149; *PL* XII.18-19; *PR* III.259; D'Ancona, pp. 403-407.

Notes

¹⁵ *FZ* 131.25; 135.11-13; 138.1, 16; *Milton* 23.45-46. Cf. *NT* II, *NT*317; *America*, Pl. 3.

¹⁶ Hertel, Pl. 142; Richardson, II, 147-48; Hilderic Friend, *Flowers and Flower Lore*, 3rd ed. (London, 1886), p. 581.

¹⁷ James Sowerby and Sir J. E. Smith, *English Botany* (London, 1790-1814) I, 8. Smith furnished the letterpress.

¹⁸ Tempest, p. 50; Boudard, II, 157, 166; Hertel, Pls. 46, 132; Gravelot, III, 33; Richardson, II, 25.

¹⁹ Blake might have seen William Speechley's *Treatise on the Culture of the Vine* (York, 1790), dedicated to the Duke of Portland and featuring plates of Basire. Plate 4, signed by Basire, shows a huge grapevine covering the rear of a mansion of Northallerton.

²⁰ See Gottfried Engelhardt, *Das Lebensbaum-Motif in der Kunst* (Steyr, Austria: Ennsthaler, 1974), p. 38, ff.

²¹ See also Blake to Anna Flaxman, 14 September 1800, in *Letters*, p. 21; and Damrosch, p. 20.

²² Curtis, *Flora Londinensis* (London, 1777-98), I, 15.

²³ See Miller, Sig. 10B, under *Periclymenum sempervirens*.

²⁴ The leaves suggest a variety between those of the Ivy-leaved morning glory (*Impomoea hederacea*) and the Glades morning glory (*Ipomoea sagittata*).

²⁵ The single leaf at the top right of "Nurse's Song" of *Experience* seems also to be that of the morning glory.

²⁶ Tempest, pp. 3, 60, 74; Hertel, Pl. 128; Richardson, II, 42; Praz, p. 217.

²⁷ *Fables of Flowers*, p. 59.

²⁸ *FQ* I.iv.22.3; cf. II.v.29.3; IV.vii.7.1-2.

²⁹ According to Miller it climbs "to the top of the highest building; but . . . the leaves fall off in autumn" (Sig. 6N, recto). For Blake's chains, see Hilton, pp. 56-78.

³⁰ Tervarent, col. 385; Rosemary Freeman, *English Emblem Books* (London: Chatto and Windus, 1948), pp. 25-29, 93-94. For discussions of the sunflower symbol and Blake's "Ah! Sun-Flower," with a bibliography of criticism and some helpful illustrations, see John E. Grant, "The Fate of Blake's Sun-Flower: A Forecast and some Conclusions," *Blake Studies*, 5 (1973), 7-50; and Mary Lynn Johnson, "Emblem and Symbol in Blake," *Huntington Library Quarterly*, 37 (1973-74), 163-70. In Stothard's illustrations for the 1794 edition of Langhorne, the ivy appears as an envious old man; the sunflower, with the bust, head, and arms of a woman; and a lovely sunflower provides an endpiece for the book.

³¹ *Emblems for Youth*, pp. 40, 87; Friend, pp. 81, 96, 143-44; D'Ancona, p. 226; Lottlisa Behling, *Die Pflanze in der Mittelalterlichen Tafelmaleri* (Weimar: Hermann Böhlaus, 1957), p. 61. The volume actually covers the 14th-16th centuries.

³² Martin Butlin suggested that the flower "probably represents sexual delight" (*William Blake*, p. 117).

³³ Here the marigold resembles the bur marigold (*Bidens cernua* or *Bidens laevis*).

³⁴ Bryant, II, Pls. 6 and 12. Cf. II, 325.

³⁵ "The germ is both *Méru* and the *Linga*: the petals and filaments are the mountains which encircle *Méru,* and are also the type of the Yoni. . . ." See "An Essay on the Sacred Isles in the West," *Asiatick Researches* 8 (1805), 273, 305. See also Sir William Jones, in ibid, 1 (1788), 243, and Edward Moor, *The Hindu Pantheon* (London, 1810), Pl. 7 and pp. 10, 29.

³⁶ *The Temple of Flora* (London, 1812), Sigs. T[2], verso; Ul, verso. In producing these lovely and original botanical prints, Thornton impoverished himself.

³⁷ In its final state Blake probably did not adapt the scene to illuminate the earlier, less significant union of the Emanation and the Shadow narrated on 19.40-47. Had Blake intended Jerusalem to replace Albion, he would probably have removed the net, certainly feminized the hair of the figure at our right. For discussion of this plate in its various states, see John E. Grant, "Two Flowers in the Garden of Experience," in *William Blake: Essays for S. Foster Damon,* pp. 354-62; David V. Erdman, "The Suppressed and Altered Passages in Blake's *Jerusalem,* in *Studies in Bibliography,* 17 (1964), 18-20; and Charles A. Ryskamp and T. V. Lange, "A Blake Discovery," *Times Literary Supplement,* 14 January 1977, pp. 40-41.

³⁸ Goltzius, I, 81, 83; Gravelot, I, 7, 17; II, 15, 103; IV, 23; Richardson, I, 108; II, 47, 95; Spenser, "Epithalamium," l. 43; *PL* IV. 698; *Hamlet* III.i.152; IV.v.158.

³⁹ This interpretation I support in my "Blake's *Dante* in a Different Light."

⁴⁰ Bunyan, p. 45; Richardson, II, 44.

⁴¹ *FZ* 16.14-15; 34.16-17, 27-28; 81.28; 81.33-82.1; Dunbar, p. 57.

⁴² For discussions of the rose, the lily, and this poem in particular, see John E. Grant, "Two Flowers," pp. 333-367.

⁴³ *Milton* 31.55; *E,* p. 859.

⁴⁴ *Milton* 31.55; *Letters,* p. 43. Whether or not Milton intended his shepherd to be declaring his love "Under the Hawthorn in the Dale" (l. 68), in his designs for "L'Allegro" Blake exhibited "The Shepherd & his Lass under a Hawthorn in the Dale" (*E,* p. 683).

⁴⁵ Tempest, p. 10; Gravelot, II, 80; IV, 47; Boudard, III, 86, 201; Richardson, II, 40; 114-15; Stewart, pp. 31-32, 119-20; Tervarent, col. 248; Chaucer, B²1651-52; "Epithalamium," ll. 43, 176, 302; *Loves's Labor Lost* V.ii.351-52; *Henry VIII* III.i.151-53; V.iv.60-61; *Cymbeline* IV.ii.202; *Comus,* ll. 861-62.

⁴⁶ Panofsky, *Netherlandish Painting,* I, 141, 333; D'Ancona, pp. 211-18.

⁴⁷ *Treatise on the Incarnation* I.13.44; cf. *Three Principles* 14.39 et passim; D'Ancona, pp. 214, 218-19; Schiller, I, 51.

⁴⁸ Panofsky, *Netherlandish Painting,* I, 333.

⁴⁹ Gerald E. Bentley, Jr., *Blake Books* (Oxford: Clarendon Press, 1977), p. 391. Similarly the stalk in "The Divine Image" is "usually green or yellow" (p. 385). The Freudian interpretation of the poem began with Joseph Wicksteed's identification of the lily stalk as a phallic symbol, in his *Blake's Innocence and Experience: A Study of the Songs and Manuscripts* (London: Dent, 1928), pp. 125-28.

⁵⁰ Sowerby also was born in 1757 and studied at the Royal Academy, his ticket

of admission dated less than two years before Blake's. Their exhibits there sometimes coincided: both exhibited, for example, in 1780 and 1784. When Blake moved to Lambeth in 1790, he was less than a quarter of a mile walk from Sowerby, who lived at 2 Mead Place.

[51] The fleur-de-lys tipped scepter appears in the right hand of the humanized sun in *The Sun at his Easter Gate,* for Milton's "L'Allegro," a design (*B,* Pl. 674) celebrating the creativity of "the bright Sun of Imagination. under the auspices of Shakespeare & Johnson" (*E,* p. 684). In *Satan in his Original Glory* (*B,* Pl. 554), however, Satan holds the scepter in his sinister hand, and the lily's head is transformed into that of a grotesque serpent.

[52] *Flora Londinensis,* opposite Pl. 302 (Fascicle V, Pl. 24).

[53] For a close reading of *Thel,* see Mary Lynn Johnson, "Beulah, 'Mne Seraphim,' and Blake's *Thel,*" in *JEGP,* 69 (1970), 258-78.

[54] *Emblems for Youth,* p. 119; *Metamorphoses* 10.725-39; *Venus and Adonis,* l. 1165, ff.

[55] D'Ancona, pp. 44-46, 287; Herbert Friedman, "The Plant Symbolism of Raphael's *Alba Madonna,*" *Gazette des Beaux-Arts,* 36 (1949), 217.

[56] *Botanical Magazine,* 2 (1788), 65.

[57] In 1794 the newly discovered Venus flytrap became a symbol of the "irritable race" of "the votaries of the Muses," in the anonymous *Sketch from the Landscape,* an attack on Richard Payne Knight's *Landscape* (Henrey, II, 543, citing p. i, "Advertisement to second issue").

Illustrations

1. *Jerusalem*, Pl. 98.
By permission of the Houghton Library, Harvard University

2. "The Tyger," *Songs of Innocence and of Experience*.
By permission of the Houghton Library, Harvard University

4. Watercolor for Young, *Night Thoughts*, p. 234.
British Museum

3. *Milton*, Pl. 46.
Library of Congress, Rosenwald Collection

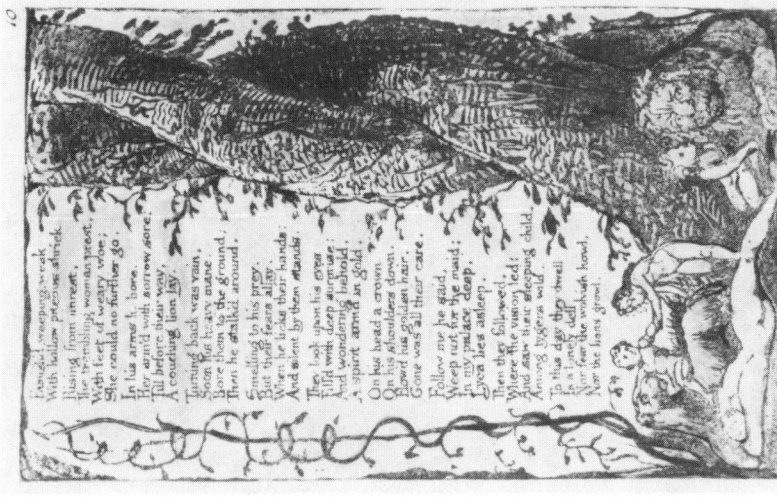

5. "The Little Girl Lost," *Songs of Innocence and of Experience.*
By permission of the Houghton Library, Harvard University

6. "The Little Girl Found," *Songs of Innocence and of Experience.*
By permission of the Houghton Library, Harvard University

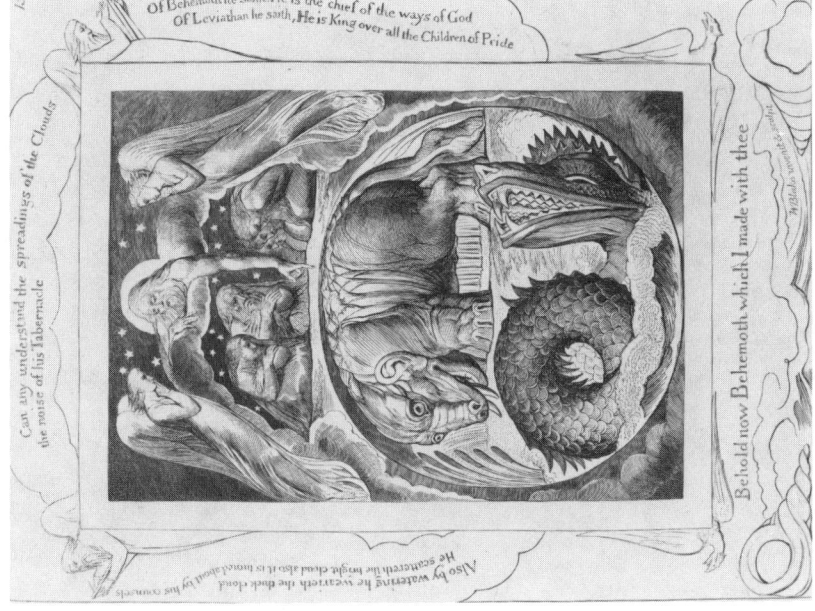

8. *Job*, Pl. 15.
By permission of the Houghton Library, Harvard University

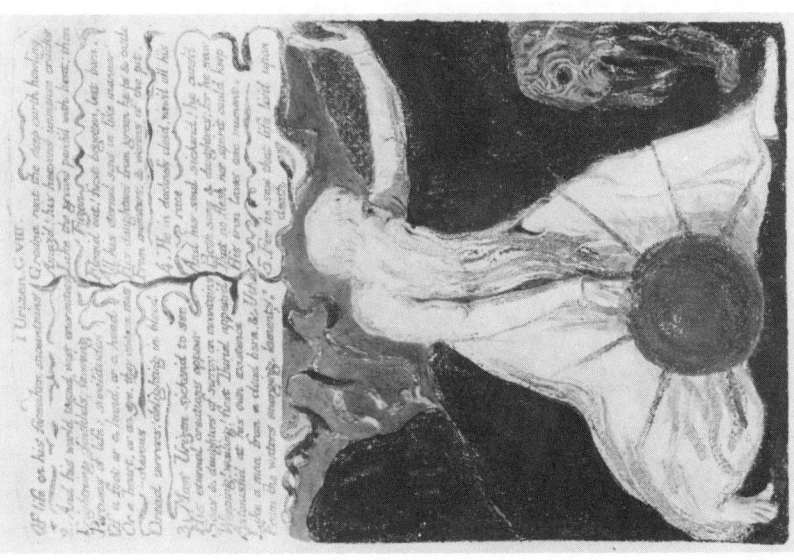

7. *The Book of Urizen*, Pl. 23.
By permission of the Houghton Library, Harvard University

9. "The Shepherd," *Songs of Innocence and of Experience.*
By permission of the Houghton Library, Harvard University

10. "The Lamb," *Songs of Innocence.*
By permission of the Houghton Library, Harvard University

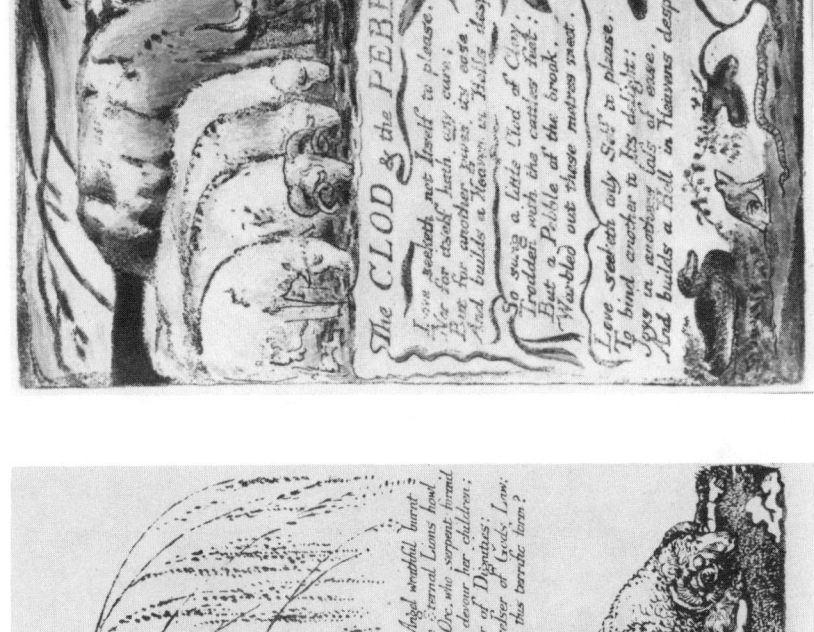

11. *America*, Pl. 7.
Library of Congress, Rosenwald Collection

12. "The Clod and the Pebble," *Songs of Innocence and of Experience*.
By permission of the Houghton Library, Harvard University

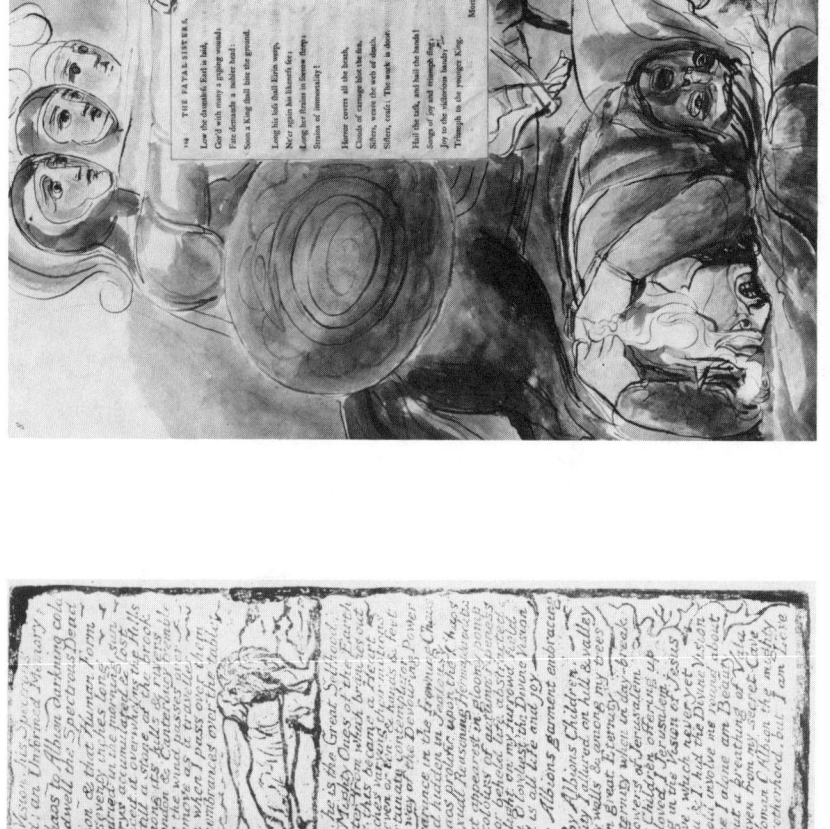

13. *Jerusalem*, Pl. 29.
By permission of the Houghton Library, Harvard University

14. Watercolor 8 for Gray, "The Fatal Sisters."
Collection of Mr. Paul Mellon

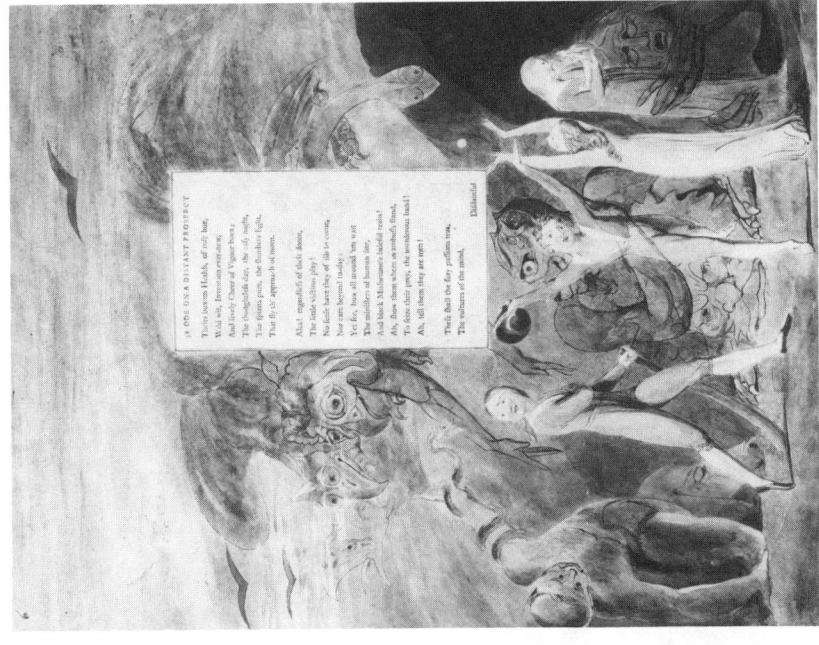

16. Watercolor 6 for Gray, "Ode on a Distant Prospect of Eton College."
Collection of Mr. Paul Mellon

15. *Jerusalem*, Pl. 35.
By permission of the Houghton Library, Harvard University

18. *America*, Pl. 11.
Library of Congress, Rosenwald Collection

17. Watercolor title page for *Poems by Mr. Gray*.
Collection of Mr. Paul Mellon

19. *Jerusalem*, Pl. 11.
By permission of the Houghton Library, Harvard University

20. *Jerusalem*, Pl. 62.
By permission of the Houghton Library, Harvard University

22. *The Marriage of Heaven and Hell*, Pl. 15.
By permission of the Houghton Library, Harvard University

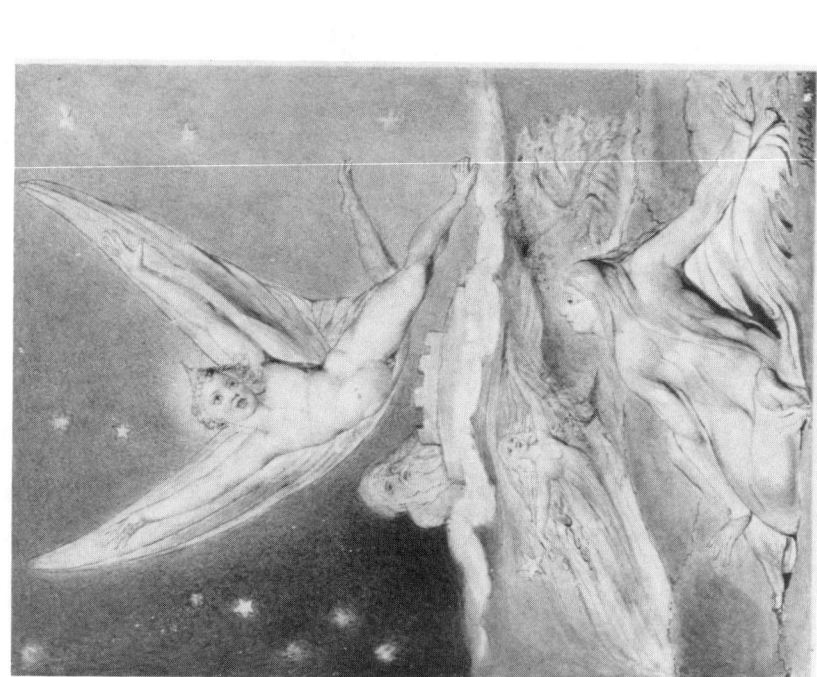

21. *Night Startled by the Lark*.
The Pierpont Morgan Library

24. *America*, Pl. 13.
Library of Congress, Rosenwald Collection

23. *Jerusalem*, Pl. 78.
By permission of the Houghton Library, Harvard University

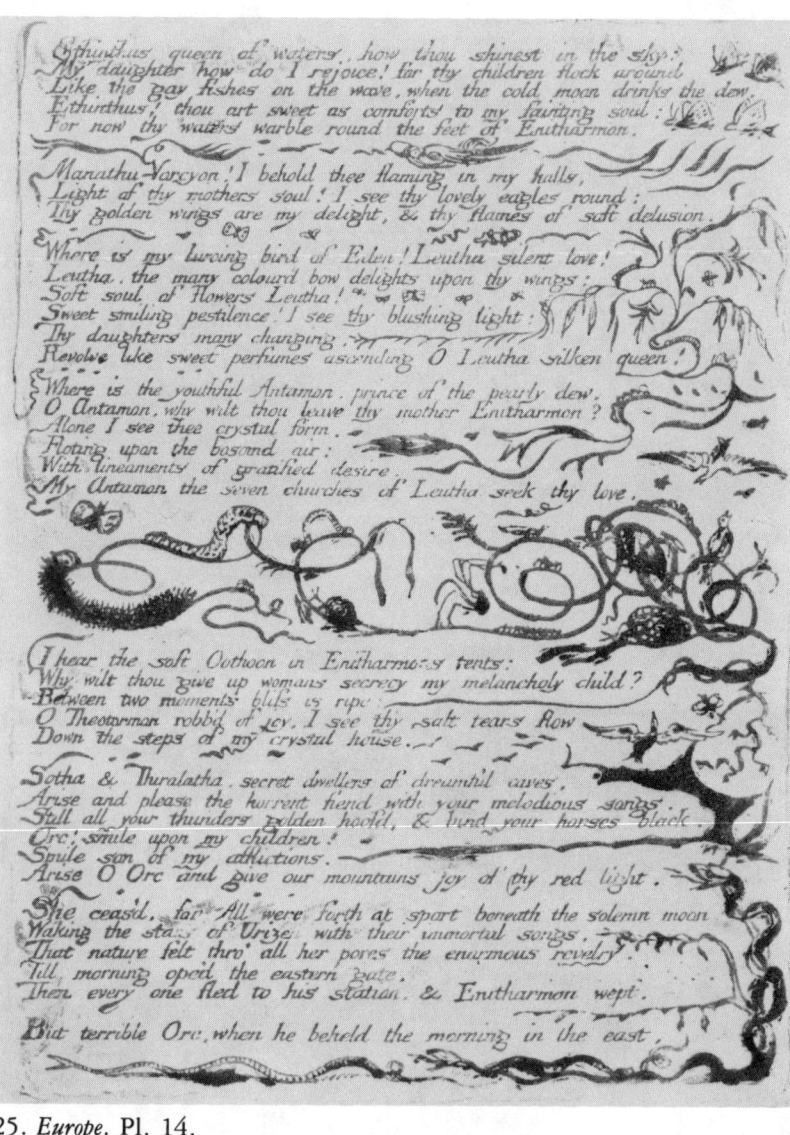

25. *Europe*, Pl. 14.
By permission of the Houghton Library, Harvard University

26. *Milton*, Pl. 42.
British Museum

27. *Visions of the Daughters of Albion*, Pl. 3.
By permission of the Houghton Library, Harvard University

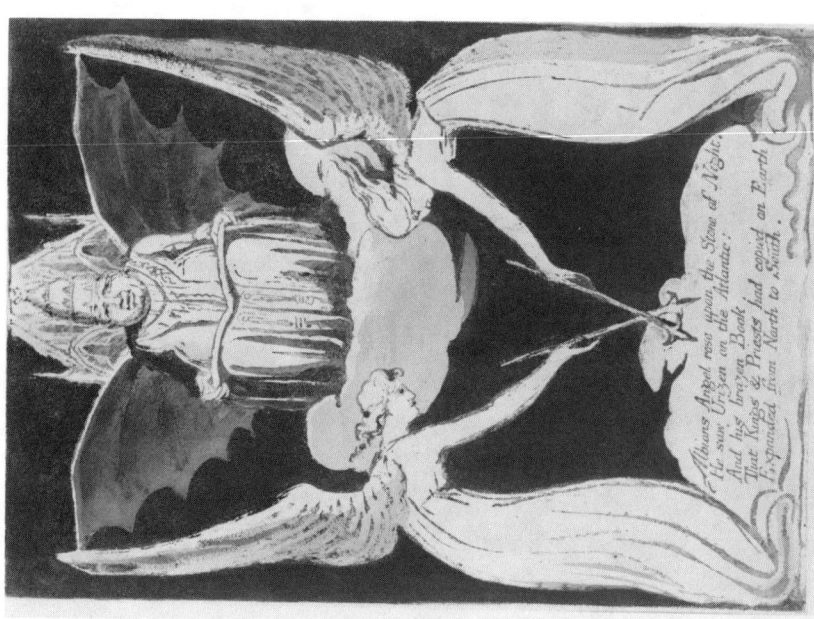

28. *Europe*, Pl. 11.
By permission of the Houghton Library, Harvard University

29. *Jerusalem*, Pl. 6.
By permission of the Houghton Library, Harvard University

30. *Jerusalem*, Pl. 33.
By permission of the Houghton Library, Harvard University

31. *The Dance of Albion.*
National Gallery of Art, Rosenwald Collection

33. For Children: The Gates of Paradise, Pl. 16.
Library of Congress, Rosenwald Collection

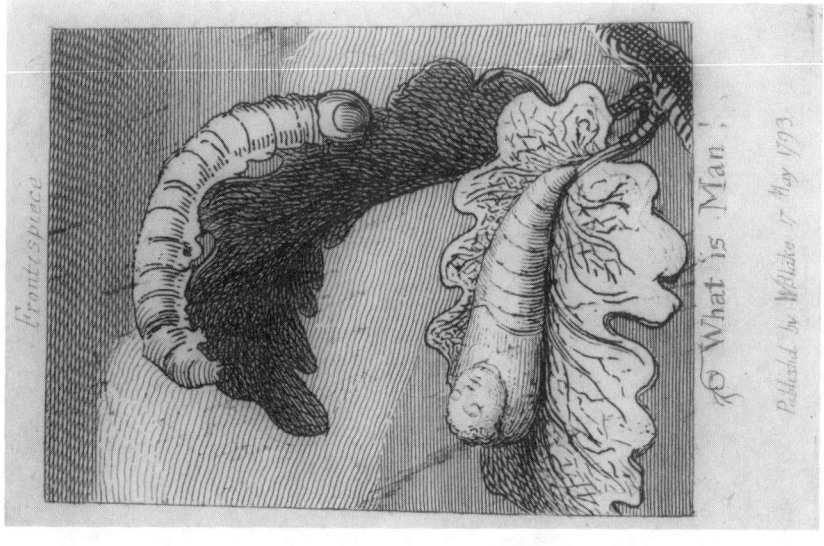

32. Frontispiece, For Children: The Gates of Paradise.
Library of Congress, Rosenwald Collection

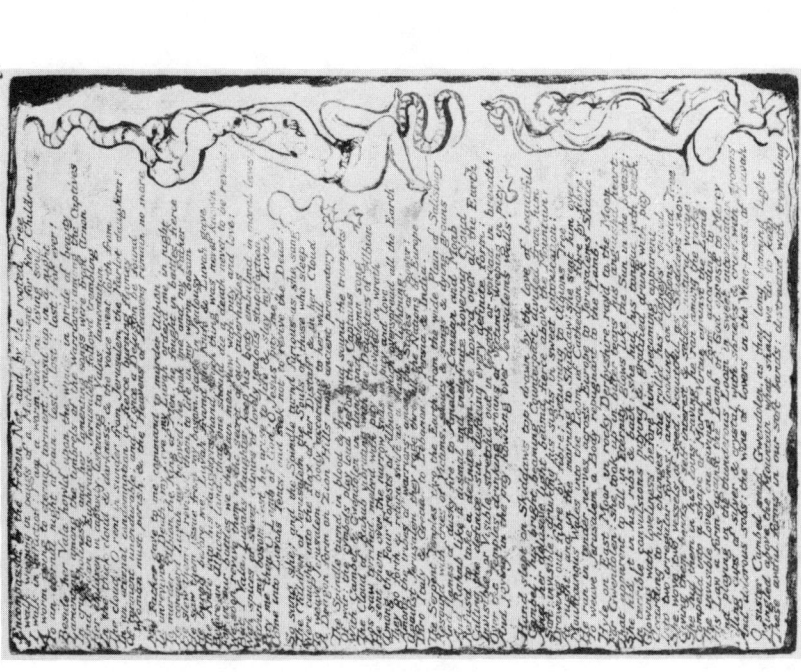

34. *Jerusalem*, Pl. 80.
By permission of the Houghton Library, Harvard University

35. *Jerusalem*, Pl. 28.
The Pierpont Morgan Library

37. "The Sick Rose," *Songs of Innocence and of Experience*.
By permission of the Houghton Library, Harvard University

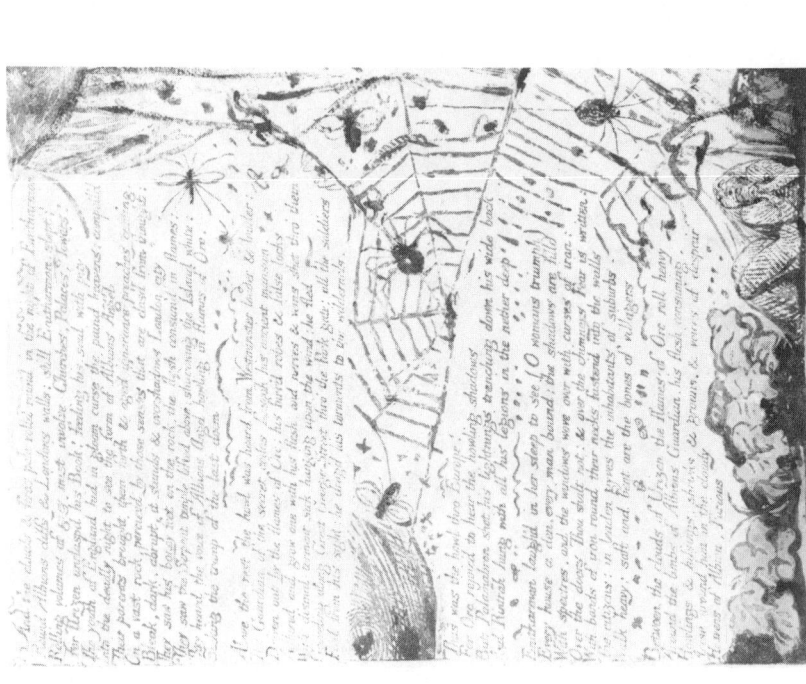

36. *Europe*, Pl. 12.
By permission of the Houghton Library, Harvard University

38. *Jerusalem*, Pl. 2.
By permission of the Houghton Library, Harvard University

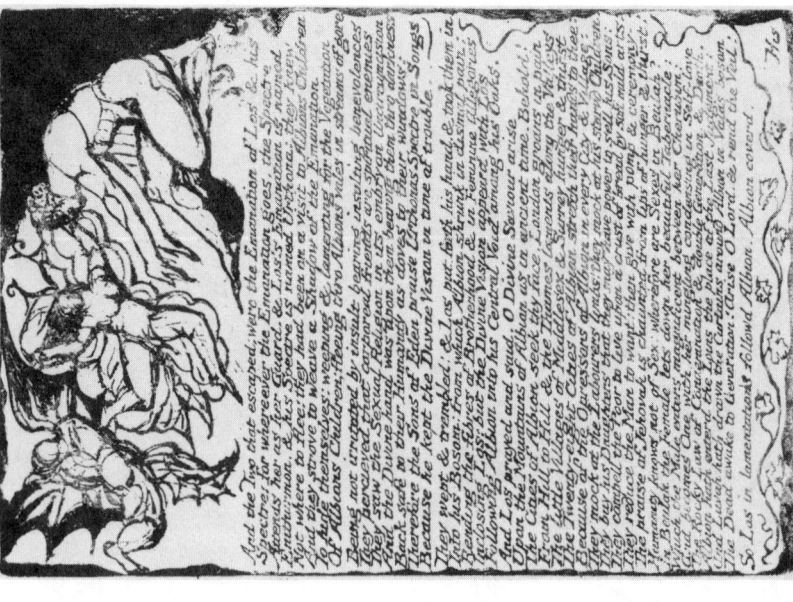

39. *Jerusalem*, Pl. 14.
By permission of the Houghton Library, Harvard University

40. *Jerusalem*, Pl. 44.
By permission of the Houghton Library, Harvard University

41. *Jerusalem*, Pl. 53.
By permission of the Houghton Library, Harvard University

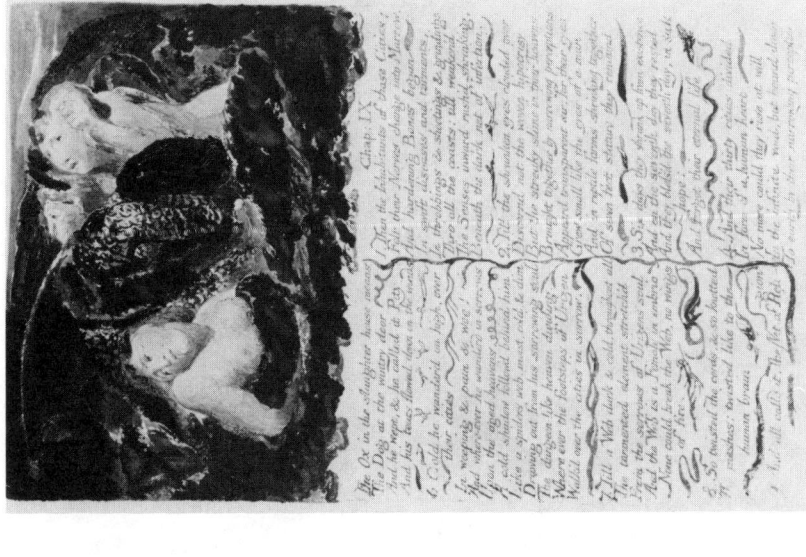

42. *Jerusalem*, Pl. 63.
By permission of the Houghton Library, Harvard University

43. *The Book of Urizen*, Pl. 25.
By permission of the Houghton Library, Harvard University

44. *Jerusalem*, Pl. 75.
By permission of the Houghton Library, Harvard University

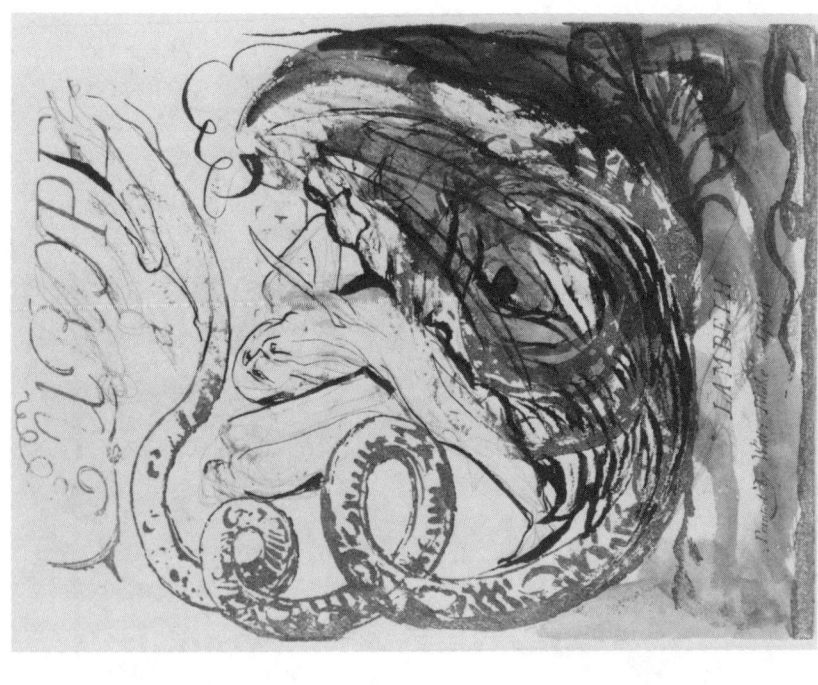

45. *Jerusalem*, Pl. 41.
By permission of the Houghton Library, Harvard University

46. *Europe*, Pl. ii. Proof in copy b.
The Pierpont Morgan Library

47. *Beatrice Addressing Dante from the Car.*
The Tate Gallery, London

48. *The Harlot and the Giant.*
National Gallery of Victoria, Felton Bequest 1920

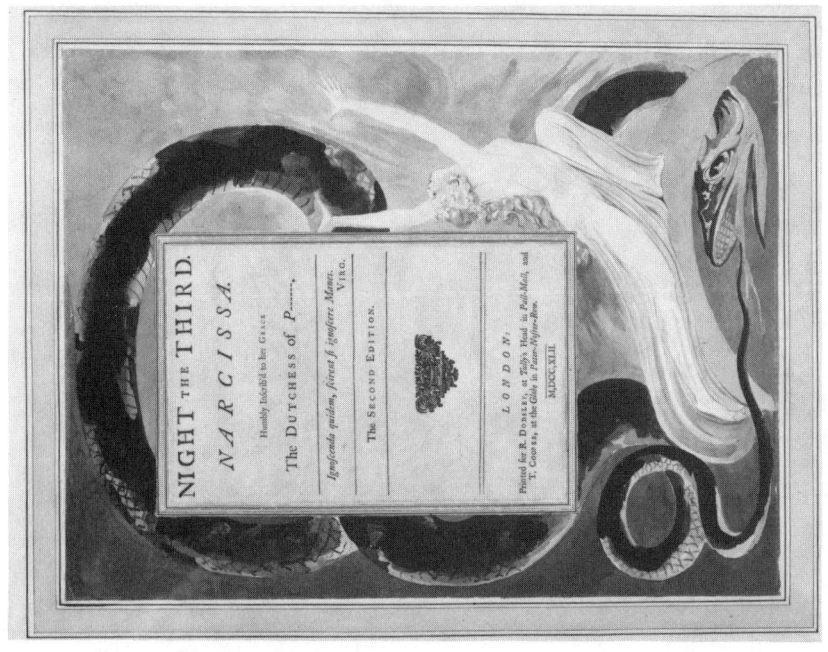

50. *Narcissa and the Ouroboros.*
British Museum

49. *The Book of Urizen*, Pl. 6.
By permission of the Houghton Library, Harvard University

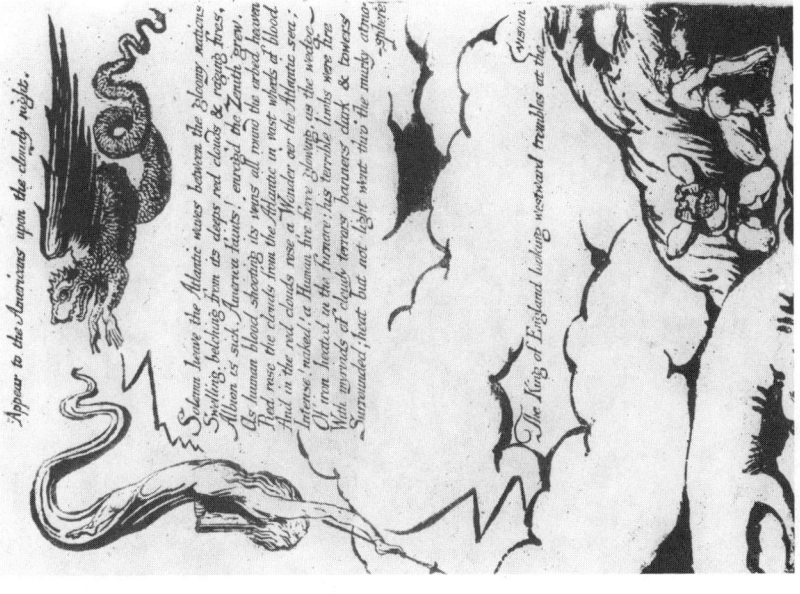

51. *Europe*, Pl. 10.
By permission of the Houghton Library, Harvard University

52. *America*, Pl. 4.
Library of Congress, Rosenwald Collection

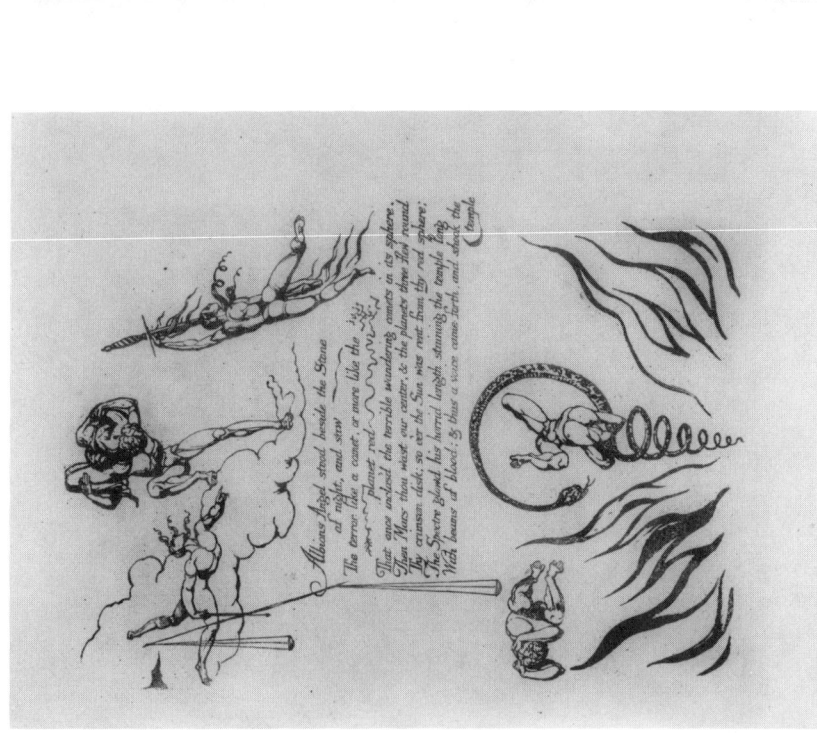

53. *America*, Pl. 5.
Library of Congress, Rosenwald Collection

54. *Jerusalem*, Pl. 40.
By permission of the Houghton Library, Harvard University

55. Watercolor 4 for Gray, "Ode on the Death of a Favourite Cat."
Collection of Mr. Paul Mellon

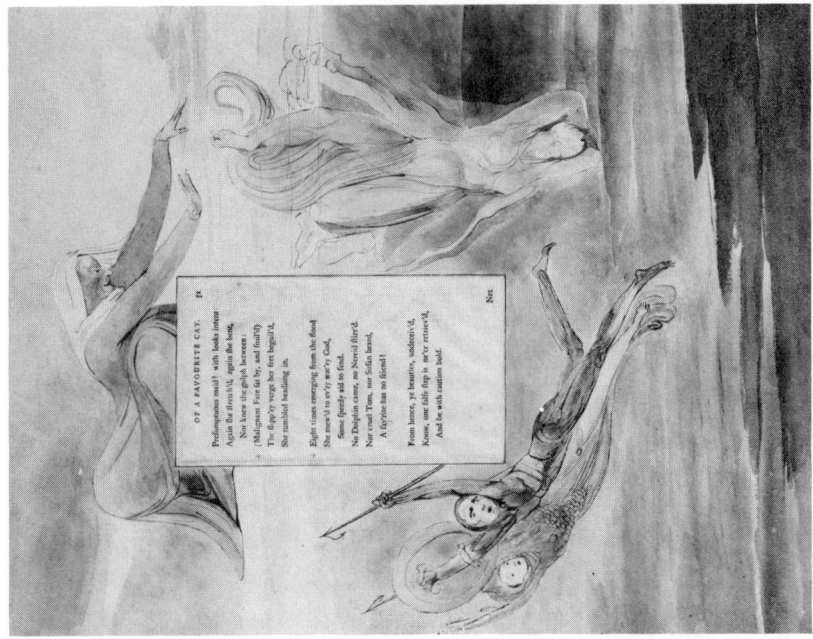

56. Watercolor 5 for Gray, "Ode on the Death of a Favourite Cat."
Collection of Mr. Paul Mellon

57. *Newton at the Bottom of the Sea of Space and Time.*
The Tate Gallery, London

58. *Jerusalem*, Pl. 92.
By permission of the Houghton Library, Harvard University

59. *The Spiritual Form of Nelson Guiding Leviathan.*
The Tate Gallery, London

60. "The Little Black Boy," Pl. 2, *Songs of Innocence and of Experience.*
By permission of the Houghton Library, Harvard University

61. *America*, Pl. 16.
Reproduced from the Collections of the Library of Congress

62. "The Ecchoing Green," Pl. 1, *Songs of Innocence and of Experience*.
By permission of the Houghton Library, Harvard University

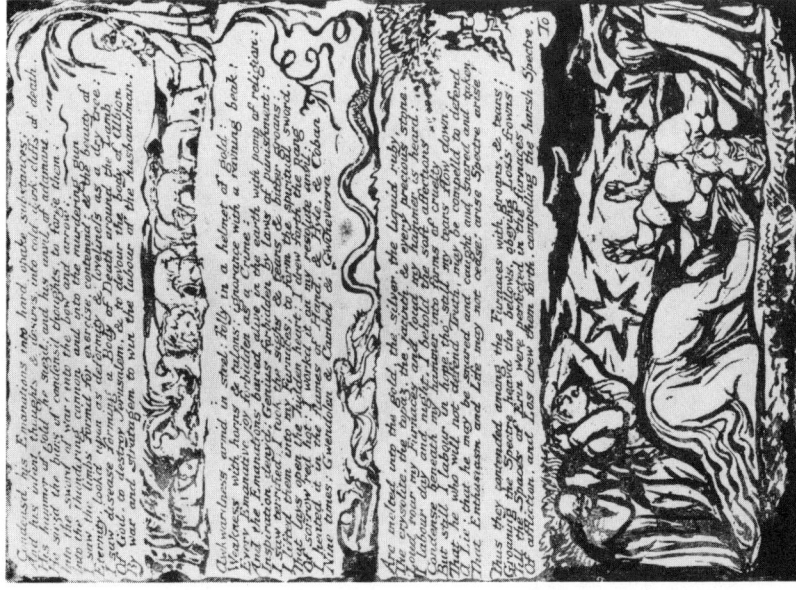

64. *Jerusalem*, Pl. 9.
By permission of the Houghton Library, Harvard University

63. *America*, Pl. 1.
Reproduced from the Collections of the Library of Congress

66. "The Angel," Songs of Innocence and of Experience.
By permission of the Houghton Library, Harvard University

65. America, Pl. 6.
Reproduced from the Collections of the Library of Congress

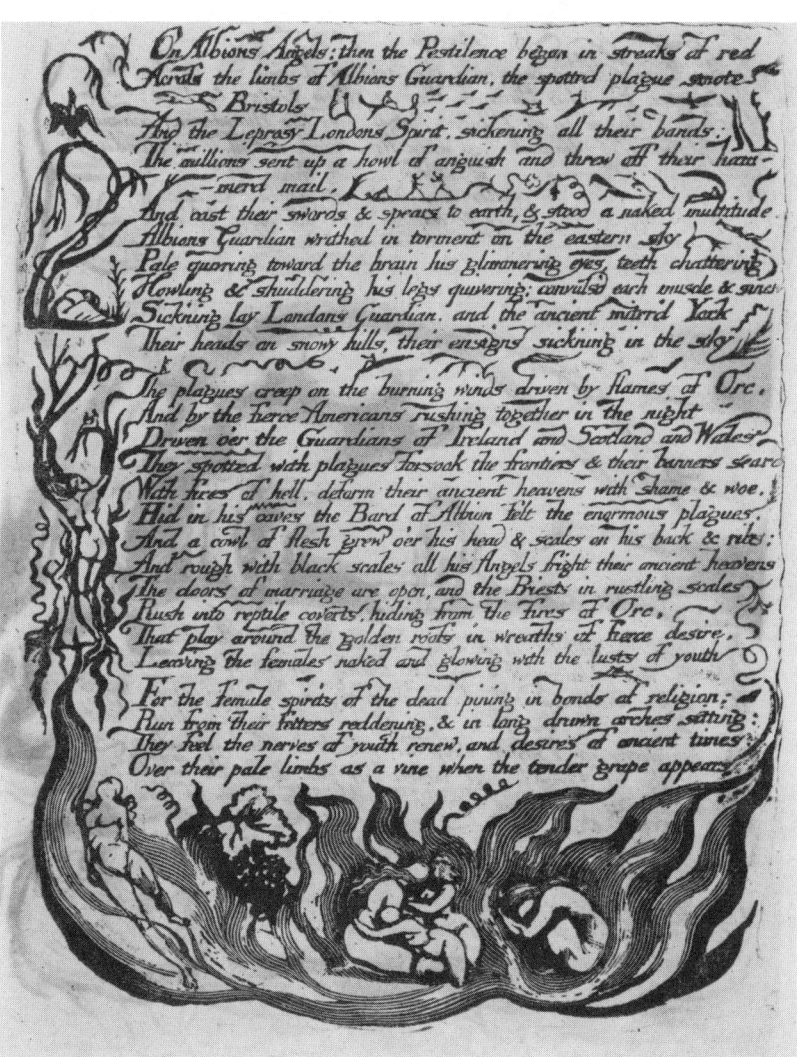

67. *America*, Pl. 15.
Reproduced from the Collections of the Library of Congress

69. "My Pretty Rose Tree," Songs of Innocence and of Experience. By permission of the Houghton Library, Harvard University

68. "Holy Thursday," Songs of Innocence and of Experience. By permission of the Houghton Library, Harvard University

70. "The Blossom," Songs of Innocence and of Experience. Library of Congress, Rosenwald Collection

71. The Botanical Magazine, Vol. I, Pl. 30. By permission of the Houghton Library, Harvard University

73. *The Book of Thel*, title page. Reproduced from the Collections of the Library of Congress

72. "The Divine Image," *Songs of Innocence and of Experience.* By permission of the Houghton Library, Harvard University

75. *The Book of Thel*, Pl. 2.
Reproduced from the Collections of the Library of Congress

74. "Infant Joy," *Songs of Innocence and of Experience.*
By permission of the Houghton Library, Harvard University

76. *The Book of Thel*, Pl. 4.
Reproduced from the Collections of the Library of Congress

77. *The Book of Thel*, Pl. 5.
Reproduced from the Collections of the Library of Congress

Index

Bracketed numbers refer to illustrations in this book. Italicized numbers refer to Blake's original plates, as numbered in Erdman's *Illuminated Blake*. For works cited in brief form, I list the first, full reference in the Key or in the notes.

Adam, 71, 78, 139, 140, 145, 151, 161

Adam and Eve Asleep, 102

Adam Naming the Beasts, 42, 143

Adder, 103, 105

Adonis, 166, 167

"Ah, Sunflower," [69], 158-59, 191n.30

Ahania, [38], 47, 95, 140, 159

Ahania, The Book of, 17, 105, 135, 140, 141, 143

Albion, asleep, [45], 95, 108, 110; attributes (banyan fig, 141-42; polypus, 127-28; sea monsters, 131; serpent, 117); as cosmic Man, 6-7; daughters of, 29, 44-45, 87-88, 93, 96, 129, 152 (*see also* Cambel; Gwendolen); epiphanies of, 39, 115; fallen and fragmented, [58], [64], 33, 67-68, 83, 155; friends of, 68; netted by Vala, [54], 124; sons of, 74, 83, 86-87, 96, 107, 129 (*see also* Hand; Hyle; Scofield); re-awakened, [26], [31], 76-77; reintegrated, 7-8; reunited with Emanation, 109; self-tortured, [20], 59, 113; submerged, [24], 123, 131; supported by Christ, [30], 83; tree of, 129, 141-42; united with Shadow, [35], [45], [54], 107-112, 124, 160-61, 192n.37; vegetating, 150

Aldegrever, Heinrich, 46, 80, 113, 186n.10. *See also* Geisberg, Max

All Religions Are One, 40, 68

Alligator, 116

Altick, Richard D., 5, 173n.4

America, 3, 25, 35, 117, 118, 121, 129-30, 143, 153; pl. *i*, 75; pl. *1*, [63], 148; pl. *3*, 181n.22; pl. *4*, [52], 116, 148; pl. *5*, [53], 119, 148; pl. 6, [65], 154; pl. *7*, [11], 39; pl. *9*, 153; pl. *11*, [18], 56, 104, 181n.22; pl. *12*, 148; pl. *13*, [24], 75, 123; pl. *14*, 106, 131, 148; pl. *15*, [67], 148, 155-56; pl. *16*, [61], 137

And She Shall be Called Woman, 144, 155

Anemone, [5], [73], [74], 166-67, 189n.21

"Angel, The," [66], 154, 155, 158

Angel of the Divine Presence, The, 149

Animal, carnivorous, 14-36, 135

(see also Bear; Behemoth; Cat; Cougar; Dog; Jaguar; Leopard; Lion; Tiger; Wolf); herbivorous, 37-52 (see also Bull; Cattle; Elephant; Goat; Hippopotamus; Horse; Lamb; Mole; Ox; Ram; Sheep; Stag); omnivorous, 52-53

Anubis, 27, 28

Apocalypse, [1], 7-8, 13, 17, 45, 72, 79, 93, 116, 121, 153

Apollo, 27, 48, 56, 148, 178n.41

Apple, 139-40; ambivalent tradition, 139; on Tree of Death and Life, 138-40; mentioned, 137, 141, 146

Arborization (human), [63], [67], 134, 137-38, 150, 156

Ariosto, Lodovico, 130

Ark, 67-68, 79; of man's body, 122

Armstrong, Edward A., 69, 182n.31

Ass, 46, 80

"Auguries of Innocence," 25, 45, 49, 65, 66, 70, 80, 92, 97, 103, 148

Bacon, Sir Francis, 143; Blake's annotations on *Essays*, 24

Baker, Henry, 126

Barbauld, Anna Letitia, 84, 102, 184n.1

Barbut, James, 127

Basire, James, 9, 10, 110, 159, 174n.20, 191n.19

Bat, 80-83; attribute of Satan and Spectre, [29], [30], 82-83; as bird, 13, 80; ears of, 81, 82; vampire bat, 81, 83; wings of, [28], [40], 50, 55, 81-82, 85, 95, 99, 169, 184n.21; mentioned, 19, 20, 51, 80, 112, 135

Bath (character in *Jerusalem*), [44], 107

Bathsheba at the Bath, 161

Beatrice, [47], [48], 27, 71, 94, 109, 138, 162

Beatrice Addressing Dante from the Car, [47], 109

Bear, 12, 14, 23, 41, 43, 50

Bee, 97-98

Beer, John, 18, 32, 176n.15

Behemoth, [8], 35-36, 76, 179n.54; mentioned, 42, 132

Behling, Lottlisa, 191n.31

Beilby, Ralph, 50, 73, 180n.23, 183n.1

Bentley, Gerald E., Jr., *Blake Records*, 183n.8; *WB's Writings*, 173n.7, 190n.31

Beulah, 67, 69, 71; daughters of, 60; edge of, 144; flowers of, 90; sleepers of, 128

Bible, 9, 13, 29, 34, 37, 48, 73, 80, 97, 98, 122, 129, 140, 143, 146, 152, 165, 170, 178n.44; Canticles (Song of Solomon), 93, 136-37, 155, 163; Deuteronomy, 9, 28; Ezekiel, 29, 109; Exodus, 17, 102, 114; Genesis, 9, 67, 106, 143; Hebrews, 151; Isaiah, 25, 51, 68, 78, 94, 104; Jeremiah, 48; Job, 34, 35, 48, 100; John, 37, 156; Leviticus, 52; Luke, 163; Matthew, 41, 61, 67, 136, 156; I Peter, 29;

Index

Psalms, 25, 46, 61, 79, 136; Revelation, 29, 94, 102, 107, 109, 114, 122, 138, 149

Bindman, David, *Blake as an Artist*, 175n.23; *Complete Graphic Works of WB (CGW)*, xv, 85, 177n.34

Birch, [2], [11], [75], [76], 39, 144-45, 168

Bird, caged, 54, 63-64, 65; carnivorous, 7, 54, 73-83 (*see also* Bat; Crow; Eagle; Owl; Raven; Vulture); granivorous, 54-72, 165 (*see also* Cock; Lark; Nightingale; Peacock; Robin; Sparrow; Swallow; Swan; Wren)

Bird of paradise, [5], [9], [11], [18], 59-61; Leutha as, 29, 60, 88; mentioned, 38, 39, 62, 99, 158, 181nn.13, 22

Blair, Robert, 91

Blake, Catherine, 190n.30

Blake, Robert, 185n.18

Blake, William, annotations of (*see* authors annotated); designs of (*see* titles except designs for Dante; Gray; Hayley; Young); as lark, 72; letters of, 153, 173n.3; Notebook of (*see* Notebook); as Quid, 63; poems of (*see* titles); self-portrait of, 185n.18

"Blossom, The" [70], 65-66, 164-65; mentioned, 61-62, 69, 139

Blunt, Anthony, 110, 178n.53, 187n.16

Boa, 39, 132

Bocchi, Achille, 174n.19

Boehme, Jacob, 6, 11-12, 32, 114, 137, 149, 173n.11; *Election of Grace*, 152; *High and Deep Searching*, 6; *Mysterium Magnum*, 11, 45, 58, 67, 79, 98, 138, 152; *Signatura Rerum*, 114; *Three Principles*, 24, 26, 31, 37, 53, 102, 103, 105, 139; *Threefold Life of Man*, 37, 105; *Treatise on the Incarnation*, 163

Book of Ahania, The (Los, Thel, Urizen). *See* Ahania; Los; Thel; Urizen

Botanical Magazine, The, [71], 6, 164

Botticelli, Sandro, 149, 161

Boudard, Jean Baptiste, 117, 174n.20, 175n.1

Boudoin, Jean, 27, 175n.1

Bourne, Vincent, 62, 169

Brahma, 134, 159

Breach in a City, A, 75

Brier, 90, 150, 151-52

Brittannia, [26], 76-77, 80

Brookes, Richard, 30, 61, 90, 118, 178n.49

Brothers Meet the Attendant Spirit, The, 110

Bruno (Blake's horse), 4, 173n.3

Bruyn, Cornelius de, 111

Bryant, Jacob, 111, 159

Buffon, George Louis Leclerc, comte de, 10, 180n.27; *Histoire Naturelle, Générale et Particuliere*, 5, 104; *Natural History (NH)*, xvi, 15, 21, 25, 30, 48, 49, 52, 81; *Histoire Naturelle des Oiseaux*, 55, 181n.4

"Buffon" (anonymous English adapter), *Natural History of Birds, Fish, Insects, and Reptiles* (BFIR), xv, 57, 61

Bull, 45-46; ambivalent tradition of, 45; attribute of Luvah and Urizen, 45-46; bull of Persepolis, 110-11, 187n.16

Bunyan, John, 10, 44, 51, 54, 62, 70, 85-86, 92, 98, 102, 103, 175n.21, 180n.11

Burdock, [65], 154

Burke, Edmund, 21

Butler, Samuel, *Hudibras*, 178n.40

Butlin, Martin, *Paintings and Drawings of WB (B)*, xv, 59; *William Blake*, 186n.12, 191n.32

Butterfly (and moth), 90-96; attribute of Emanation, [38], [39], [41], 92-96, 160; Ealing's Glory, [38], 95; Io, or Peacock, [38], 92, 93-94; Pearl Border Fritallary, 95; mentioned, 8, 39, 82, 84, 85, 86, 88

Butts, Thomas, 153

By the Waters of Babylon, 146

Cambel, [34], 87, 101, 156

Cankerworm, [37], 89, 162

Canterbury Pilgrims, 66

Cary, Henry Francis, 29, 186n.14

Cat, [55], [56], 16, 20, 124

Caterpillar, [25], [32], [37], 88-90; mentioned, 8, 75, 78, 84, 85, 99, 123. See also Cankerworm

Cattle, [12], 43-46. See also Bull; Ox

Cerberus, [3], 26-27, 28, 135

Characters in Spenser's Faerie Queene, 30

Chaucer, Geoffrey, 5, 9, 25, 30, 46, 57, 58, 66, 73, 178n.46

Cherub, Covering, 115, 116

Chew, Samuel C., 178n.36

Chicken, 27, 85-86; head of, [45], 108

Christ, Jesus (Biblical), Communion of, 153, 156; Passion of, 64, 95, 139, 146, 149, 151, 152, 157, 161, 163, 167; mentioned, 29, 37, 41, 42, 59, 61, 144, 159;

———(Blake's), attributes (anemone, 167; grape, 156; Gryphon, [47], 109; lamb, 37, 38, 40-41, 87, 179n.6; lily, [60], [72], 161, 163-66; lily of the valley, 166; palm, 149; thorn, 152; thyme, 151; Tree of Life, 144; wheat and bread, 153, 154, 156; willow, 137, 146); as child, 38-39, 157, 166; crucified, 59, 95; the Good Shepherd, [60], 37, 39, 41, 137, 179n.5; Passion of, 147, 157, 161; as scapegoat or false Christ, 40, 113-14, 179n.6; supporter and redeemer of Albion, [30], 83, 95, 115; the Universal Humanity, 39; mentioned, 8, 41, 60, 66, 68, 149, 159, 170

———(traditional), 43, 64, 137, 139, 153, 165

Christ Blessing the Little Children, 189n.18

Christ Child Asleep on a Cross, The, 146, 163

Index

Christ Offering to Redeem Man, 184n.21
Christ Refusing the Banquet, 124
Christ's Entry into Jerusalem, 149
Christ's Troubled Dream, 32
Chrysalis, [31], [32], 84-85, 86, 90, 94; chrysalis-embryo, 86, 87, 161
Church, Anglican, 82; as civilization, 71; Protestant, 72; Roman Catholic, 109-110; spiritual, 109
Cicero, Marcus Tullius, 142
Circe, 52, 150
Clay, [77], 21-22, 43-45, 168
Clematis, Entire-leaved (Virgin's Bower), [77], 168
"Clod and the Pebble, The," [12], 43-45, 102, 147, 171
Cobra, 118
Cock, 57-58, 78, 112
Coleridge, Samuel Taylor, 68
Collins, William, 64
Comus Disguised as a Rustic, 159
Comus with his Revellers, 14, 24, 46, 53
Comus with the Lady Spellbound, 50, 58, 78
Convolvus, [65], 154. *See also* Morning Glory
Corn. *See* Wheat
"Corpse-plant," [77], 169
Correspondence (spiritual), Blake's 6-9; Boehme's, 11; Swedenborg's, 12, 123
Cotton, Nathaniel, 70

Cougar, 14, 15
Cow. *See* Cattle
Cowper, William, 9, 14, 24, 48, 51, 56, 58, 62, 67, 70, 90, 113, 143, 144, 176n.5
Cowslip, English (marigold), 159
"Cradle Song," 67
Cranach, Lucas the Elder, 138
─────── the Younger, 138, 164
Creation of Eve, The, 60, 189n.21
Crocodile, attribute of the Selfhood and Urizen, 18, 116; teeth of, 16; mentioned, 42
Cross, the, 59, 138, 139, 144, 156. *See also* Christ, Jesus, the Passion of
Crow, 78, 79
Cumberland, George, 174n.19
Curtis, William, 4; *Botanical Magazine*, [72], 6, 157, 164, 168; *Flora Londinensis*, 166, 179n.4

Dalila, 17-18, 32. *See also* Delilah.
Damrosch, Leopold, Jr., 170, 173n.10
Dance of Albion, The (*Albion Rose*), [31], 85
D'Ancona (Levi D'Ancona, Mirella), 146, 149, 155, 157, 165, 188n.3
Dante Alighieri, 9, 73, 109-110, 178n.39, 186n.14; *Inferno*, 20, 25-26, 27, 29, 82, 103, 104, 135, 137; Design 1, 30, 148, 151; Design 2, 148; Design 3, 30; Design 8, 148; Design 24, 134, 138; Design 25, 138; Design 59, 26, 28; *Purgatory*, 71,

73, 94, 138, 161-62; Designs 85-87, 148; Design 88 (*Beatrice Addressing Dante from the Car*), [47], 109; Design 89 (*The Harlot and the Giant*), [48], 109-110, 138, 152; *Paradise,* 161; Design 99, 161

—————(character in *Divine Comedy*), [47], 27, 71, 109, 151, 162

Daphne, [67], 134, 156

Darwin, Erasmus, 5, 141, 154, 157, 159, 166-67, 188n.12

Death (character in *Paradise Lost*), 26, 106, 186n.10

"Death and Burial of Cock Robin, The," 61, 65, 182n.30

Death of Abel, The, 107

Delilah, 124. *See also* Dalila

Descriptive Catalogue, A, 5, 12, 35, 41, 46. *See also* "A Vision"

Devil, the, 29. *See also* Satan

Devil Rebuked, The, 184n.21

Diana, 43, 100, 110

Direction, symbolism of: down, [9], [49], [52], [53], 38; left (sinister), [2], [7], [19], [45], [46], [48], 19, 33, 41, 42, 54, 108, 109, 110, 112, 126, 138, 161, 185n.18, 193n.51; right, [5], [17], [18], [19], [47], [48], [65], 38, 41, 42, 54, 56, 57, 95, 138, 154, 158, 161, 185n.18, 193n.51; up, [5], [9], [17], [65], 38, 55, 73, 154, 158

"Divine Image, A," 22

"Divine Image, The," [72], 22, 165, 192n.49

Dog, 26-27; as companion, [61], 25, 138, 177n.34; Fenris, 178n.38; as hellhound, [4], 26, 27; of Leutha, 28-29; of Nimrod, 28; as scavenger, 25-26; as sexuality, 28-29; as stupidity and Selfhood, 11, 24, 26-27, 102, 178n.40

Dolphin, 121, 187n.1

Donne, John, 138, 150, 190n.3

Donovan, Edward, 6, 185nn.13, 15

Dove, [9], 66-68; contraries (crow, 79; eagle, 75; raven, 79; serpent, 114); Holy Dove, 60, 67; of love, 66-67; of peace and divine grace, 67; mentioned, 38, 58, 59, 122

Dragon, altars of, 117; attribute of (Rahab, [44], 107; Satan, [44], [48], 106-107, 114, 179n.6, 186n.11; Urizen and his daughters, [43], [52], 116); creative, 103-104; dragon-man, 103; Hydra of Lerna, 27; Spenser's Error, 135; wings of, 115; mentioned, 30, 105, 112

Dragonfly, [36], 92, 96-97

Drayton, Michael, 64, 125, 126, 130, 182n.26

Duppa, Richard, 160

Dürer, Albrecht, 9, 45, 80; *Fall of Man,* 139; *Madonna of the Siskin,* 166; *Melencholia I,* 74-75; *Rhinoceros,* 36; *The Small Passion,* 139

Eagle, 73-77; ambivalent, 19, 78, 170; attribute of Orc and the Shadow, [26], 24, 103; benign,

73-75, 79; contrary of mole, 51-52; eagle-vulture, [27], 78, 83; of empire, [8], [24], 56, 75-76, 97, 99, 170; head of, [23], 74; malign, [24], 19, 56, 75-76, 78; of nature, [25], 88, 99, 123; with serpent, [22], 73-74, 103; mentioned, 6, 55, 57, 79, 88, 109, 121-22

"Earth's Answer," 117, 155

Earthworm, [63], 86-87, 100-101, 148; as fallen man, 100-101, 112. *See also* Worm

"Ecchoing Green, The," 70; pl. 1, [62], 142, 157; pl. 2, 154, 155

"Edward III," 57, 149

Edwards, George, 5-6, 60

Eel, [19], 126

Eft, [65], 154

Eglantine, 158. *See also* Honeysuckle

Eichler, Gottfried, 153, 174-75n.20

Elephant, 28, 34, 50

Elm, 145-46; entwisted pair, [6], 31, 139; with vine, 145, 155

Emanation, butterfly as attribute, [38]-[40], 82, 91, 92-96; controlling space, [39], 94, 115; divided from Humanity, [24], 32, 33, 95, 115; as medium for Humanities, 72; reclaimed by Humanity, [41], 7, 27, 96, 109; renouncing Shadow, 68, 71, 77; with Shadow, 161, 192n.37; mentioned, 75

Emblems for Youth, 166, 181nn.3, 13

Empire, attributes of: birds of prey, 75, 97; eagle, 75, 77, 97, 170; forest, 135; insects, 99; lion and wolf, 25, 32, 77; serpent, 99; spider, 99; sparrow, 63

England (Shadow of Albion), 76, 115. *See also* Brittannia

Enion, butterfly and Golden Emperor moth as attributes, [38], 95; reunited with Tharmas, 93; separated from Tharmas, 39, 139; mentioned, 67, 153

Enitharmon, as Beatrice, 109; as butterfly, [38]-[40], 95; distortions of, 60-61, 75, 88, 99, 100, 123, 152, 169; as female will and nature, 32, 75, 108, 135, 163; with Los, [40], [63], 7, 68, 109, 154, 162

Enitharmon as Iris, 59

Enoch, The Book of, Blake's drawings for, 124

Erdman, David V., 85; *Complete Poetry and Prose of WB (E)*, xv; *Illuminated Blake (IB)*, xv, 43, 54, 57, 79, 112, 168, 181-82n.22; *Prophet against Empire*, 176n.12

Essick, Robert, 114, 187n.21

Eternals, 90, 148. *See also* Immortals

Europe, 17, 29, 32, 60, 99, 108, 134, 135, 143, 163; pl. *ii*, [46], 27, 108-109, 110; pl. *1*, 82, 99, 154; pl. *3*, 149; pl. *9*, 158; pl. *10*, [51], 113, 116; pl. *11*, [28], 82, 117; pl. *12*, [36], 88, 99, 144, 185n.24; pl. *13*, 88, 99; pl. *14*, [25], 55, 75, 78, 88, 99, 123, 169; pl. *15*, 88, 144, 158

Eve, [64], 71, 102, 139, 140, 145, 151, 154, 161
Eve Tempted by the Serpent, 138-39, 140
Evelyn, John, 189-90nn.27, 30
Experience, arborization in, 134, 144, 156; accepted, 104, 145-46; attributes (dry or dead tree, 136; ivy, 158; reptiles, 102, 104; willow, 145; yew, 147); divided state in, 8; rejected, 104, 166, 168; vegetation in, 159; mentioned, 13, 17, 19, 32, 52, 58, 74, 143, 147, 153
Expulsion, The, 140, 151, 152
Ezekiel's Wheels, 109

"Fairy, The," 61
Fall, the, 152; division into sexes, 161; of the Four Zoas, [49], [58], 47, 112, 127; as separation, 6-7, 11, 121; of Tharmas, 121, 139; Tree of, 138-44
Fall of Eve, The, 107
Fall of Man, The, 19, 78, 138
Female, "nameless, shadowy," 134, 135
Female will, 29, 43, 63; Enitharmon as, 32, 75, 123; renunciation of, 77, 87, 95
Fig, 138, 140-41; banyan fig, 141-42; of peace and prosperity, 140
Fish, [19], [24], [54], 122-26; fins of, 124-25; scales of, [55], [56], 124, 187n.2; fish-woman, [19], [55], [56], 124-26, 147; mentioned, 78, 88, 99, 121
"Flame plant," 164

Flaxman, Anna F., 177n.29, 191n.21
Flaxman, John, 110
Flea, 82
Flowers, 136, 150, 158-69. See also Anemone; Fuschia; Lily; Lily of the valley; Marigold; Poppy; Rose; Sunflower; Water Lily
Fly, [25], [36], 8, 75, 92, 97, 99. See also Butterfly; Dragonfly; Moth
"Fly, The," 91, 145
For Children: The Gates of Paradise. See *The Gates of Paradise*
Forest, 17, 32, 135
Four Zoas, The (FZ), xv, 7, 16, 26, 28, 32-33, 34, 39, 40, 41, 43, 45, 47, 49, 50, 56, 58-59, 67, 74, 76, 78, 79, 90, 92, 98, 100-101, 116, 118, 119-20, 121, 125, 127, 127-28, 131, 135, 137, 139, 141, 142, 149, 151, 153, 160, 162, 182n.39; p. 14, 186n.8; p. 70, 116; p. 124, 159
Franklin, Benjamin, 56
Freher, Dionysius, 58, 114, 149, 152, 166, 181n.12
French Revolution, The, 32, 73, 75, 99, 102, 118, 135, 155
Freud, Sigmund, 61, 192n.49
Friedmann, Herbert, 62, 193n.55
Friend, Hilderic, 191n.16
Frog, [1], [12], [65], 44, 80, 102; as reptile, 102; of the Selfhood, 18. See also Toad
Frye, Northrop, xix, 10, 18, 22-23, 175n.23

Index

Fuschia, 4, 168-69

Fuseli, Henry, 4, 8, 22, 84, 173n.5

Furies, 115, 147

"Garden of Love, The," 90, 117, 152

Gates of Paradise, The, 10; pl. *i*, [32], 85; pl. *1*, 147, 150; pl. *6*, 85; pl. *7*, 91; pl. *15*, 86; pl. *16*, [33], 86, 87; pl. *19*, 82, 107; Keys, 85, 86, 117, 150

Gay, John, 10, 50, 179n.10

Geisberg, Max, 178n.45

Genesis (Blake's Illustrated), 43, 74

George III, [28], 35, 82, 153

Ghost of Abel, The, 30

Ghost of a Flea, The, 82

Giant (of the Whore of Babylon), [48], 107, 109-110, 152

Gilpin, William, 142

Goat, 12, 23, 41-42, 45, 155, 170. *See also* Scapegoat

God, as Christ the Good Shepherd, 137; and dove, 60, 67-68; Eyes of, 71; loving, 61, 67, 137; omnipotent, 100; of the Ten Commandments, 105, 117

"Golden Net, The," 162-63

Goldfinch, 63-64, 165

Goldsmith, Oliver, "The Deserted Village," 14; *The History of the Earth*, 11, 13, 15, 20, 21, 25, 42, 50, 52, 58, 59, 61, 73, 81, 84, 88, 96, 98, 122, 123, 126, 127, 176n.8, 177n.26

Golgonooza, 71, 95, 151

Goltzius, Hendrik, 9, 23, 25, 83, 177n.26; *Casting out Evil*, 46; *Night*, 112

Grampus, 130-31

Grant, John, 82, 192n.37

Grant, Ms. John. *See* Johnson, Mary Lynn

Grapes, 54, 60

Grapevine, benign, [62], [65], [67], 155-56; divine, 156-57; malign, 155; mentioned, 39, 95, 140, 142-43, 145, 154, 157

Grass, Spring, 39, 179n.4

Gravelot (Hubert-François Bourguignon), 10, 117, 151, 174n.20

Gray, Thomas, *Poems by Mr. Gray*, 177n.29, 178n.38; watercolor title page, [17], 56, 77; "The Bard," 24; Design 2, 76; Design 9, 49; "Elegy," Design 4, 147; Design 10, 189n.18; "The Fatal Sisters," Design 7, 49; Design 8, [14], 49; Design 10, 49; "Ode for Music," Design 4, 159; "Ode on the Death of a Favourite Cat," 124; Design 4, [55], 124; Design 5, [56], 124; "Ode on a Distant Prospect," 53, 77, 105; Design 6, [16], 53, 77, 105; "Ode to Spring," 96, 157; Design 3, 157; Design 5, 96; Design 6, 92, 96; "Progress of Poetry," 56

Great Dragon and the Woman Clothed with the Sun, The, 184n.21, 186n.11

Great Red Dragon and the Beast from the Sea, The, 107, 186n.11

Guyon, or Guion, Jeanne Marie, 62

Gwendolen, Blake's, [34], 45, 87, 100, 125, 156; Milton's, 125

"Gwin, King of Norway," 75

Hades, 130, 147, 148

Hancarville, Pierre François Hughes, 111

Hand, dragon and polypus as attributes, 107, 129; mentioned, 40, 87, 108, 156, 161

Harlot, The, 152. *See also* Whore of Babylon

Harlot of the Giant, The, [48], 109-110, 138, 152

Hawthorn, [69], 162, 192n.44

Hayley, William, his *Ballads*, 25, 50, 177n.34; Blake's designs for ("The Dog and the Crocodile," 25,; "The Dog Defending his Dead Master," 25; "The Elephant," 19, 50); Blake's portraits for, 142, 148, 158, 188n.8; Blake's subjection to, 153; edition of Cowper, 62, 143

He Cast Him into the Bottomless Pit, 186n.11

Hecate, 80

Henrey, Blanche, 173n.2

Herbs, 150-51. *See also* Mandrake; Thyme

Hercules, 27, 35

Hertel, Georg, 153, 174n.20, 175n.1, 187n.2

Hill, John, 141

Hilton, Nelson, 184n.17

Hippopotamus, 34-35

Hog. *See* Swine

Holtzwart, Mathias, 126-27

Holy Family, The, or Christ in the Lap of Truth, 163, 167

"Holy Thursday," (*Experience*), [68], 144, 152, 153, 158

Homer, 18, 52, 130

Honeysuckle, [62], 38, 142, 157, 161, 165, 168

Horace (Quintus Horatius Flaccus), 56, 57

Horse, 46-50; batwinged, [15], 50, 82; of instruction, 17, 33, 47, 170; of intellect, 47; of light, 33, 47, 49; of passion, 48. *See also* Warhorse

"Human Abstract, The," 79, 97, 141, 145

Humanity, divided from Emanation, [24], 68, 95, 115, 160; the Divine Humanity, [72] 109, 165; reawakened, 122; sleep of, 108; mentioned, 71, 75

Hunter, Alexander, 189-90nn. 27, 30

Hunter, Henry, 11

Hunter, William, 5

Huquier, Gabriel, 10

Hyle, 40, 87, 140, 156, 161

Hymn of Christ and the Apostles, The, 149

"I Saw a Chapel," 53, 117

Ignoge, 125

Ijim, 8, 32, 106

Immortals, 101. *See also* Eternals

"Infant Joy," [74], 165, 167

Index

"Infant Sorrow," 117, 156

Ingersoll, Ernest, 182n.25

Innocence, attributes: bird of paradise, 60; serpentine vines, 157; shade trees, 136-37; sheep and lambs, 37-38; songbirds, 39, 61; swan, 55

Innocence, Higher, 31, 34, 56, 60, 74, 104, 146

Insect, 84-101; chrysalis, 84, 90; metamorphosis, 84-88. *For winged state see* Bee; Butterfly; Dragonfly; Moth. *See also* Cankerworm; Caterpillar; Earthworm; Spider

Isis, 159, 160

"Island in the Moon, An," 63, 82

Ivy, [66], 41, 158, 171, 191n.30

Jacob's Ladder (plant), 164

Jaguar, 15

Jehovah, 137. *See also* God

Jellyfish, 127. *See also* Medusa

Jerusalem (protagonist of the poem), [58]; asleep, [30], 83; as bride of the Lamb, 40; as butterfly, [38], [39], 93-94; as shepherdess, 39; vegetation of, 163; mentioned, 87, 100, 192n.37

Jerusalem, 3, 6, 16, 24, 25, 28, 29, 35, 39, 40, 41, 44-45, 45, 50, 67-68, 72, 76, 76-77, 79, 80, 82, 85, 86-88, 91, 93-96, 98, 100, 115, 116, 117-118, 122, 124-25, 127, 129, 132, 134, 140, 141-42, 143-44, 151, 152, 153, 155, 156, 160-61, 161; pl. 2, [38], 67, 82, 93-96; pl. 3, 42; pl. 4, 108; pl. 6, [29], 82-83; pl. 9, [64], 154; pl. *11*, [19], 57, 124-25, 126, 147; pl. *13*, 92, 96; pl. *14*, [39], 94; pl. *15*, 150, 152; pl. *18*, 161; pl. *23*, 95, 159, 163; pl. *24*, 67; pl. *25*, 6; pl. *26*, 108; pl. *27*, 164; pl. *28*, [35], 87, 126, 160-61, 192n.37; pl. *29*, [13], 45; pl. *33*, [30], 78, 83, 95, 149; pl. *34*, 158; pl. *35*, [15], 50, 82; pl. *36*, 154; pl. *37*, 122; pl. *39*, 67-68; pl. *40*, [54], 72, 124, 126, 150, 152; pl. *41*, 107-112, 186n.12; pl. *44*, [40], 91, 95; pl. *48*, 60; pl. *50*, 107; pl. *51*, 95, 108; pl. *53*, [41], 95, 160; pl. *62*, [20], 59, 113; pl. *63*, [42], 100; pl. *65*, 158; pl. *71*, 55; pl. *72*, 105; pl. *75*, [44], 107; pl. *76*, 59, 95; pl. *78*, [23], 74; pl. *79*, 60; pl. *80*, [34], 87, 100; pl. *82*, 87; pl. *85*, 11; pl. *92*, [58], 127; pl. *98*, [1], 7-8, 121

Jessamine, [69], [72], 162, 165

Jesus. *See* Christ, Jesus

Job (Biblical character), 140, 142, 161, 163

Job (Blake's), 34, 48; pl. 2, 59; pl. 3, 184n.21; pl. 4, 142, 184n.21; pl. 5, 152; pl. 6, 184n.21; pl. 8, 152; pl. 10, 79, 80, 184n.21; pl. 11, 117; pl. 14, 110, 131; pl. 15, [8], 34, 35-36, 126, 132-33; pl. 18, 153; pl. 19, 140, 153, 161, 163; pl. 20, 161

John, Saint, the Evangelist, [23], [47], 73, 74

John, Saint, the Visionary, [23], 74

John the Baptist, 136, 146, 157, 165, 166
Johnson, Mary Lynn (Ms. John Grant), 193n.53
Johnson, Samuel, 82, 165
Jones, Sir William, 160
Jonson, Ben, 56, 78
Journal of the Warburg and Courtauld Institutes (JWCI), xvi
Jove, 75. See also Zeus
Judas Betrays Him, 149
Judgment of Paris, The, 28, 139
Jung, Carl G., 177n.25

Kauvar, Elaine M., xix, 145, 164, 166, 188n.19
Keynes, Sir Geoffrey, 81, 110; ed. *Letters of WB*, 173n.3
Killer whale. See Grampus
"King Edward the Third," 31, 97
Klingender, Francis, 9
Kostelanetz, Anne T. (Ms. Anne Mellor), 78, 146, 179n.3

Lacépède, Bernard Germain Etiénne, comte de, 113, 116, 118, 131, 187n.19
Lack, David Lambert, 182n.30
Lamb, 37-40; contrary of (lion, 30; tiger, 19, 22; wolf, 23, 24, 25); Lamb of God, 40, 87; symbol of Innocence, [10], [12], 8, 12, 22, 34, 37-38, 38, 55, 67; mentioned, 78, 179nn.3, 5
"Lamb, The," [10], 37, 38, 39, 157
Lamprey, [19], 126

"Land of Dreams, The," 66, 163
Langhorne, John, 10, 158, 163, 191n.30
Laocoön, The (Blake's engraving), 138
Lark, 69-72; as divine inspiration, 70-72, 77; as dweller in the skies, 70; as herald of the morn, [21], 69; as messenger of Los, 151; song of, 69-70
Latham, John, 79
"Laughing Song," 54, 55, 189n.18
Laurel, 134, 148
Lavater, Johann Caspar, *Aphorisms*, Blake's annotations on, 24; *Essays on Physiognomy*, Holcroft trans., 16, 176n.10; Hunter trans., 11, 16, 24, 30-31, 32, 35, 45, 50, 51, 53, 57, 66, 75, 81, 84, 90-91, 104, 117, 122-23, 174n.13
Leclerc, George Louis, comte de Buffon. See Buffon
Leopard, 14, 18, 31, 33, 42
Leutha, attributes (dog, 28, 29; dragon, 105; marigold, 28, 159; moth, 93); and bird of paradise, 29, 60, 88
Levi D'Ancona, Mirella. See D'Ancona
Leviathan, [8], [59], 35, 76, 116, 131-133
"Lilly, The," [69], 162, 163
Lily, 163-64; attribute of Christ, [70], 159, 163-64; emblem of marriage, 64, 161; Fairy lily, 163; fleur-de-lys, 193n.51; Lily of Havilah (Vala), [35], 161; Meadow lily, 163; scarlet lily of

Index

the Passion, 161, 164; Turk's Cap lily, [70]-[72], 164, 165; Zephyr lily, 163; mentioned, 48, 65, 150, 162, 166, 192nn.42, 49

Lily of the valley, [75]-[77], 137, 166, 168

Lindberg, Bo, 184n.7

Von Linné, Carl, 5, 13, 131

Linnell, John, 23, 187n.16

Lion, 29-34; ambivalent tradition of, 29-30, 170; attribute of (Christ, 29, 109; Orc and Satan, 29, 130; the Selfhood, 18, 32-33; Urizen, [7], 32-33, 50); in England, 30, 57, 178n.48; of Innocence, 34, 74; Milton's, 19, 30; nose of, 32; Redeemed, [6], 17, 31, 59; rehumanized, 7; skin of, 30; symbol of empire, 25, 99; wrath of, 16-17, 55, 170; mentioned, 42, 52, 116, 122, 135, 155

"Little Black Boy, The," 137; pl. 2, [60], 137, 163, 166

"Little Boy Lost, A," 158

"Little Boy Lost, The," 55

"Little Girl Found, The," [6], 31, 104, 139, 145

"Little Girl Lost, A," 60, 90, 145, 155, 167

"Little Girl Lost, The," [5], 31, 60, 104, 137

"Little Vagabond, The," 54, 60

Lizard, 39, 80

Locke, John, 47

Los, attributes (eagle head, [23], 74; horse, 47; lark, 71-72, 151; thyme, 151); as Blake, 72; children or sons of, 92, 134; creator and shaper, 22, 83, 87, 96, 127, 154; his epiphanies of Jerusalem and the Covering Cherub, 93, 115; fall of, [49], 112; furnaces of, 156; gate of, 80, 82; as the Good Shepherd, 41; as imagination, 29, 92; opposer of Milton and Orc, [63], 134, 148; receiver of the Stigmata, 95; reunited with Emanation, [40], 7, 68, 95, 109; separated from Emanation, [39], 83; with Spectre, [29], [40], 83; winepress of, 3, 156; mentioned, 35, 39, 45, 162

Los, The Book of, 22, 99, 127

Lotus, 159-61; oriental lotus (tamara), 159, 192n.35. *See also* Water lily

Lucifer, 51, 82, 187n.3. *See also* Satan

Luke, Saint, [47], 43

Luther, Martin, 72, 186n.11

Luvah, attributes (bull, 45-46; horse, 47, 48; thyme, 151; warhorse, 49; wild beasts, 33); Emanation of, 95; mantle of, 40; Spectre of 29, 46; winepress of, 7, 49, 156

Lyca, [5], [6]; attributes (anemone, 167; bird of paradise, 60, 158; blossoming vine, 158; Redeemed wild animals, 31, 74, 104); traverser of Experience, 145-46

Madonna and Child, [74], 62, 65, 66, 139, 164-65, 167; *Mater Dolorosa*, [70], 65, 165

Mandrake, 147, 150

Marigold, 159, 160, 163, 191nn.32, 33

Marine Life, 121-33. *See also* Eel; Fish; Grampus; Lamprey; Leviathan; Polypus; Sea-serpent; Shellfish; Squid; Whale

Mark, Saint, [47], 29

Marotti, Arthur F., 14, 30, 176n.3

Marriage of Heaven and Hell, The (*MHH*), xvi, 3, 12, 16, 25, 32, 41, 50, 54, 56, 58, 73-74, 77, 79, 97-98, 98, 103, 132, 169, 170; pl. *4*, 48; pl. *5*, 50; pl. *8*, 43, 54, 149, 155; pl. *10*, 81; pl. *15*, [22], 73, 103; pl. *22*, 43, 104; pl. *24*, 48

Mary the Virgin, 93, 159, 161, 163, 165, 166. *See also* Madonna and child

"Mary," 162, 163

Mason, William, 142

Maty, Henry, 111

Maurice, Thomas, 160

Medusa (polypus), [57], 127

Melancholy, 110

Mellor, Ms. *See* Kostelanetz, Anne K.

"Mental Traveller, The," 24, 43, 52, 152

Michelangelo Buonarroti, 9, 140, 160

Miller, Philip, 151, 190n.5

Milton, John, 9, 10, 27, 30, 32, 48, 52, 69, 72, 157, 159, 176n.4, 188n.8; "L'Allegro," 69, 192n.44, 193n.51; *Comus*, 14, 23, 41, 52, 110, 125, 135; *History of Britain*, 124-25; "Lycidas," 151; "On the Morning of Christ's Nativity," 67; Blake's design for, 186n.11; "Il Penseroso," 110; *Paradise Lost*, (*PL*), xvi, 14, 19, 20, 23, 26, 28-29, 30, 42, 46, 48, 71, 75, 102, 103, 106, 116, 139, 140, 141, 145, 152, 155, 162, 176n.4; Paradise Regained (*PR*), xvi, 30; *Samson Agonistes*, 30. *For Blake's other designs, see title*

————, as hero of *Milton*, [3], [26], 27, 68, 72, 77, 109, 135, 162

Milton, 3, 12, 24, 27, 29, 48, 58, 67, 68, 69, 70-71, 84-85, 89, 92, 93, 94, 96-97, 97, 100, 105, 109, 117, 128, 135, 144, 151, 153, 155, 157, 162, 173n.1; pl. *12*, 159; pl. *19*, 134; pl. *30*, 96; pl. *32*, 185n.18; pl. *37*, 185n.18; pl. *40*, 72; pl. *42*, [26], 77; pl. *46*, [3], 26-27; pl. *49*, 153; pl. *50*, 153

Miner, Paul, 188n.10

Mirth, 82

Mole, 51-52

Monocarp, [77], 168

Moor, Edward, 192n.35

Morning glory, 154, 158, 165, 191nn.24, 25

Moses, 17, 114

Moses at the Burning Bush, 143

Moses Erecting the Brazen Serpent, 114

Moth, [31], 85, 88, 90-95, 99; Enion as Golden Emperor moth, [38], 93, 95; "many-feathered

Index

moth," 94, 185n.15; "white-feathered moth," 185n.15. *See also* Butterfly

"My Pretty Rose Tree," [69], 152, 162, 192n.42

Myrtle, 156

Nanavutty, Ms. Piloo, 144, 174n.19

Narcissus, 166, 168

Nature, attributes (polypus, 128; serpent, 112-113; stag, 43); Covering Cherub of, 115; domination or spell of, 7, 27, 29, 75, 86, 88, 112, 123, 147, 150, 152, 155, 160; Enitharmon as goddess of, 32; as Female Will, 32, 43; rejection of, 7, 77, 87; as "Shadowy daughter of Urthona," 118; as "Shadowy Mother," 128; Vala as goddess of, 95, 100, 108, 160-61; mentioned, 20, 143

Net, of mystery, 141; of religion, 100, 134, 144; of Vala, [35], [54], 124, 160, 192n.37

Nettle, 150, 153

Newt, 18, 102, 103, 121

Newton, Sir Isaac, [57], 5, 62, 123, 127, 169

Newton at the Bottom of the Sea of Space and Time, [57], 127

Nicholson, William, 4

Niebuhr, Carsten, 111

"Night," 18

Night Startled by the Lark, [21], 69

Nightingale, 62, 68-69, 71

Nimrod, 28

Noah, 67

Notebook (Blake's), *Notebook of WB*, ed. Erdman, 20, 21, 63, 175n.21; cited in *E*, 41, 53, 58, 62, 63, 124, 141, 163

Number of the Beast is 666, The, 107, 179n.6, 186n.11

"Nurse's Song" (*Experience*), 155, 191n.25

"Nurse's Song" (*Innocence*), 147

Oak, 142-44; bare oak, forest, or grove, 143-44; dry oak or fallen leaves, [11], [36], [68], 144; single, shady oak, [62], 142-43, 189nn.15, 18; oak of weeping, [30], 83, 134, 143

Oberon and Titania on a Lily, 163

Octopus, [58], 126, 127

Ololon, with Blake, 72; as Milton's Emanation and quest, [26], 27, 77, 109, 162; as sacrificial dove, 68, 69, 71, 94, 182n.39; mentioned, 128, 134

"On Another's Sorrow," 60, 66

Oothoon, attributes (lamb, 55; marigold, 29, 159; nightingale, 69; swan, 55); as victim of society, [24], [27], 74, 75, 78; mentioned, 51, 54, 70, 86, 99

Orc (son of Los), attributes (hellhound, 28; lion, 135; orc or grampus, 130-31; polypus, 128; sea-monster, 131; serpent, [53], 116, 118-19; warhorse, 48; whale, 130; wild beasts, 33); with bulls of Luvah, 46; in French Revolution, 17, 155; as foetus or worm, [63], 148; manacled by Los, [63], 148; as Spectre of Luvah, 29, 46

———————(grampus), 130-31

———————(giant or monster), 130

Orcus, 126-27, 130

Orpheus, 27, 56

Osiris, 160

Ott, Judith, 74-75

Ounce, 14, 42

Our Lady with the Infant Jesus, 146, 157, 165, 167

Ouroboros, [20], [45], [46], [48], [50], [53], 108, 109, 112-14

Overthrow of Apollo, The, 178n.41

Ovid (Publius Ovidius Naso), 9, 27, 80, 102, 145, 147, 158

Owen, Charles, 118, 132

Owl, 80; attribute of Selfhood or Shadow, 24, 135; malign, 20, 78, stupid, 19, 76, 79, 80; mentioned, 13, 81, 112

Ox, 12, 45, 49; attribute of Vala, 107-108, 110-11

Paine, Thomas, 56

Palambron, 48, 105

Paley, Morton D., 175n.23

Palm, 149; of suffering, [30], 83, 134, 144

Palmer, Samuel, 74

Panofsky, Erwin, xix, 10; *Early Netherlandish Painting*, 19, 176n.17

Paris (mythological), 28-29, 139

Parisi, Frank M. 184n.6

Pars, Henry, 9

Partridge, 61

Pasqueflower, or Passion flower, 167. *See also* Anemone

Passion (Christ's). *See under* Christ, Jesus

Paulson, Ronald, 6

Peacock, 58-59; fan of feathers, [20], 46, 113; mentioned, 21, 170

Pebble, 43-44

Pennant, Thomas, 52, 56, 79, 80, 126, 180n.27

Percy, Thomas, 6, 64, 182n.28

Pers, Dirck, 177n.26, 187n.2

Physiognomy, 9, 11. *See also* Lavater, Johann Caspar

Pig. *See* Swine

Pigeon, 59, 61

Pigler, A., 180n.28

Pindar, 56

Pitt, William the Younger, 35

Plants, 150-169. *See under* Flowers; Hawthorn; Herbs; Vines; Weeds

Plato, 9, 56

Pliny the Elder (Gaius Plinius Secundus), 9, 127, 131, 132, 144, 151, 158, 166, 174n.15

Poetical Sketches, 64, 135, 142, 147, 148, 163, 169, 179n.3

"Poison Tree, A," 137, 139

Polypus, 126-29, 188n.10; freshwater polyp, 126, 169; Medusa, [57], 127; squid or octopus, [58], 126, 127-28

Pope, Alexander, 14, 24, 25, 50, 80, 143, 154, 176n.5

Index

Poppy, 112, 138, 153-54
Post, G. E., 178n.43
Praz, Mario, 10, 174n.16

Quarles, Frances, 63, 137, 139, 174n.19, 175n.21, 182n.23

Rahab, [44], 6, 40, 96, 107
Rahner, Hugo, 150, 189n.25
Raine, Kathleen, 74, 144, 175n.23
Ram, [11], 12, 150
Raphael Sanzio, 9, 149, 160; *The Judgment of Paris*, 28; *The Holy Family under an Oak*, 189n.15; *Madonna of the Goldfinch*, 165
Raphael Warns Adam and Eve, 60, 140
Raven, 78-79, 99, 121-22
Ray, John, 52
Repose, The, 149, 167
Reptiles, 102-120; species of, 102, 103. *See also* Alligator; Crocodile; Frog; Lizard; Newt; Serpent
Richardson, George, 10, 11, 35, 61, 80, 117, 150, 174nn.18, 19, 175n.1, 177n.26
Rintrah, 32, 135
Ripa, Caesare, 10, 174n.19. *See also his editors:* Boudoin, Jean; Hertel, Georg; Pers, Dirck; Richardson, George; Tempest, P.
Robin, 61, 64-66, 153, 165, 182nn.27, 28
Roe, Albert S., 178n.39, 186n.12
Romano, Guilio, 9, 189n.15
Rose, Edward J., 184n.6

Rose, [36], 161-62; false, [61], 138; of love and marriage, 64, 89-90; mentioned, 98, 163, 192n.42
Rose tree (hawthorn), [69], 162
Rowland, Beryl, 178n.37
Royal Academy (London), 5, 9, 192-93n.50; Library, 5, 10, 35, 104, 118, 174n.19, 188n.11; Library Catalogue, 173n.8
Sabrina, [19], 57, 124-26, 171, 187n.6
Sabrina Disenchanting the Lady, 126
Salemi, Joseph S., 174n.19
Sambucus, Joannes, 51, 59, 180n.26
Samson, 27, 32, 85, 124
"Samson," 17, 32
Satan (Biblical), attributes: dragon, 106, 107, 114, 186n.11; lion, 29, 170; serpent, 106, 109
———(Blake's), attributes (bat, 81, 82, 184n.21; dragon, [44], 106, 107; serpent, 106, 114); Emanation of, 29, 93, 106; hypocrisy of, 117; as limit of opaqueness, 82; seat of, 71; as Spectre of Albion, 101; as Spectre of Luvah, 40, 46; as Spectre of Urizen, 45, 47, 108-109; State of Satan, 114, 120; watch-friends of, [15], 50, 82; mentioned, 47, 105, 142, 193n.51
———(Milton's), attributes (cormorant, 130; lion, 32, 130; serpent, 103, 130; toad, 102, 130); degeneration of, 119; and Sin, 29, 105, 106, 186n.10

_____(mythical and other literary), attributes: bat, 80-81, 82; dog, 26; goat, 41; serpent, 107, 113

Satan Comes to the Gates of Hell, 26, 106

Satan Exulting over Adam and Eve, 184n.21

Satan Exulting over Eve, 140

Satan in Council, 184n.21

Satan in his Original Glory, 107, 193n.51

Satan Smiting Job with Boils, 184n.21

Satan Watching the Endearments of Adam and Eve, 161, 166, 184n.21

Satan's Entry into Paradise, 107

Satyr, 41, 170

Scapegoat, 40

Schiller, Gertrud, 188n.6

"School Boy, The," 64, 69, 137, 156

Scofield, 108, 151

Scorpion, 12, 34, 99, 104, 117, 118

Sea of Space and Time, [57], 68, 121-22, 127, 128, 131

Sea-serpent, [24], [54], 123, 126, 131, 132, 133

Selfhood, attributes (bat, 81-83, 135; Behemoth, 35; carnivores, 33-34, 135; dragon, 107, 115; forest, 135; goat, 42; lion, 18, 33, 34; scorpion, 34; serpent, 18, 59, 107, 114-16, 117, 152; tiger, 17, 18, 23, 33, 34; toad, 18; warhorse, 33; wolf, 24, 83); domination of, 8, 42; Ijim as, 32; rejection of, 8, 68, 71, 91, 92-93, 95; Tiriel as, 18; mentioned, 90. *See also* Spectre

Serpent, [1], [16], [25], 103-107; airborne, 104; attribute of (Orc, 130; Satan, 107-108, 113, 130, 138, 140, 143, 154; Vala, [45], 108; Urizen, [46], 108-109); Brazen Serpent, [20], 59, 113-14; eagle-serpent, [22], 73-74; of empire, 32, 97, 99; of the Fall, [64], 152, 154; of Higher Innocence, [18], 56, 104; human-headed, [53], 119; of materialism, [49], 27, 112; Milton's serpent of Sin, 30, 106; of nature, [25], [45], [46], [50], [51], 88, 108, 111, 112-13; of the passions, 74; as phallic symbol, 104; Prester serpent, 118; priests, 117-18; of the Selfhood, 18, 34, 59, 114-16, 121; tails, [28], 117; temples, 117; mentioned, 8, 68, 121-22, 138, 155, 186n.8, 193n.51. *See also* Adder; Boa; Dragon; Ouroboros; Viper

Shadow, attributes in eagle, owl, and wolf, 24; and nature, 112, 115, 143; rejected by Emanation, 77; State of, 125; symbols of rejection in butterfly and dove, 68, 92-96; united with Emanation, 161; mentioned, 76, 77, 108, 185n.19, 192n.37

Shakespeare, William, [19], 9, 45, 47, 56, 57, 62, 68, 79, 80, 90, 126, 129, 142, 157, 175n.2; *As*

You Like It, 61; *Coriolanus,* 14, 142; *Cymbeline,* 64, 70; *Comedy of Errors,* 58, 145; *Hamlet,* 61, 70; 1 *Henry IV,* 88; 1, *Henry VI,* 58, 3 *Henry VI,* 14, 30; *King Lear,* 14, 26, 77, 78, 102, 114; *Macbeth,* 81, 147; *MND,* 151, 163; *Othello,* 41, 146; *Richard III,* 98; *Sonnets,* 70, 136, 169; *Tempest,* 81, 158; *Titus Andronicus,* 26, 77, *Troilus and Cressida,* 46, 50, 58, 61; *Twelfth Night,* 26, 89, 147, 161; *Venus and Adonis,* 166. For Blake's designs, see title

Shaw, George, 131

Shellfish, [8], [24], [35], 123, 126, 160, 187n.6

Sheep, [9], [10], [12], [61], [64], 12, 38-39, 41, 42, 43, 138, 179nn.3, 6

Shepherd, [9], [61], [64], 37-39, 138, 179n.5; the Good Shepherd, 37, 39, 41

"Shepherd, The," [9], 38, 157

Shepherd and his Lass, The, 192n.44

"Sick Rose, The," [37], 89, 162

Sin, Biblical, 106, 151, 152; Blake's Leutha as, 29, 105; Milton's character, 26, 28, 29, 105, 106, 186n.10

Sins, Seven Deadly, as birds of prey, 73; as Seven Diseases of Man, 73, 118. *See also under* Spenser, Edmund, *Faerie Queene*

Smith, Sir James Edward, 6, 154, 191n.17

Snake. *See* Serpent

Song of Los, The, pl. 3, 39, 96; pl. 4, 79; pl. 5, 163

Songbird, 38, 54-55, 61-72, 79. *See also* Lark; Nightingale; Robin; Sparrow; Swallow; Wren

Songs of Experience, 136, 137. *See also titles*

Songs of Innocence, 38, 60, 136, 137, 157; Introduction, 38, 63, 156; frontispiece, 40; title page, 139, 146. *See also titles*

Songs of Innocence and of Experience, 3, 10, 136; frontispiece, 40, 158; title page, 140

Sowerby, James, 192-93n.50; designs for *Botanical Magazine,* [71], 164, 165; *English Botany,* 6, 191n.17

Sparrow, 61-62, 63, 65, 153, 169

Spectre, aggression of, 132; attributes (bat, [29], 81, 83, 85, 95; Behemoth, 35, 132; dragon, 106; Leviathan, 35, 132; lion, 32; marine life, 122; moth, 85; serpent, [20], 106-107, 119-20; Tree of Death, 144; wolf, 25, 83); dominating Albion, 101; dominating Jerusalem, [30], 83; dominating mankind, 122; dominating Milton, 48; dominating Rintrah, 32, 135; dominating Urizen, 45, 108; malignancy of, 119; as nature worship, 112, 113, 143; rejected, 68, 122; as Satan, 29, 82, 101, 106, 114; spiritual blindness of, 82, 83, 119; mentioned, 58, 100, 107, 108. *See also* Selfhood

Speechley, William, 191n.19

Spenser, Edmund, 9, 50, 56, 62, 89; *The Faerie Queene (FQ),* xv, 14, 26, 30, 45, 81, 89, 130,

135, 138, 139, 142, 145, 153-54, 161; the Seven Deadly Sins in: envy as wolf and toad, 23, 102; gluttony as swine and ivy, 52, 158; lechery as goat, 41; pride as peacock, 58; wrath as lion, 30

Spider, [1], [25], [36], 98-100; bush-spider, 98; of empire, 97, 99; as insect, 13, 98; of nature, 88; web, [36], 98-99; mentioned, 8, 91, 121

Spirit of Plato, The, 124

Spirit Vaulting, A, 47

Spiritual Form of Nelson Guiding Leviathan, The, [59], 132

Spiritual Form of Pitt Guiding Behemoth, The, 35

Spiritual Preceptor, The, 12, 46

"Spring," 37, 57, 69, 70, 189n.18; pl. 2, 39

Squid, 126, 127

Stag, 42-43

State, 42, 120

Stedman, John Gabriel, 15, 81, 98, 116-17, 132, 176n.9

Stewart, Stanley, 139, 188n.4

Stothard, Thomas, 91, 94, 111, 158, 191n.30

Strutt, Joseph, *Sports and Pastimes*, 173n.7

Stubbs, George, 4, 19

Sun at his Eastern Gate, The, 193n.51

Sunflower, [41], [69], 150, 158-59, 191n.30

Sunshine Holiday, 189n.18

Swallow, [18], 56, 61, 62-63, 68, 181n.21

Swan, 55-57; of Avon, [19], 56, 57, 126; emblem of beauty and innocence, 55-56; emblem of music and poetry, [17], [18], 56, 77; king of waterfowl and seducer of Leda, 55

Swedenborg, Emanuel, 12-13, 31, 34, 42, 57, 59, 156, 157, 174n.12, 185n.21; *Angelic Love and Wisdom*, 123, 126; *Apocalypse Explained* (AE), xv, 31, 35, 37, 40, 46, 79, 122, 123, 132, 140, 143, 149; *Apocalypse Revealed* (AR), xv, 20, 26, 59, 81, 140; *Arcana Coelestia* (AC), xv, 12, 24, 26, 37-38, 38, 41, 46, 54, 73, 80, 103, 105, 112, 114, 129, 135, 136, 143, 149, 151, 152, 154, 156; *Conjugial Love*, 57, 136, 138, 181n.9; *Divine Love and Wisdom*, 59, 136, 176n.11; *Divine Providence*, 98, 140, 152, 185n.23; *Heaven and Hell*, 6, 174n.12, 184n.2, 185n.21; *True Christian Religion* (TCR), xvi, 12, 18, 24, 46, 47, 67, 84, 102, 176n.14

Sweet William, [68], 158

Swift, Jonathan, 16, 53

Swinburne, Algernon Charles, 23

Swine, [16], 5, 23, 41, 52-53, 173n.7

Tayler, Irene, 178n.38

Tempest, P., 10, 174n.18

Temptation and Fall of Eve, The, 140, 152

Tervarent, Guy de, 43, 108, 177n.33, 187n.2

Tharmas, 39, 121, 127, 139, 160, 182n.39

Thel, attribute (narcissus), 168; discussed, [73], [75]-[77], 166-69; mentioned, 31, 104, 145, 160

Thel, The Book of, 3, 39, 44, 48, 51, 104, 160, 166-69, 193n.53; pl. *ii*, [73], 167, pl. *2*, [75], 145, 168; pl. *4*, [76], 168; pl. *5*, [77], 168, pl. *6*, 104

Theotormon, 29, 55, 58, 74, 159

There Is No Natural Religion, 137, 146

Thistle, [65], 121, 152-53, 154

Thomson, James, 50, 71, 177n.29

Thorn, [61], 98, 138, 152

Thornton, Robert John, 159, 192n.36

Thyme, 151

Tiger, attribute of (Orc, 38, 46; the Selfhood, 18, 23, 33, 36, 170-71; Urizen, 33, 41, 50, 135); fangs of, 16, 19; its ferocity and cruelty, 8-9, 12, 14-18, 23, 30, 32, 42, 55, 88, 99, 155, 170, 175n.1, 177n.26; illustrations of, 16; snout of, 15-16; sublimity of, 21; symmetry of, 19, 21, of wrath, 16-17, 33, 47; mentioned, 4, 7, 31, 135, 145, 177n.24. *See also* "The Tyger"

Tiger-cat, 15

Tiriel, attributes (lion, 18; newt, 18, 102; serpent, 106, 114; tiger, 18; toad, 18, 102); as Selfhood, 18, 114; his sons, 106; mentioned, 14, 32, 100

Tiriel, 14, 18, 28, 32, 100, 102, 106, 114, 130

Tirzah, 6, 16, 27, 86, 96, 140

Titania, Oberon, and Puck, with Fairies Dancing, 4

"To the Evening Star," 135

"To Nobodaddy," 117

"To Tirzah," 140

Toad, 102-103; attribute of Satan and Tiriel, 18, 102; malice of, [65], 98, 152, 154; as reptile, 102; spiritual blindness of, 80; mentioned, 8, 31

Tree, 134-149; bare, barren, dead, or diseased, [61], [68], 18, 19, 135, 136, 137-38, 140-41, 144; deciduous, 138-47 (*see also* Apple; Birch, Elm; Fig; Oak; Willow); evergreen, 147-49 (*see also* Laurel; Palm; Yew); of Death and Life, [48], 138-44; of Good and Evil, 105, 118, 119, 138-44, 152, 155; hanging, 144; of Jesse, 63, 154, 156; of mystery or religion, 79, 100, 120, 139-40, 141; upside down, 134

Trimmer, Sarah, 65, 182n.29

"Tyger, The," [2], 18-23; eye of Tyger, 20-21; imbrutement of, 32; like lion of *Urizen*, 33; snout of, 16; stupidity of, 19; symmetry of, 19, 21; mentioned, 17, 135, 145, 170-71, 176n.16. *See also* Tiger

Ulro, 34, 51, 108, 151

Upas, 141

Urizen, attributes (banyan fig, 141; bat, [28], 82; bear, 41, 43; blighted tree, 137; bull, [13], 45; Cerberus, [3], 26-27; crocodile, 116; dragon, [52], 116; eagle, 74; elephant, 42, 50; forest, 135; horse, 42, 47, 49; lion, [7], 32-33, 42; oak, 143; polypus, 127, satyr, 41, 43; serpent, [46], 108-109, 110, 112; spider, 99-100; stag, 42; tiger, 41, 42; wolf, 41, 42, 50); daughters of, [43], 105, 186n.8; dominated by Spectre, Satan, 45, 47, 108; as explorer, [7], 33; opponent of Orc, 119-20, 137; sentimentalist, 25; mentioned, 17, 83, 127, 159

Urizen, The Book of, 22, 25, 99, 119, 135; pl. *6,* [49], 112; pls. *19, 20,* 148; pl. *23,* [7], 33-34; pl. *25,* [43], 105; pl. *28,* 99

Urthona, the shadowy daughter of, 118, 130. *For* Urthona, *see* Los

Vala, as Albion's Shadow, [45], 6, 107-112; as goddess of nature, [41], [42], 100, 110, 150, 160; as Lily of Havilah, [35], 160, 161; as Luvah's Emanation, [38], [41], 95, 160; her net, [35], [54], 124, 150, 160; her Triumph, [45], 183-89; her union with Orc, 119-20; her veil, 134, 160

Vala. See The Four Zoas

Vegetation (human), 150, 159, 163, 169

Van Veen, Octavio, 10

Venus, 29, 66, 139, 161, 167

Venus fly trap, 169, 193n.57

Vine, 154-58, cut or falling, [64], [65], [68], 154, 158; independent, [11], [66], [76], 154, 155, 168; serpentine, [10], [67], 157, 171; unidentifiable, 157. *See also* Grapevine; Honeysuckle; Ivy; Morning glory

Viper, attribute of Orc, 118-19; creative, [22], 74, 103; crest of, 113; of fraud and malice, 11, 103, 105, 106

Virgil (Publius Vergilius Maro), 56, 151

Virgin and Child, 165

Virgin and Child in Egypt, The, 149

Virgin Hushing the Young Baptist, The, 92, 165

Virginia creeper, or climber, 158, 168, 191n.29

"Vision of the Last Judgment, A," 138, 142, 148-49, 156, 186n.11

Vision of the Last Judgment, The, 186n.11

Visions of the Daughters of Albion (VDA), xvi, 20, 26, 29, 51, 54, 55, 69, 70, 74, 77, 78, 99, 135, 153; pl. *iii,* 159; pl. *3,* [27], 78, 83

Vulture, [16], 77-78; beak of, 83; of the deep, [24], 75, 78; eagle-vulture, [27], 78, 83; of empire, 97; of the mind, [16], 77, 105; of nature, [25], 88, 99, 123, mentioned, 19, 55, 76, 170

Wardle, Judith, 92, 175n.21

Index

Warhorse, [14], [15], 28, 33, 46, 48-50; attribute of Orc, 48, 49, 180n.21

Water lily (lotus), [35], 159-61

Watts, Isaac, 26, 97, 124, 178n.38

Weed, 19, 80, 151-53. *See also* Brier; Burdock; Nettle; Thistle; Thorn

Whale, 129-30

Wheat (or "corn"), 49, 70, 153, 158

White, Gilbert, 142, 147, 181n.21, 189n.18

Whore (of Babylon), [48], 107, 109, 186n.11

Whore of Babylon, The, 186n.11

Wicksteed, Joseph, 185n.16, 192n.49

Wilford, Capt. F., 159

Willow, 146-47; of Experience, 145; of sterility, [19], [66], [73], 57, 146, 154, 166, 189n.27; of suffering, [60], 44, 57, 137, 149; weeping willow, [5], 146-47

"Willow-Tree, The," 146

"Willow, Willow, Willow," 146

Wimberly, Lowery Charles, 145, 189n.23

Wolf, 23-25; attribute of (Satan, 24; the Spectre, 18, 83; Urizen, 41, 42, 50); batwinged, 83; companion of the tiger, 14; contrary of the lamb, 75; embodiment of cruelty, greed, and envy, 12, 17, 24, 31, 32, 37, 170, 177n.26; of empire, 24, 25, 32, 76; of famine, 76; of the female will and nature, 52, 76; mentioned, 30, 98, 135, 177n.32

Woolstonecraft, Mary, 65

Wordsworth, William, 17, 176n.13; Blake's annotations on *Poems*, 5

Worm, [1], [12], 100-101; as chrysalis, 90; as insect, 13, 98; as larva, 88; symbol of misanthropic man, [42], 100; worm-embryo, [33]-[35], 86, 87, 100, 119, 168; mentioned, 8, 44, 121. *See also* Cankerworm; Earthworm

Wren, 66

Wynne, John Huddleston, *Choice Emblems*, 42, 91, 97, 145, 175n.21, 177n.33, 182n.28; *Fables of Flowers*, 10, 151, 158, 163, 166, 167, 168, 190n.4

Yew, 147-148; of death, [63], 106, 147-48, 189-90n.30

Young, Edward, *Night Thoughts (NT)* (*references cite Blake's watercolors and usually Young's verses*), xvi; p. 17, 90; p. 51, 162; 184n.9; p. 63, 145, 179n.5; p. 78 (*Narcissa and the Ouroboros*), [50], 112; p. 79, 112; p. 89, 159; p. 91, 82; p. 117, 28; p. 119, 140; p. 163, 113; p. 181, 92; p. 189, 146; p. 199, 80; p. 205, 162; p. 234, [4], 27; p. 246, 32; p. 257, 113; p. 258, 134; p. 307, 54; p. 309, 53; p. 340, 179n.5; p. 345, 186n.11; p. 346, 139; p. 349, 132; p. 358, 106; p. 361, 88; p. 368, 106; p. 378, 179n.5,

189n.18; p. 381, 153; p. 409, 82, 184n.9; p. 440, 162; p. 478, 184n.9; p. 492, 145; p. 508, 51; p. 512, 156-57; p. 513, 179n.5; p. 521, 80

Zeus, 55, 73, 116

Zoas, the Four, 94, 109; their separation and fall, [49], [58], 112, 127. *See also* Los; Luvah; Tharmas; Urizen